The Last Golden Smile

A Narrative of War and Peace

Al Karasa

Llumina
Press

Photographs from author's collection

Cover photograph:
Office of War Information image LC-USW33-021089-C
Library of Congress Prints and Photographs Division
Washington, D.C. 20540

ISBN: 978-1-62550-483-8

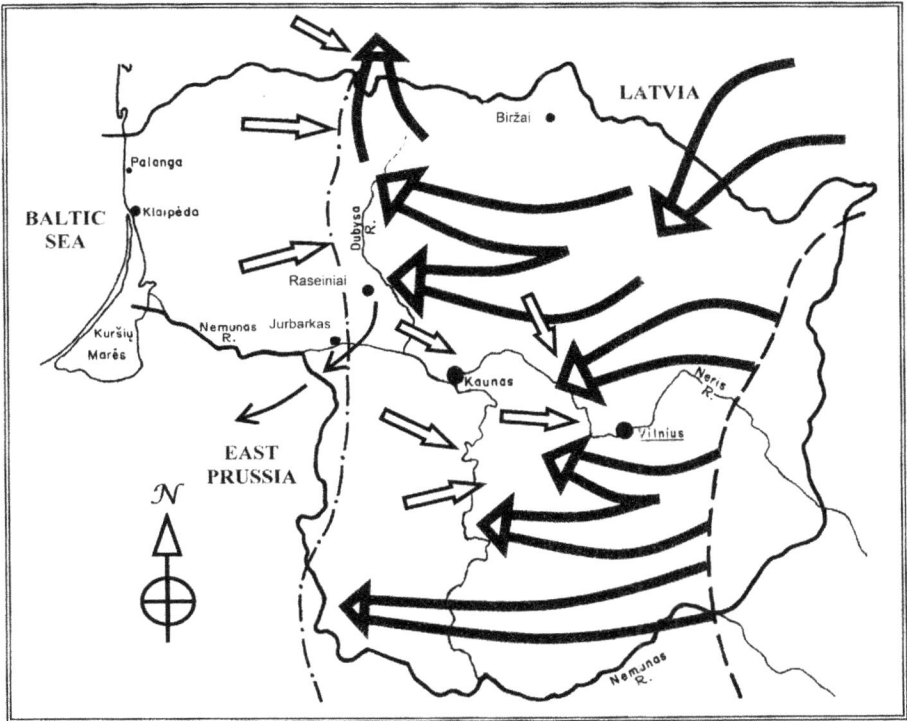

——— Lithuanian border	⮕ Russian attacks, July 3 - Aug 28
– – – – Front line, July 3	⇨ German counterstrikes
–·–·– Front line, Aug 28	
⟶ Author's departure, July 11, and border crossing August 3	

War zone during author's departure from Raseiniai, 1944

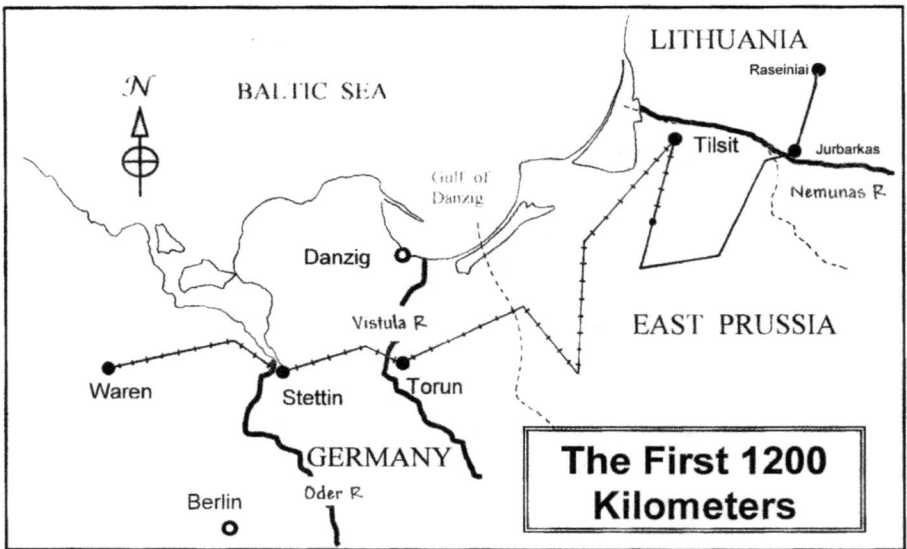

The First 1200 Kilometers

LITHUANIA

BALTIC SEA

Raseiniai

Tilsit

Jurbarkas

Gulf of Danzig

Nemunas R

Danzig

EAST PRUSSIA

Vistula R

Waren

Stettin

Torun

GERMANY

Berlin

Oder R

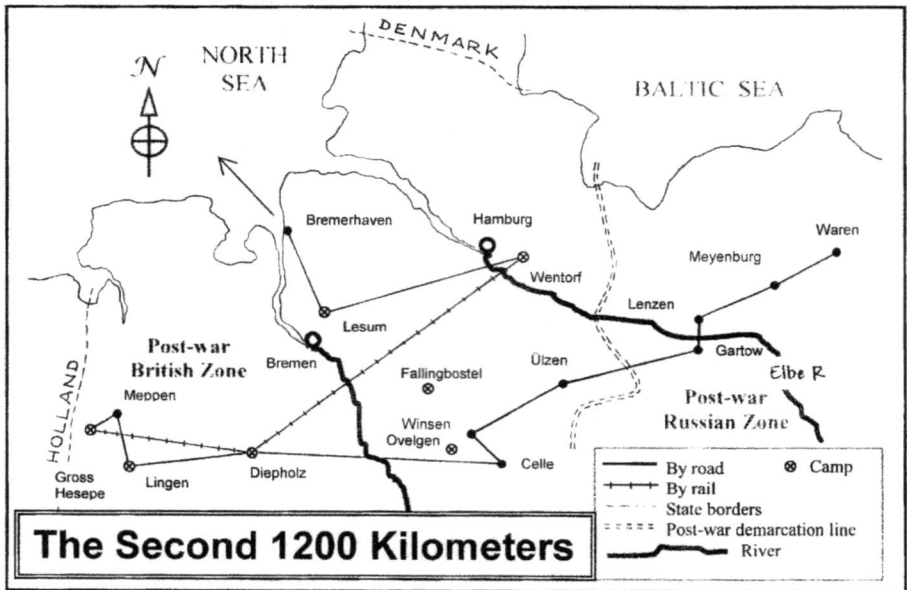

The Second 1200 Kilometers

DENMARK

NORTH SEA

BALTIC SEA

Bremerhaven

Hamburg

Waren

Meyenburg

Wentorf

Lenzen

Lesum

Post-war British Zone

Bremen

Fallingbostel

Ülzen

Gartow

Elbe R

Meppen

Post-war Russian Zone

HOLLAND

Winsen Ovelgen

Gross Hesepe

Lingen

Diepholz

Celle

——— By road	⊗ Camp
+—+—+ By rail	
- - - State borders	
===== Post-war demarcation line	
━━━ River	

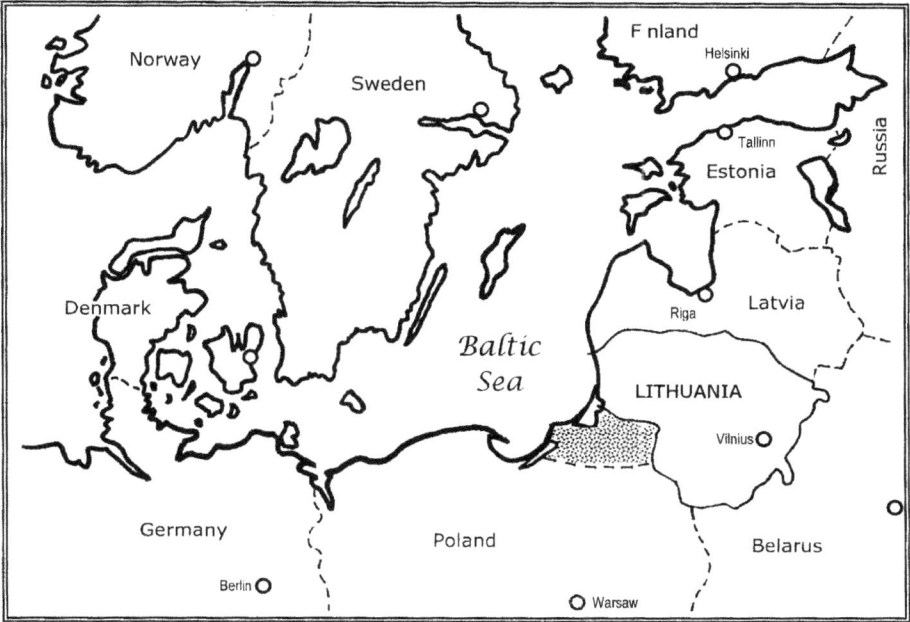

THE BALTIC AREA TODAY

Approx. scale 100 km / 100 mi

▬▬ Coastline	○ State capitals
─── Lithuanian borders	▨ Kaliningrad
- - - - Other national borders	(under Russian occupation)

Norway, Sweden, Finland, Helsinki, Estonia, Tallinn, Russia, Denmark, Riga, Latvia, Baltic Sea, LITHUANIA, Vilnius, Germany, Poland, Belarus, Berlin, Warsaw

The Last Golden Smile

A Narrative of War and Peace

To the memory of my father,
whose undying sense of duty, perseverance
and honor in the face of adversity,
saw me through disasters
which I could not have survived without him.

Acknowledgements

There never was a conscious plan to write a memoir. Brewing in my head were just stories. Disconnected. Disordered. Two realms of thought, a half-century apart, crossed paths with unrelenting similitude — the joys of one forever linked to the tragedies of the other. Nevertheless, putting pen to paper was encouraged by friends who knew something of my past but never heard the stories. But such self-centered story telling was anathema to my inbred skepticism. I am in their debt that my skepticism was turned around. The result is in these pages.

In addition, I am grateful to members of my family in Lithuania who corresponded with me over the years and helped fill the gaps in my story which escaped early edits. My thanks also extend to fellow survivors of the war who agreed to be interviewed and contributed much to my appreciation of wartime conditions in other parts of Europe, which I did not experience first hand.

This note would be incomplete without my expression of profound gratitude to my father, the late Colonel Motiejus Karaša, whose journals were the inspiration for the first draft.

"… as much as I scrabble through the ruins of my memories,
I find that time, that other time,
fresh and untouched by forgetfulness…"

Ida Fink

Prologue

Leaving home. Taking only what could be carried. Not knowing when we would return, if ever. It was the choice made by millions, a choice imposed by war. The alternative was death. Maybe worse. The unknown was better.

In his lifetime, my father made this choice three times. I was more fortunate. It happened to me only once. And I was young enough to ignore the full impact of my displacement. The miracle of freedom would not come for another ten years. But the miracle of survival would repeat itself many times over. To account for this, it is tempting to set it at the doorstep of fate, divine intervention, luck. But that wouldn't be accurate. Better to examine how the survivors themselves effected these events, to tell their story.

It is said that to learn a new language quickly one must go where the known language is unavailable. Such circumstance followed me all the years of my youth, and into my adult life. I received my primary education in the country of my birth. The rest of my teaching fell to remarkable people in four other countries and three languages unknown to me at the time.

You may think this is unusual, but it was de rigueur to many European children of World War Two. We became autodidacts when our teachers were taken away, murdered, or disappeared without trace. Formal education came to a sudden and violent end when Russian troops crossed our borders.

It is remarkable that so much literature in print, video and film has been produced about the Holocaust and other Nazi crimes against humanity, and so very little about the equally heinous crimes perpetrated by Soviet Russia not only during the same war years, but long after the war ended. It is remarkable because the Russian counterpart took ten times the number of lives and still continues today.

My reason in having begun the manuscript for this book was born of this anomaly. Written more than a half-century after the events it describes, it suffers from limitations of human memory as any such work must. But memory is most faithful to life changing events, and all of them in this story were life changing. Some things never fade from a child's memory. Some things stay there for all time. In this book, I make no distinction between the two. They are inseparable. They connect me to the time and place of today through things that mirror those memories and trigger some which I thought I had forgotten.

This work began with disconnected vignettes and flashbacks into sights and sounds of operatic grandeur, pageantry, prosperity, splendor, conflict, destruction, death and chaos. When assembled in proper order, they conspire to tell a story.

Substantiated by relatives who indulged me in my inquiries, confirmed by acquaintances and fellow refugees, and by my father's journals which served to explain events beyond my comprehension, the story is also my own. It is one readily applicable to the thousands who fled the brewing hell Europe was to become. Ostensibly torn apart beyond recall, many families survived the conflagration that was the war of the century. Some, only in part. Ours was one of those.

By the time of Allied landings in Normandy, Nazi Germany was in retreat, all but crushed by the Soviet juggernaut. The war was nearly over. We knew nothing of Pearl Harbor, of America's entry into the war. To our concerns, the Second World War in Europe was won and lost on the Eastern Front of hostilities between Hitler and Stalin. There was unspeakable evil on both sides, each one claiming good.

Did that mean evil was winning?

We thought so.

The savagery and frenzy of destruction which swept through our homes could not be conceived as anything but evil. And it returned. More than once.

We fled.

For the Russians were to be feared. They locked sane dissidents in lunatic asylums, they sent thousands to Gulag's Siberian slave labor camps, they routinely practiced horrific torture on resistance fighters, assassinated and blackmailed political opponents. They have shown themselves as the most ruthless, the most unscrupulous instrument of tyranny and oppression the world has ever known.

Mountains of rubble, where once great cities stood, were everywhere. Farms and estates in the country were laid to waste. The detritus of war included homeless throngs in their millions. We blended in with the rubble. It made us indistinguishable from one another. We survived by perseverance, stubbornness and will. Lives were rebuilt. But they would never be the same.

*"Facts do not cease to exist
because they are ignored."*

Aldous Huxley

Misconceptions

Pervasive Soviet propaganda and the Russian penchant for rewriting history are responsible for many misconceptions about the Second World War in Europe. Repeated for so many years, the Russian version has taken root in the West and is only now attracting the attention of historians as needing correction.

Start of the war is often quoted as the Nazi invasion of Poland. What of the invasion of Poland from the east at the same time by Russia, while the German/Russian non-aggression pact was still in effect? In the West, this is never mentioned in the same context, in spite of the fact that Poland was divided between them.

Worse yet is what is being taught in American schools and noted at the new World War Two Memorial in Washington, DC. where 1941-1945 is quoted as the war period.

1941 is not the year World War Two started. 1941 is the year United States joined in the Pacific. It was three more years before Americans reached Europe. The war was already half over.

Regarding the plight of civilians, the West is focused on the Holocaust, and ignores the Russian parallel. No case was ever presented against Russian use of liberated Nazi concentration camps. They were not destroyed. Russians used them for the same purpose long after the war ended.

The impact of previous wars, even 1914-1918, was mainly felt by soldiers on the battlefield. In World War Two, however, for every soldier in the field there were at least ten civilians, who were not directly involved, but suffered the horrors of war and its aftermath.This was a war like no other.

Stalin's regime was a mass-murdering monster from which Hitler sought to learn human extermination methods already developed in Russia, where concentration camps had been functioning since 1917. The Nazis took the Russian model and developed it into a super-efficient killing machine. But the largest concentration camp in Europe was not German. It was Vorkuta, in the northern reaches of the Ural Mountains of Russia, where recorded winter temperatures were beyond human endurance — as low as -80°F.

In addition to many smaller ones, there were 476 principal Gulag camps scattered throughout Russia, some of which were still functioning in the 1980s. No one from the West was allowed in, and the rare escapees were not believed until 1998 when Gulag archival files were opened for research. Until then, the world believed only Nazis ran concentration camps.

Neither the SS nor the NKVD kept accurate records, but death count in Nazi camps is believed to have been more than three million. The Russian counterpart is estimated at ten times that, with an additional three million after the war ended. This does not take into account those who perished in Gulag concentration camps before World War Two began.

Understanding of the military aspects of the war is not much better. Americans will point to Normandy as the biggest and most decisive military action of the war in Europe. But they will be mistaken. The most devastating losses inflicted on Nazi Germany came from the east. First was Hitler's disaster at Stalingrad, and then the colossus of the Battle of Kursk, the biggest battle ever fought in the history of mankind.

The scope of death and destruction in World War Two staggers the imagination. An estimated 52 million lives were lost in the 21 countries involved. Of those, 32 million were civilians. In Europe alone, 13 million children were orphaned and abandoned. Over four million German soldiers lost their lives along with an equal number of German civilians. More than 12 million fell victim to Nazi genocide. In Western Europe 390,000 British troops perished in the fighting alongside the 285,000 Americans and 42,000 Canadians. Russia mobilized 34 million and lost a combined total of 27 million people of which 16 million were non-combatants.

There were 30 million homeless refugees in Europe when the war ended.

Such losses are beyond civilized comprehension. They leave us in rueful silence.

The Last Golden Smile

Gypsy

Best Man. A privilege. An honor. My best friend is getting married and I am his Best Man. It is a laudable American custom, for this is an American wedding, a wedding 9,000 miles from home, in a land still foreign in our minds, but already ours in our hearts.

Our friendship was born here. Here are our homes now, our hopes. The occasion is festive, the first of many more to come. We celebrate life whenever we can. Our celebrations need no other reason. This time it is the wedding, the first of many more to come.

Children scamper about the ballroom floor, always the first to dance. The men are loud and boisterous with happiness for the newly wed pair. The women are aglow in their finery and cast flirtatious glances as prelude to more. The flowing gowns, the silky bows, the gems that sparkle in their hair, all attest to the festive air. It is an American wedding indeed. Here, women ask men to dance.

And I don't dance.

But there once was a woman who asked and, with her, I danced.

* * *

Watching people without their knowledge was one of those things not to be done. I knew that. Mother drilled it into me long ago. But here I was, not meaning to spy on anyone, when I heard strange hissing noises and then someone humming a tune. The door was open, as doors always were in this house.

I had to look.

With her side to me stood a woman at an ironing board. She sipped some water from a glass, puckered her lips and blew a fine spray over the white linen on the board. She licked her finger to test the iron with a quick touch before gliding it smoothly over the steaming surface.

And then she hummed — in rhythm with her ironing strokes.

1

That was before I knew who she was.

After I learned, and visited her often, there was another time when I found the door open.

Johannes Brahms. It was his music, although I didn't know it at the time, to which she danced. I walked in unannounced. I heard the gramophone playing behind the half open door and walked in. Her full, wide skirt fluttered round her as she spun in stocking feet on the polished parquet floor. Her eyes were closed. She didn't see me standing there, and I didn't dare move for fear of interrupting. She was so immersed in what she was doing, interruption was unthinkable. I was frozen in place, mesmerized by the music and by my godmother's dance.

She danced alone. For herself. I was an intruder.

The music stopped. She opened her eyes and saw me.

"Hullo!" she said. Her voice was always lilting, like the music just ended. Her smile flashed her gold tooth. It always intrigued me — that smile, framing the golden tooth. I know my face tingled — sure sign I would blush. Why? I didn't know. Perhaps because I interrupted, eavesdropped.

"*Ateik,*" come here, she beckoned as she walked to the gramophone and reset the needle back to the record's outer edge. I stepped closer as the music began anew, feeling embarrassed, not knowing why.

"Here. Let me show you." She took my hand. Her touch was gentle but firm. I didn't dare refuse. "Like this." She showed a step and bid me to follow. She took my other hand. We were face-to-face, holding hands, side stepping to the music's every other beat. Slowly.

Shakily at first, my feet followed her steps, and soon she changed them to fall closer to the rhythm Johannes Brahms intended. It felt better the longer we danced. The dance was Hungarian, she said. The music swept its sound up and down, filling the room with its festive mood. We moved with its changing rhythms and my own mood changed.

This was fun! Before the needle reached the record label and before the music stopped, I had relaxed and lost my apprehension.

"*Vėl?*" again? she asked. I nodded without hesitation. She flashed her golden smile and reset the needle on the gramophone.

We danced.

The long established preconception of my godmother was being thoroughly trounced. I was seeing her in a new light. She had seemed beyond reach when I grew old enough to know who she was. Aloof, aristocratic airs, romantic notions, my mother said. Dvorak, Liszt and Brahms — their music always filled her home. Hers was a world of fairytales, a world my nanny read to me about. A world I didn't know could be. And yet, my godmother lived in it even then. It was a fantasy come true.

This was the first time I was allowed to stay more than a day. She showed me photographs of her grandfather's house. An old house, overgrown with ivy vine and surrounded by tall, slender poplars. She had grown up there.

One of the photos showed a strange inscription above a large fireplace. Learning to read was a welcome challenge in school, but I couldn't read it. I made out the letters, but the words made no sense. Carved in wood, in letters filled with gold, was this passage:

Na may kharunde kai tshi khal tut.

Then it dawned on me why I couldn't read it.

"Is that a foreign language?" I asked.

"Yes. Romani."

"Romani? What's that?"

"It's a Gypsy language they speak in Hungary," she explained.

"What does it mean?"

"Oh, it's just a saying the Gypsies have."

"What?" I persisted.

"Don't scratch where it doesn't itch."

"What?" I didn't know I was scratching.

"That's what it means."

I was confused, but she offered no explanation.

"You'll understand when you get older." She smiled her golden smile.

I wasn't satisfied with that. It raised questions I didn't know how to ask. But I didn't want to try her patience. Was Romani among the languages she spoke? I was sure she was Hungarian — a Gypsy, no less. This notion pursued me to my teens. She wasn't, of course. Her family was much like mine. My parents saw hers as our own.

3

But I still see her black mesh gloves over delicate hands and her broad-brimmed sun hat, all very different from what other women wore. There was an elegance about her I might have appreciated had I been older. And I still see her loosely combed red hair; when other women wore theirs in severe, tightly bound buns; her sparkling emerald green eyes, and her golden smile. A Hungarian Gypsy if there ever was, a true exotic. And the first beautiful woman I remember.

I looked to her to fulfill fairytale fantasies and to flatter me with unreserved admiration for my most insignificant deeds, accomplishments made significant by her praise.

There were other visits, other dances, lessons not learned in school, stories as varied as those father told me, but of a different world — a world, I suspected, father did not know. She spoke in a poetic tongue, a language I should not have understood, but did because of the way the stories were told — her hands drawing pictures in the air as she spoke. And always the music, sounds I never heard beyond her parlor, away from the grand piano sparkling there under the kaleidoscope of a huge crystal chandelier. She played it with a loving care, like that first time I saw her dance, for herself. But I was a participant now, no longer an intruder.

Her piano was the biggest and grandest musical instrument I had ever seen. The noble sound it made followed me all the way home after each visit. I wanted to understand how it made the sounds she evoked. She showed me. We plucked its strings with our fingers and watched the hammers rebound. We touched them gently to feel as well as hear the sound they made. It was a revelation of how all string instruments worked, even those which did not make music.

I learned new things in her company, things I could not learn elsewhere. It provoked questions I would not have dared ask anyone else for fear they were foolish, and some I never considered. But she never treated me like a child. I was her equal in her company. I could ask anything that came to mind and knew she would grant me a considered reply, childish question or not.

When I stayed longer, she showed me more of the estate. Her home was surrounded by open meadows fringed in airy groves of birch and spruce. Sometimes, when summer weather gave the cue, she packed a picnic basket and we strode out of the house on our way to one of her favorite spots on the bank of a meadow stream shaded by willows. There, smoked eel would be consumed with pungent rye bread, still warm from the oven, and goat's cheese. Honey glazed banana slices delighted my pallet for dessert one day. It was meant to be a surprise. But, as something extraordinary often emerged like magic from her kitchen, the banana did not surprise me. I didn't know what it was. I had never seen one and her attempt to describe what it looked like whole, in trees, escaped me.

After we closed the picnic basket, we played. A short stick was as good as a ball. We counted the spins it made when tossed into the air and caught on its way down. We tossed it between us without spinning to make it easier for the catcher. One stick in hand we batted at another, a shorter one, trying to keep it in the air as long as we could. She showed me how to weave a willow branch into a wheel with criss-crossed spokes made from the sticks. The rounder we made it, the farther it rolled down the hill.

Balancing tests demanding dexterity and concentration were always fun. A heavy stick, longer than my own height, was best. Balancing it vertically on the palm of my hand was easy. Doing so on my chin made me dizzy. If this was not challenging enough, we did it with feet rooted in place. The sky would rotate crazily beyond the end of the wobbling stick, stabbing the clouds, until either the stick fell or I did.

These skills were not wasted. Schoolmates took to them with glee when I introduced these stick games at mid-day recess in the schoolyard. I also gained their respect for my expertise which they equaled only after much frustrating practice.

Sometimes we lay in the meadow, looking up at the clouds drifting by. I fashioned each one into whatever struck my fancy. There was a cave, and a snow capped mountain, a train engine blowing off steam.

Without a word spoken, my godmother knew what I was doing, what I was thinking. To her, my imagination was transparent.

"There!" she pointed. "A pig with a curly tail. See?"

I didn't. But I picked the wrong cloud. When I saw it, I was amazed she was doing the same thing. As I followed it, the shape dissolved into a unicorn. Now I had something to show *her*.

"Look! A unicorn," I exclaimed.

She saw it, and she smiled her golden smile.

One day the circus came to town. It was a traveling show in wagons drawn by horses which performed in the ring as mounts for riders of unbelievable skill. The only other animals were dancing bears. But there were clowns and acrobats, trapeze artists, jugglers and ropewalkers. In the biggest tent I had ever seen, pretty girls cart wheeled in the sawdust and built human pyramids six high. I laughed at the clowns until my sides hurt. I held my breath with the crowd for the man on the high wire, and I gasped with relief when flying hands caught the trapeze. At those moments the band was still and silent. But at others the horns, the bows and drums made a glorious noise. The shivers it sent up my spine made me wish it would never end. But when it did, there was another thrill awaiting my awe.

It was the first big entertainment I had ever seen, and my godmother's smile never faded that day.

Other days were spent in study of things outside my school curriculum and in making new friends I would not have met elsewhere.

Sometimes I was taken along when she traveled. I saw rivers and valleys far from home, and forests so dense no sunlight ever reached the ground. I saw cities with streets so filled with carriages and cars, that to cross them on foot was to run a gauntlet. I knew then there was a world outside my realm of understanding. I also knew I would step beyond that line as soon as I was smart enough to know how.

Sometimes she came along when I traveled with my parents on vacations to Finland, Sweden's islands, or to Zarasai and its endless lakes. One year we went to Nida, the small Lithuanian town on the sand spit separating Kuršių Marės (Courland Lagoon) from the Baltic Sea. It was there I learned how difficult it is to climb a sand dune. Father and I took forever to reach the top. When I could no longer cope, he carried me. At the top was our reward. Views of the sea to the west and the lagoon to the east were nothing short of spectacular. Nida is known worldwide for its dunes. They are 60 meters (200 feet) high, the largest in Europe.

Best were vacations in Palanga on the Baltic Sea. There I could play and run on the beach to my heart's content. New friends were made in the surf who kept company the whole week or two we stayed there. I found strange treasures washed up by the tide and heard stories about the sea and the beach where I walked.

On this beach, King Mindaugas rode to meet the defeated Grand Master of the Teutonic Order and threaten him with annihilation if his order refused to leave Lithuanian land — the fate already visited on the Schwertbrüder Order at Durbė in 1236. Mindaugas may have been a fearsome pagan in animal furs, but he was an astute ruler, respected throughout Europe, who united the warring tribes of Lithuania and forged them into a single Christian nation. In 1253 Pope Innocent IV had him crowned the first King of Lithuania.

Kęstutis, the 14th century Grand Duke and ruler of Lithuania, came here to visit the sea. He fell in love with one of the keepers of eternal flame on this beach. Birutė was the most beautiful girl his eyes had ever seen. He was a man of action and lived by his own rules. He claimed Birutė for his own, took her to his castle without elders' blessing, and made her his queen. They ruled together and continued the dynasty which ruled Lithuania for 400 years and made her the largest country in Europe.

The country King Mindaugas had forged would be attacked and savaged repeatedly by enemy troops for the next seven centuries, and even removed from the map of Europe following World War Two. Throughout these trials, she survived, retained her national identity, and rose from the ashes of war in 1990 to celebrate her millennium in 2009. Her history, full of patriotic uprisings against foreign rule, is testament to our proud, fiercely nationalistic people, who are never more so than when threatened by foreign oppression.

I learned all this later, in school. Here, on the beach, I heard the stories from my father. They were stories I should have expected from a patriot, a soldier. But when they came from my godmother's lips, they took on a more meaningful air. She brought King Mindaugas to life. She spoke of his great castles in my birthplace of Samogitia and in far off Naugardukas when it became part of his realm. She spoke of the great hunts to which he invited not only the neighboring Poles, but also the Mongols of the Golden Horde — eastern enemies of both (*know thine enemy as you know yourself* would become a familiar adage to me in later years). She spoke of others who followed our first king, and praised Traidenis, the warlike ruler who made our country strong. She spoke of the sons of Grand Duke Gediminas who fought by their father's side and of his granddaughters who married into the ruling families of Hungary, Brandenburg, and Byzantium.

Her stories reinforced everything I learned in school and everything I heard from my father. They fused together the loose threads of my early education. I looked with eagerness to my next visit, and the next. They were more frequent as time went on. And, as time went on, I came to feel at home away from home. I reveled in her stories and in her company. At least until my ninth birthday. Then, there was war and she was lost to me forever.

I never learned what became of her. And I no longer danced.

"We cannot direct the wind,
but we can adjust the sails."

Bertha Calloway

Wind

Pursuit of ventures whose success depends on weather should be avoided. Where I heard this advice I don't remember, but I disagree.

Waiting for wind is seldom unpleasant. If I am with friends, it is an opportunity to share quiet reflection or revel in their story telling. If I am alone, it is that rare chance to look inward, within myself, undisturbed, uninterrupted, or to marvel at nature's wonders without distraction.

When wind comes, my work begins. The mainsail must be tended first. Then, the drifter, for in small wind or the calm waiting for it to come, the jib is sentenced to the sail locker below. A furling headsail is beyond my means. Instead, I change sails. My boat is small. Her modest accommodations leave no room for refinement. But she serves me well. Our experiences can make good stories, but only on the rare occasion when we are surprised or unprepared, and something goes wrong. The rest are stories for my ears alone. They have no meaning to those not on board. But that's alright. Some stories are only meant for one, not many. They are the ones in greatest abundance. Even those to be shared must be lived first, or else they lack substance.

A brisk morning sail is a rare treat in the protected waters where we spend the most time. Wind takes a rest or perhaps oversleeps after an active night. Once the sun strikes the sea in storm season, the wind sleeps no longer. It is then that share-worthy stories begin. But I shun the storm season. My modest boat either lacks courage or has little faith in my sailing skills. I forgive her this slight for we have shared — the boat and I — stories intended for one, not many.

The way of the wind is fleeting. It comes. It goes. How it will change is not for me to predict. I am here only to benefit from the change, or to lose by it. I try to choose my time on the water with an eye to the wind. More often than not, I err. Sometimes there is a pattern. When I find it, it is a gift.

Cool evenings in the spring and fall are best. Wind is more dependable and we ride the swells in its wake with little effort. These peaceful times produce no stories. Stories need action, excitement, mystery, surprise. It is what makes them share-worthy.

Stories

Shoes. Wooden ones. For horses. Horseshoes made of wood. No, no, not horseshoes for pitching in horseshoe pits. Horseshoes for horses. Nailed to their hooves just like the metal ones. Only these were wood, used on horses for hire so as to discourage theft. Wooden shoes might not last seven miles — manageable distance for a posse to catch a horse thief.

It is one of many stories I heard as a child. This one, like the others, is true. And, like the others, it was told to me by my father. The horses for hire were those in Tomsk, a town of refugees and fugitives of the Revolution, a town in central Siberia. Father knew the story first hand — he made the horseshoes. His experiences were the root of each and every story. I didn't know that when I heard them. They were just stories then. I would find out only decades later and half a world away.

Meanwhile, I made some stories of my own.

* * *

It was improper behavior to spy on neighbors even as innocently as to satisfy a childish curiosity. I knew that. I was forbidden to climb the high stone wall to peer into the courtyard next door not only because mother was certain I would break my neck, but also because it was rude to trespass, if only with one's eyes, on property considered the House of God. But the temptation to discover the mystery of what lay behind the wall was strong, made stronger still by frequent glimpses of men garbed in black robes, with long black beards under round-topped, wide-brimmed hats, who came to our door on countless occasions and brought fresh bagels. And bagels — boiled, not baked — I still find a rare delicacy.

Over the wall I went. Well... not quite over. The vine I tried to climb, ever so slowly did it tear away from the gray stone, ever so slowly did I tumble down not having reached half the wall's height. Overshadowed by embarrassment, what pain there was I

11

didn't feel it. I could not go in the house, bruised and cut as I was. My transgression would be discovered sure as the next dawn. And it *was* near dawn before I found myself facing the consequences of my deed.

But before this moment of truth came, hours passed in fear of being discovered. In the darkness of the sauna hut where I hid I agonized over what I knew must come. Punishment — its degree an overbearing mystery. Father was away. And that was bad. Grandma once told me, that if my father wasn't there to punish me when I did wrong, the devil would. Not God, but the devil himself!

The hut seemed darker then, when I remembered her warning.

Long before dawn would wake the day, I tired, and calmed, and slept. By then, of course, it was too late. While I dozed in the sauna hut behind the apple orchard, waiting for my courage to return, mother began a search of friends' and neighbors' homes to find me. Well into nightfall this continued, and then I saw a light approaching the hut. The courage I had waited for had never come, and now I was to be discovered.

The door opened. Three faces lit by oil lamps peered into my hideout. They were filled with worry and concern. Mother was there as well as grandma, and with them was an old man I had never seen. His beard was long and black and the wide brim of his hat cast flickering shadows over his face — a face I couldn't see, but could well imagine. He was, of course, the devil grandma said would come.

My fear was stifling. I could not speak. Questions were asked I would not answer, would not admit my misdeed. I waited for the punishment to come. I closed my eyes, held my breath and clenched my teeth preparing for the worst.

But nothing happened.

Soft voices spoke gently to me and strong arms picked me up. I felt myself being carried through the dark orchard and into the house. Mother cleaned my wounds but could not get a word out of me about how I got them. I was so ashamed. Ashamed of having disobeyed my father's words. More so, the punishment I knew I deserved hadn't come.

Next day, the old man returned. I hid. But I listened as I peeked around the doorway into the sitting room. He saw me.

I ran. Mother called and I had to find the courage to return. Disregarding her call was not an option. I would not have dared. But courage, again, was slow in coming. I forced myself to stop, and somehow willed my steps back to the sitting room.

It wasn't all that bad. He brought bagels. Still warm. Steaming. Sliced and spread with a thin coat of honey, served with milk, a fresh bagel was my favorite snack. The old man joined me. He told me how bagels were made. I was fascinated. He offered to show me. Next door. On the other side of the stone wall!

Now, my punishment would come. I wanted to run. To hide. Again, it was too late. All three of us, grandma the man and I, were already walking out the door, each holding my hand. I was between them. Trapped. There was no escape.

Again, it wasn't all that bad. Visiting the synagogue next door was privilege undeserved. I learned how boiled bagels were made, the complexities of which; but for the aroma of fresh dough in the kitchen and the slippery film of flour on the long, narrow tables; I've long since forgotten. But I still remember the old man's tired eyes, his soft low voice, and how there was no mystery at all behind the great stone wall. I also remember telling my father about bagel making and my visit to the synagogue when he came home next day. But I carefully neglected to mention my unsuccessful attempt at finding out about bagels on my own.

Although not my first childhood memory, the episode was the first significant one I remember. Significant because it was the first story I ever told my father.

Stories I considered even more important were those about my father from the time before I saw the light of day. But they were hard to come by. When those rare occasions landed in my lap, the stories usually came from Mr. Gantautas.

Antanas Gantautas was my father's best friend. I knew him as *Ponas Uoga* (Mister Berry), a name I gave him as a child does to identify people by their deeds. It was also what I came to call him to his face, and to his delight. With each visit he brought me fresh blackberries, sometimes raspberries, cherries, blueberries or currants. With sugar and milk, they were a special treat. I also looked forward to his visits for the stories he told.

He was a career army officer, like my father, and he was also a motorcyclist. They were friends before either one married and years before I was born. His stories were short glimpses into adventures he and my father shared before my time, adventures seldom talked about.

One of these was about the crossing of a deep ravine by way of a very narrow footbridge. It called for a slow approach on their motorcycles, down the steep hill to the bridge. My mother, riding pillion, didn't like the look of things and jumped off before crossing. My father didn't notice she was missing until they were on the other side. Ponas Uoga never let him live it down. It was one of those rare stories I heard before the war came. Then, the stories changed. And I was not allowed to hear them.

One winter's day I had an unforgettable treat. Three days after Christmas, godmother came to visit. Her husband, who was always away at work when I visited, and a stranger to me, came with her. He provided the special holiday treat.

"Can you drive horses?" he asked me.

"No."

"Would you like to learn?"

Sure, I said. And I meant it, never mind I had never been near a horse.

He was not only mysterious, he was also smart. If he couldn't teach me to drive horses, no one could. And nothing pleased me more than learning new things. Their visit was to pick me up for an extended stay at their estate. I was not due back at school until after New Year's Day. That meant four days in the country!

But that was nothing compared to driving horses.

Outside was a strong black mare hitched to a sleigh. The sleigh was mottled brown and trimmed in bright red leather. Mother bundled me up in my fur-collared coat with a wool scarf round my neck and a knitted hat pulled over my ears. I wore a pair of quilted trousers tucked into tall, heelless boots.

"Ready?" he asked with a smile as bright as godmother's. With sheepskins covering our knees, I sat on the single bench seat between him and godmother. I nodded.

He slapped the reins on the mare's rump and the sleigh jerked into motion. Bells round her bow collar rang as we glided away, waving to mother at our gate. It was still snowing lightly, the last of three days' heavy snow. I had to squint to keep the fine flakes out of my eyes. The runners sang a swishing song, throwing two plumes of snow spray behind us. That, and the bells. There was no other sound. The mare's hoof beats were muffled by the snow.

I was handed the reins when we left the city and were gliding along at speeds greater than a wheeled wagon could reach. I felt the rhythmic tug through my mittens and was shown how to keep the mare going straight. That was easy. When it was time to turn, I had help. Godmother was laughing. I didn't think it was funny. This was serious business. What if my coach let go of the reins?

But he didn't let go until we were going straight again.

Wow! This was fun. Soon, I learned to hold the reins in one hand and use the other as a shield over my forehead to keep the snow out of my eyes. That's when I saw the fine, sparkling snow spray rising behind the mare's hoofs and disappearing between the runners. It was a silvery dust that rose in waves just short of reaching our faces. It landed on the sheepskins and was instantly blown away by the wind.

When we arrived, the snow had stopped. When the sleigh stopped, it was quiet. In the silence only the steam from the mare's nostrils made noise as it froze in the air into ice fog. The ride was too short. I wanted more. But I learned to drive a sleigh. Now I had another story to tell.

⚜

Wind

The breeze whispers, barely ruffling the young, tender leaves of early spring growth. Its silent caress is ignored by branches closer to the trunk. It is morning. Early. I watch the balloon drift imperceptibly higher over the trees — too far to see the faces of people in its basket. I wait. When its direction is more marked, I start the engine and proceed.

This is a balloon chase. I've done this many times. On spotting one up in the air I follow its path as closely as the road network permits. Sometimes the road is little more than a well-worn firebreak. Sometimes there is no road at all. That's when I lose the balloon altogether. But while I can, I follow its course in the hope of seeing it land.

Today, I am in luck. Wind is so light, keeping up is effortless. There is no time lost in waiting to confirm the balloon's course change. A few more turns along another road and I am back under its lazy shadow. It drifts off and there is another side road to the left. I turn. I lose sight of the balloon when it sails behind intervening woods or loses altitude too low to see beyond a hill's horizon. But soon its rainbow stripes, diffused in the morning haze, appear once more before it dips out of sight.

Sometimes I wait, sometimes I follow. This can continue for hours, but usually ends sooner when roads in direction needed do not exist, or the balloon lands out of sight.

It is behind tall trees and very low now. Perhaps I'll miss the landing, or the flyers will be gone by the time the road to take me there is found. But patience bears fruit. Its domed top reappears just above the tree line for a moment — long enough to betray its course — and I start off again. I'm closer now, and if my car had a hardtop I would not be able to see it. But I can look straight up. And there it is, close enough to see faces in the large wicker basket. I stop and turn off the key.

"Are you following us?" comes a call from above.

The car engine is silent and we speak in normal tones.

"Yes," I reply. "This light breeze makes it easy."

"When will you land?" I ask. They cannot tell me where. Only the wind knows that.

"Fifteen minutes more. Then we look for a field."

"Good luck," I say and step out of the car to wave.

"Will you join us?" they ask.

"Yes. I would like that," I say. "Thank you." This is a rare treat — invitation to share the traditional bottle of champagne at the end of a hot air balloon flight.

They drift away, I get back in the car and follow.

Half hour later, we are in an open field, freshly ploughed and fertilized for planting. The air is pungent. But no one complains as we sip the champagne and celebrate the landing.

New friends are sometimes made in the most unexpected ways. And friends have always been my priceless teachers. I learn about myself from them, but more important, I learn about the world we live in, the world of balloons in this case.

City Boy

"I wish I could go with you tomorrow," my godmother said. "It will be so much fun meeting your cousins. I haven't seen them since they were babies. You will have a great time."

I was not convinced. I had never been to a farm, had no idea what could happen to me there. Goats were bad enough, I knew. We kept one in Raseiniai, the small city where we lived. The milk and cheese were welcome, but getting butted from behind for no good reason was maddening. Chickens were more peaceful. Collecting eggs in the chicken coop wasn't all that bad even if I did have to hold my nose.

But farms? They had geese and ducks, dogs, cats and who knows what. Pigs, horses. Probably cows. I had learned to stay clear of the goat, but what would I do when faced with an angry bull?

Father made plans to take me along to visit his brother, my uncle Jonas. Uncle Petras and his family would also be there. They lived some 300 kilometers north of us, near the Latvian border, where my father was born. There, too, lived the rest of my father's family. I did not know anyone there. I had met uncle Jurgis' sons once, but I didn't remember them. Both were much older, ten years or more.

The three cousins on mother's side, I knew well. Uncle Mike's and uncle Kostas' families also lived in Raseiniai. I grew up with them. Arūnas, the older, attended the same school. Only uncle Kostas' daughter, Violeta, remained an enigma. But then, she was the only girl. Boy! was I in for a surprise at the farm.

We would travel by train — another new experience. But this I looked forward to. Travel, by any means, was an adventure. I wasn't so sure about farms.

"You will see country you've never seen," godmother said, smiling her golden smile. "The train is fast and you will see much more than you can in the city. Your cousins will want to know all

19

about it — your train trip, and about the city. They've probably never been on a train. They want to meet you, you know. They'll show you the farm and teach you new games."

Her gold tooth always held my attention when she smiled, and she smiled often. She was the only person I ever knew with a gold tooth. She must be rich, I thought, to have one. But her smile was more than golden, more than rich. She never failed to persuade me when she put her mind to it. Her perseverance, determination and devotion in all things, in fact, was testament to the respect she garnered among all who knew her well. I didn't. Not then. But it would come in time. And she would have my respect and admiration for all time.

Now, her efforts to put me at ease about the coming trip bore fruit before my visit ended. Only shy apprehension remained — about the farm, not the trip — for this was my first, and I looked forward to it with impatience. I didn't know then how many more trips I would take with godmother when I grew older, how many countries I would visit, how many wonders I would see.

Godmother had a gift for me before my visit ended.

"You'll need this tomorrow," she said as she handed me a small suitcase. "Here, put these keys in your pocket. Don't lose them."

I had never seen such a suitcase. It was about one quarter scale — exactly my size. Corners studded with leather reinforcements, a hinged carry handle and a snap lock with keyhole in front. A perfect miniature of the suitcase my father packed when he traveled.

"It is yours to keep," she added. "You'll need it later."

I was thrilled. My own suitcase! I didn't know what to say. Muttering my thanks, I already planned what would be packed in it before tomorrow's trip.

"It will keep your things safe on the train." She read my mind. And she smiled her golden smile.

Little did I know my godmother's wonderful gift would accompany me half way around the world. Little did I know it would be with me the whole way across Europe and cross an ocean in the years to come. And I would keep it with me for all

20

time. Little did I know it would one day be the only tangible reminder of her golden smile.

I opened it now to its checkered lining. There was a pocket in the lid for small things, small things my mind already listed for tomorrow. It really was just like the one my father had. It did not surprise me that she knew about the trip tomorrow. Always considered one of the family, she was also part of many things my parents planned for me.

"You'll have a great time. Trains are fun," she said.

Little did I know the many trains I would soon share with her to places I could only imagine, and those I could not. Little did she know the trains I would ride through a war's wasteland without her.

But now her enthusiasm was contagious. I looked forward to tomorrow, never mind the mystery of my first visit to a farm.

So, off we went, father and I. The train station in Vidukle was twenty kilometers away. It would take hours by horse and carriage, so father hired a taxi and I had my first ride in an automobile.

The small railroad station was noisy, but not very crowded. The noise echoed from the high ceiling of the airy building. People sat on slatted wood benches, their luggage on the floor at their feet. Others were at the ticket windows or standing in small groups, talking. Kiosks filled with knick-knacks, newspapers and books were all along the wall opposite the railroad tracks. Some even sold toys. They got my attention first, but father said there was no time for toys. I agreed. There was already more here than I could comprehend. At any rate, I felt that toys were now beneath me. After all, I was a traveler now, much too grown up for toys. My own suitcase in hand, I marched beside my father, as tall as he in my mind's eye.

Godmother was right. And we hadn't even boarded the train.

* * *

The woman sitting opposite father and me was knitting. Her head was down, chin on her chest, her hands moving methodically with the blue yarn as she worked. She never looked up. A thin strand of hair kept falling over her eye causing annoyed swipes with her hand to move it aside. She wore a hat rimmed in flowers and a vest over a dress striped in green. Her jacket was on her lap. Except for her hands she never moved. Her severe concentration seemed threatening. I was afraid to do something interruptive, and also kept still. I wanted to be somewhere else.

But I was safe. Father sat beside me and spoke occasionally with the man next to the knitter. He was her husband, and they were traveling as far as Šeduva, 100 kilometers short of Biržai, our destination. Much of the rest of their conversation was beyond my grasp.

Thoughts about what I should expect in Biržai already filled my mind and the foreboding knitter was forgotten. My cousins in Raseiniai were younger than I and, having shared infancy with them, they were no mystery — Violeta excepted. But she was only a girl. Older. Intimidating. But only a girl. Nevertheless, I watched her with deep envy. I envied her age. I wanted to be older — a grownup. I wanted to know what she knew. I wanted to know more. There was a certain guile in her I could not penetrate. She was the only girl in the close knit group of my other cousins, two close friends and me, with whom I spent most of my time playing. Perhaps she posed a challenge. Although I teased her no less than my cohorts, I already appreciated that she was different. Whether this was because she was a girl, I was not prepared to question. I just wanted to know more than she did, and was forever frustrated by her response that I was only a little whelp and didn't know anything.

My schoolmates were merely that — schoolmates — and their influence was insignificant at the time. Interaction with cousins and neighbors was largely trouble free. The adults — parents, uncles and aunts — were never far away. We played games long known to us and comfortable in their familiarity. Our elders were obeyed without question. It never occurred to us to challenge them. Rewards for this were frequent and ongoing. We enjoyed their love and attention. Their gifts were cherished whether in the form of toys, entertainments, or questions answered to build knowledge of the world around us. Even speaking only when spoken to, as we had been taught to do when with adults, had its advantages. And knowing more than our playmates was never a bad thing.

From time to time a special treat would come our way. One such, several times each year, was provided by uncle Mike's bees. He kept more than a dozen hives and cared for bees as one of his hobbies. We would all don head nets and carry a smoking wand to the hives. Once the bees calmed, honeycombs would be pulled out one by one, and carried in huge bowls to the house. While rendering the honey from the combs, we always got bite size pieces cut off to eat like candy. We chewed each piece to a soft waxy pulp. Spitting it out was a contest. We'd line up behind the porch railing and see who could spit the farthest. Size and consistency of the chewed wax was the important factor in winning. I didn't do badly, but never beat Arūnas, even though he was younger than I.

Violeta never participated, nor did she ever make fun of us when we did. She would just stand there, on the porch, watch and not say anything. She loved the honey as much as any of us, but spitting the wax the farthest was apparently not among her goals. It seemed to us, when it comes to honey, eating and spitting belong together. But Violeta always found a way of getting rid of the wax without anyone noticing how she did it. I was sure she swallowed it. But the only girl cousin I knew was a mystery. Perhaps it was only because she was older. Whatever it was, we boys all shared this opinion of her and I hoped my cousins on the farm were boys. I didn't know and it never occurred to me to ask.

The train stopped briefly in Šeduva. The knitter and her husband got off. Only father and I were in the compartment. I was relieved.

There were more hills after Šeduva. The country drifting by the train window was more interesting now. Forests were thinner and there were more farms. Endless fields of rye swayed in the wind in ocean-like waves like those I saw at Kuršiu Marės on our Baltic Sea vacation, an annual event since I was three. As I watched them glide by the window, I formed visions of what uncle Jonas' farm might be like and wondered if he kept bees on the farm. Maybe they made more honey than uncle Mike's.

We passed a pig farm. There was a big, black and white hog and little pink piglets rousting about in fenced pens right next to the rail line. I thought I could hear them. They didn't look all that great. I hoped uncle Jonas didn't have pigs.

"Don't be shy when you meet your cousins," my farther coached me. "They'll want to know about the city. None of them have seen one. Tell them what you know. Don't guess and tell them something that's not true. Come to me."

"Why haven't they seen a city?" I thought everyone knew about cities; only farms were unknown.

"They have their own school, and when they're not in school there is much work on the farm. There is no time."

"Don't they ever go places by train?"

"Only your uncle does. The children stay home."

Now it was clear this was a special treat. Even more special than uncle Mike's bees.

I wondered if I should ask questions about the farm. But why would I? I'll be there. I'll see for myself soon enough. Maybe I can ask my cousins. Will I know what to ask?

The train trundled along as morning passed into noon. The monotonous click-clack drone of wheels passing over rail joints soon lulled me to sleep. Pigs, goats, cows and horses changed places in my dream.

I felt a nudge to my shoulder and woke with a start.

"Hungry?" my father asked. "Here. Eat your bun. Here, a cucumber and blueberry tart with goat's cheese." He set the picnic basket on the seat between us and removed a jar of buttermilk, my favorite drink. I hadn't eaten since early breakfast. Dozing off on the train helped awaken the hungries. I ate with gusto.

When I was younger, going to bed for sleep at the end of each day was a frustration. What if I missed something important while I slept? Then I might know less than my peers. Now, as we neared Biržai, I slept again. But I already knew more than my cousins in Raseiniai, wondered if Violeta knew about farms. I'd have to ask her when we get home. It's just that she was always so difficult to talk to. She seemed standoffish and unsociable when it came to playing with us boys. I guess it was because we teased her unmercifully whenever one of the adults commented what a pretty girl she was. But then, she was only a girl, and older. Sometimes, when we gathered for uncle Mike's honey, she brought along a schoolmate. He was older than any of us and knew even more. Maybe I'd ask him. He was more approachable than Violeta. Perhaps, when I return, I'll know more about farms than they do. They might ask questions. What if I can't give the right answers? What then?

At father's next nudge to wake me we had arrived, and I no longer wondered what I had missed while sleeping.

Uncle Petras met us on the siding. He was older than my father, a slightly built man with a severe limp, who appeared to be in poor health and didn't have much to say. I thought there was something forbidding about him and later made it a point to stay out of his way. He led us to his hay wagon for our drive to his oldest brother's farm. I stood behind him and father, both seated on the driver's bench-seat. My short arms barely reached the high, slatted wagon sides. The slats were far enough apart that I would surely fly right through between them if thrown sideways.

Once we left the railroad siding, my suspicions were confirmed. I was jostled about mercilessly from side to side the whole way to the farm in the bumpy going. I held on tight, teeth clenched in anticipation of the worst, feet planted in a determined stance to stay on board the bucking hay wagon. Two furry-hoofed horses pulled us along at a slow, determined pace. Nothing like the briskly stepping horses and fast carriages I was used to at home. The animals were huge, as was the wagon. I wondered if all things on farms were bigger than they were in town.

No one greeted us. Farmers were busy people, just as my father said. Aunt Ona told us that her daughter, my oldest cousin, was away. She is the one I was destined never to meet. Because of her absence and uncle Petras' failing health, all his three daughters were helping at the farm. Uncle Jonas was working in the fields. That's why his younger brother came to the train station to pick us up. Visitors were no reason to interrupt farm work.

By long standing tradition the oldest son inherited the farm. Others, who were not needed there, were expected to make their own way elsewhere. My father was the youngest of eight, born five years apart. The first four died in infancy beginning in 1865. Of the four following, Jurgis went on to engineering and my father to pressed military service for the Czar, and Lithuania's Armed Forces later, when the Revolution ended and national sovereignty was restored.

Before Jonas and Petras took over my grandfather's farm, they went to America in 1910 to "make their fortune". They worked two years in the Pennsylvania coal mines and returned home well fed (so father claimed) but without any fortune.

Many disinherited sons went to America with the same goal in mind. Most of them never returned. Lithuanian coal miners' descendents still live in large numbers in the Scranton-Wilkes Barre coal mining country. Their Lithuanian communities still support their own churches and function as a respected ethnic minority in the area. But my two uncles chose to return and stayed on the farm when my grandfather died in 1918.

They were the last two uncles I had yet to meet. Now that I had, I didn't quite know what to make of them. They didn't look like my idea of coal miners, or farmers, for all that; not that I knew what coal miners or farmers looked like. Remembering godmother's words, I was more keen on meeting my cousins.

When the time came I wished I had stayed home.

There were no introductions. I was sent to the barn to help milk the cows. When I got there, the girl sitting on the milking taboret turned around. "Where did you come from?" she asked.

First I was speechless. Staring. When at last I found my tongue, I said I came from the train station.

"Who are you? What are you doing here?"

"I came to visit. They sent me here to help." I felt like a fool.

She stared at me with a questioning look in her eye. She was at least ten years my senior. Her look was what I was used to seeing in grownups. I was about to turn and run.

"Sit over there," she pointed to a hay bale and went back to milking the cow. But soon she talked while she worked.

"You must be uncle Motiejus' boy. Papa said he'd fetch you from the station."

And that is how I met the first country cousin. And she was a girl! And older. Almost a grownup. Now I knew I was leaving.

I stood to go.

"Get me that pail." It was a command. I reacted as I would to an adult, and immediately regretted it. But I did get the pail before I left the barn. As I walked out the door I heard whispered voices. Then two girls nearer my age blocked the way.

"Ha! Ha!" they laughed. "Where did you come from? What are you doing here?"

Apparently they had been listening and already knew who I was. This was deliberate teasing and was making me angry, but I had no idea who they were. I walked around them and ran back to the house.

A gaggle of geese was in my way. They hissed and chased me, pecking at my heels. The girls laughed loud enough to attract the adults' attention. I was mortified.

Father stood on the front stoop, watching. "Why you run from your cousins?" he asked.

I hung my head in shame and humiliation. There they were, my cousins, all girls! I hoped we would leave soon.

It was not to be.

On the third day of our visit a pig was to be slaughtered. This would have shocked me earlier, but by then I had learned to hiss back at the geese and gather cow chips and horse dung for fertilizer mix. If this had been winter, they would be used for fuel to heat the house. Boy! you think holding my nose to collect hen eggs was bad? How bad could pig slaughter be?

So far, no games like godmother promised. But this was about to change. Right after breakfast, we dressed in burlap, my two cousins and I. They were very serious about the whole thing. They seemed to know what they were doing, so I followed their lead.

"We have to catch the pig," Vida, the younger and two years my senior, explained. Dana said nothing, but took me by the hand out to the barnyard. I tried shaking her off, but she wouldn't let go. Girls!..

The pig was corralled in a large pen filled with sand. Uncle Jonas stood by the large wooden tripod in the center with a knife in one hand and a big wooden mallet in the other. The adults had gathered to watch. I wasn't sure I wanted to see this. Olė, the milkmaid cousin, poured something all over the pig. It squealed. So did the milkmaid. Girls!..

On her signal, Dana dragged me over the pen rail and we three charged the pig. Olė laughed with the grownups.

Once in the sand, I did my best to catch the slippery pig. I never knew pigs were so fast. I touched it once, that's all. I couldn't keep up with the girls. After many unsuccessful attempts, they cornered the pig at last and jumped on top of it, screaming and hollering and laughing all at once as they wrestled it down into the sand. I fell exhausted over their combined heap, trying to do my part.

The girls were strong. And they were quick. And I just ran around not knowing what to do until they pinned the pig to the ground. I doubt if my city cousins could have done it. I was impressed. If Dana would just have stopped taking me by the hand like a baby, we could have been friends. But Vida and I got along fine the rest of the day and the next. It's when I learned I could actually be friends with a girl. Wow!

"Don't you know how to make a straw whistle?" Vida quizzed me.

I shook my head. I never heard of such a thing.

"I do," and she showed me. After a few aborted tries, I made my own straw whistle, and even learned to how to use it. It worked!

Now, I owed her.

"I have a train. Dad made it for me," I countered.

It meant nothing to her. I picked up a stick and drew a train in the sand.

"What does it do?" she asked. I explained. She didn't understand. So, I told her about my train trip to Biržai.

"You're lying! Your dad can't make a train like that."

"No, no. It's a wooden toy train."

She was still puzzled. But now, we were pals.

Olė, the milkmaid, was beyond my years and I saw little of her our few days on the farm. As with uncle Jurgis' two sons, whom I had met earlier, the difference in ages made it difficult to find common ground. In my view, his sons were already adults. Narimantas was twelve years my senior and his brother Algirdas even older. Such was my luck with country cousins.

But my lasting memory of uncle Jonas' farm was the time shared with Vida in a field of sunflowers. We chased each other through Queen Anne's Lace underfoot, blowing our straw whistles until we fell breathless to the ground, huffing and puffing among the huge stalks in a forest of flowers bigger than our heads.

"They turn to face the sun, you know." Vida had a way of coming up with the strangest comments right out of the blue.

"What?"

"The sunflowers. You know? They always face the sun, and they bow down and close up after dark."

"Aw. You're crazy." I couldn't believe such nonsense. But Vida convinced me that sunflowers were living things, like all plants, and did stuff I never imagined.

I didn't think I would tell my city cousins about that one. It was one of those stories meant for one pair of ears, not many.

* * *

We took the train home the day before Friday, and Friday was a special day. When father was away, Grandma Marcė sometimes went to the farmers' market, often enough to have made a lasting impression on me. She walked across half the city to get there. It took most of the day. The little two-wheel cart was full when she started back and there would be baskets in the kitchen, filled with produce to be sorted, when I came home from school. Although I never volunteered, I didn't mind helping her with this task. It was another opportunity to learn things.

Marcė was a proxy grandmother to me — proxy, because she raised my mother after she had been orphaned early in life. She was my mother's aunt. Educated in Poland, she spoke the language fluently and was said to be more Polish than Lithuanian. But she refused to teach me Polish. I remember her as a strict disciplinarian, but always gentle and kind to me. She lived with us in Raseiniai and looked after me while my parents worked. From her I learned how to take care of our goat and collect eggs from the chicken coop. It was not uncommon for city dwellers to keep small farm animals. We had a constant supply of goat's milk and eggs.

I worked with her, sorting and cleaning the produce, until the time for homework was at hand. But Fridays I skipped homework whenever I could. There was, after all, a two-day respite before it was needed on Monday. Elementary school homework did not take much time and market day was a reminder that I could put it off.

Some Fridays father was at home, and on those days I went to market. Huddled on the back of his bicycle, I rode with him the distance grandma took hours to cover. A large reed basket was tied to the handlebar and I had a net bag in my lap.

The smell of potatoes, freshly dug from the earth, greeted my nostrils first as we entered the huge tent. They soon mixed with the aroma of fresh fruit lined up in rows on the counter. Squash of all kinds was laid out next to cucumbers and beets. When fishermen were there, the air was filled with ghostly fog from the ice covering their catch. The chatter of people crowded around the stalls mixed with the clucking hens, kept in cages where they laid eggs to be sold still warm to the touch. Dried pear slices, strung on long strings, swung gently from the overhead frames supported by tall trestles loaded with plucked and beheaded fowl, hung from string loops around their necks. Brown skinned smoked hams, the size of my upper leg, were suspended from sharp shiny hooks.

Much of this was still fresh in my mind from my uncle's farm. It felt good to be here, to know what to ask now that I had seen a farm where this great cornucopia of food came from. Tomas, the man who sold us ham, smiled broadly when my father told him I was at my uncle's farm the day before and knew where ham came from. I remembered the greased pig we chased in the pen and wondered who would buy its ham. I told him all about the slaughter and my part in catching the pig.

His wife Vanda sold bread at the same stall. Mother baked bread at home, so we never needed more. But Vanda always had a sweet roll reserved for me. This time, however, there was no pastry. This time, she had a special treat. She handed me a candied nut ball on a stick, wrapped in a wax paper cone.

I never left the farmer's market empty handed. There was always a special treat of one kind or another. Aldona, a widowed farmer who had been a friend of our family for years, was a sharecropper on Tomas and Vanda's farm. She wasn't there that Friday, but when alternating market days with Vanda, she often had a trick to show me which I would learn by repetition and dazzle my city cousins later. Some of my favorites were string designs weaved around my fingers to be made into unexpected patterns or tied into what looked like tangles and untied again with a quick move. All her tricks were slight of hand devices which required practice, so once I learned them, my audience could not repeat them even after discovery of how they were done. I valued this knowledge highly and looked forward to Fridays when I would see her again.

Wind

"Don't be in a hurry to get old. Play as long as you can" were words spoken to me, in response to my wish to be older and wiser, by the Gypsy with the Golden Smile before I understood what those words meant. Now that I do, I play — her advice taken — my games most likely not what she had in mind.

* * *

The angry roar is welcome. It conveys the health of my racecar. The riotous sound is not yet lost in the wake behind us. A few seconds later, when I come boiling out of the corner, it will be beyond my earshot. I will no longer know how well it sounds. Only by the seat of my pants will I be able to tell if the engine's heart skips a beat. Wind takes the upper hand in the open cockpit at speed and little else is heard until it relinquishes its claim to prominence when we slow down for the next corner.

But no matter. The car is a joy whether I feel it with my ears or by the seat of my pants. More often it is both. It is best then — the reward for driving a hard-edged car well.

Sometimes there is an urge to try something new. Perhaps delay the shut-off point a yard or two. Then the sound returns later, a fraction of a second — no more — and there is less time to react to the corner and clip its apex the moment it is due. The degree of wind interference with the exhaust note tells me if my speed is proper or if I've overstepped the bounds of better judgment.

I know what happens if I am late and miss the apex. I also know what happens if I'm early. But it's a mystery how it will go if I shut off and clip the apex as prescribed, but at a higher speed than prudent. Then wind can no longer help us, my car and me. Either we make it or we don't. If we don't, I will embarrass myself and insult my car — we slide or we spin. That's unacceptable. Better not to try more than one unknown at a time, for it is the unknown we fear most.

Sometimes the certainty of disaster induces preconceived fear. And sometimes it can be anticipated. Mine came in a friendly race with those who belong in that place where hard-edged cars dwell, and I did not anticipate it.

* * *

The grid has been set. We are lined up on the black ribbon of the macadam road, ready for the start. Twenty-eight of us in alternating rows of three and four. That I am in the first row is a miracle. My qualifying time has put me there. I drove my racecar like the wind, in tune with every move it made, with every weave through the fast corners, with every rise and fall of the undulating road. I'm not afraid of speed, only of standing still.

We await the green flag now, engines coming up to higher pitch as time draws near. Excitement of the chase is there. It is visceral, primal, elemental.

The starter's hand is in the air, index finger extended to remind us only ten seconds remain.

Then, the flag is up.

It drops.

My clutch foot slides off the pedal and I squeeze the power on, careful not to spin wheels. I lift to shift into the next gear, and ...

The engine dies!

The angry roar is gone, replaced by sounds of other cars leaving me behind. Trying to restart is fruitless.

The finger in the air flashes before my eyes. My ten seconds are gone. I sit up and put my arms up in the air — the signal that I will not move.

And then, I am afraid.

The packed crowd of drivers are passing left and right. I feel their wind as they flash by in clouds of smoke and waves of noise enough to wake the dead. The ground shakes. And I'm afraid.

They're gone as quickly as they came. Not one comes close enough to hit me. The fear of standing still subsides. At last I breathe again. My arms are still above my head, frozen in the sudden silence. But the fear is past.

Fear

My earliest recollection of fear is a dream. No... a nightmare. My grandmother died, or so it seemed when I awoke. In tears. It was so real. I visited her grave and she spoke to me. But I knew she was very much alive. Our last meeting was only days before. I could not tell my dream for fear it might come true. It must have shown, for mother worried and coaxed me into telling.

She kept it from me at the time — motherly concern I'm sure — but I learned later that grandma Marcė had died indeed, and on the very night I had my frightful dream. By then, because of war, we were already far away. She could not be persuaded to leave her home, and chose to stay, when father thought it best to move the family westward, away from what was later called "the blood flood", a term the invading Red Army richly deserved. The things I remember of that time still find a haven in my mind. They live within, immune to all eviction efforts.

This was the Russians' second coming. The first, three years before, I remember mainly because father wasn't home. We used my mother's maiden name more often than his, naïve of us though it may have been. To help insure our safety, father went a step further. His security had to be deeper than ours. He had been a colonel in the Lithuanian Army and now held high rank in the National Guard. He was also responsible for army recruitment before the Russians came, and continued this work after. Such posts were specifically targeted by the Soviet regime.

Russian suspicion of father's activities was confirmed by a co-worker. He was arrested by the NKVD (the later KGB), but held only long enough to sign an agreement to work as informant against my father. This he did under threats of harm to his family if he refused. The next morning he told my father what he had done. With this simple act, he risked his life to save another, just as he had saved the lives of his children by agreeing to carry out

NKVD demands. That man's selfless, honorable act gave my father time to make arrangements for going underground.

Farms and businesses were expropriated without compensation. Shopkeepers were being harassed as capitalists. People were being arrested without explanation. But the NKVD had not yet penetrated the underground resistance. Safeguards, such as members knowing only the local organization, and covers of normal occupation, denied them the critical information Russians needed to find their targets.

Going to ground was the most intelligent option for my father.

The question of armed resistance came to mind in some circles, but Lithuania's Army was never large enough to oppose a threat of such proportion and the German occupation had dispersed our armed forces and detained the officers. Opposition would have been ineffective and would have cost thousands more lives.

Neutrality was a considered stance during the German *Blitzkrieg* of 1940, but Soviet invasion gave scant opportunity for declaration. As a consequence, former members of our armed forces were hunted down during the second Russian invasion as they were during the first. Those not imprisoned, were deported to slave labor camps in Siberia. Officers were less fortunate. The Geneva Convention was never signed by Russia and was anathema to the Red Army. Lithuanian officers, who failed to escape, were subjected to all manner of horrors under the NKVD. Their mere survival during Nazi occupation arbitrarily rendered them collaborators and enemies of the state in Soviet eyes.

My father knew, along with every Lithuanian of his generation, Russian methods of occupation were an extension of the savagery that was the Bolshevik Revolution. Young men were pressed into the Czar's army before it began. Despite Czarist Russia's prohibition of books and all other Lithuanian publications, the literacy rate was 92%. In Russia it was 45%. It meant Lithuanian recruits were candidates for the officer corps. They were the first to suffer retribution when the Czar's defenses were broken. The *Immortals* and the *White Guard*, with which my father served, disintegrated. For every mark of rank on their shoulder boards, captured officers had a horseshoe nail driven into their shoulders.

By way of one of those miracles of survival, father evaded capture and rode to join a Lithuanian battalion forming to return home from central Siberia where they had been fighting the Bolsheviks. Delayed by a fierce winter storm, he was a day late. The day before, Russian troops overpowered the Lithuanians. Stripped of all their clothing, they were chased naked into a snowy field by mounted Russian cavalry armed with sabers, and hacked to pieces as they ran.

Now, their first invasion three years earlier, already showed their methods hadn't changed in the years since the Revolution, nor would they change after Nazi Germany's defeat.

Our neighbor came with bad news. Her husband had just returned from NKVD interrogation concerning their two children. Something happened in school, she said. Someone had turned them in. She wept, but her tears were cold with hatred. Their children were reported to have talked about going to church. That was enough to deport all four to Siberia.

The next day, the family was loaded onto trucks and disappeared.

The anxious cries of another neighbor are still fresh in my ears, her anguish vivid in remembrance. She rushed to our door for help no one could render.

"They took him away", she sobbed. "They're packing them into boxcars like cattle. Simukas, my Simukas! They took him." She wept uncontrollably, her whole body consumed with pain. "He has no food. I wanted to give him his gloves. They threw them away." She still held the gloves in her hands, shaking like leaves in the wind.

At the railroad station in Viduklė, the same one where father and I departed for my first visit to a farm, innocent people were shoved and prodded with bayonets into railroad cattle cars, packed in as many as could stand upright, shoulder to shoulder, with only the clothes they wore. Men, women and children, separated and together, were taken away by the thousands. No food, sanitation, or heat was provided. Many died long before the trains reached their frozen Siberian destinations.

This was the transport method later copied by Hitler to move masses of people to concentration camps in his attempts to wipe out the Jews. But the Russian counterpart came first. This model for Hitler was swift and sweeping with no regard to race or ethnic origin. Victims were chosen based merely on their work and cultural affiliation, including social clubs, church functions, government occupations, ownership of large farms or small businesses in the city, theater arts, and whatever else could be drummed up to include people in the deportation lists.

That we were not among them was a miracle. Father learned that our names were on a later list of those to be transported to Siberia, a list not yet released to the executors of those orders. His work, as an anonymous bookkeeper at a country girls' school on Adakavas estate, delayed inclusion in those lists. He stayed at a different home each night and carried his work with him. The school paid for his services off the record and did not know where he was staying on any particular night.

Among those who sheltered him was a Lithuanian Army lieutenant whom he knew well. He had connections to the underground resistance movement. Intelligence secured through those sources made it possible for father to avoid being in the wrong place at the wrong time. In return, he contributed to secret underground publications striving to inform the public about Russian lies and expose Soviet propaganda. The underground also provided means of communication between us, but we never knew where he stayed at any particular time. No one betrayed him.

Had we been on one of the deportation lists during that period, we most likely would have been separated. That we weren't was another miracle of survival. The lists contained the names of 800,000 people. But the Russians ran out of time. War returned to our homeland.

Before we buried our valuables, before we packed and said good-byes, were nights of fireworks we watched in awe and apprehension. I felt the apprehension not because I understood, but because it was so obviously real in the faces of adults around me.

I felt their fear. And so, I felt my own.

The sky lit up in flashes white and orange. Through a maze of madly crisscrossing search light beams aircraft dived headlong toward the ground, their sirens wailing their eerie howl. Dive-bombers (Stuka, I was told) did their work this way perhaps to strike fear into their targets even before the bombs struck. This was no ordinary bombing. This was a battle being fought on the ground, ground no longer far away. Not close enough to feel the shock, only to hear and see the flash of explosions, it was enough to understand why adult conversation was filled with apprehension and alarm, but not quite enough to separate fireworks from destruction in a child's mind.

Father already knew what must be done to protect us. But he wanted me to understand why we must go, leave home, leave school, leave friends behind, leave grandma and my Gypsy with the Golden Smile. I failed to fathom why they wouldn't come with us just as I failed to fathom why all this was happening to our family, our neighbors, our friends. But one day, I overheard a conversation. The woman said she would rather kill her own children than let them fall into Russian hands. It chilled me. I asked no more questions.

My father had spoken to me about war. I did not believe him. Then came the morning which would stay in my mind for all time. It was never his intention to have my earlier questions answered in the way they were, in the way I would never forget. Understanding would come later.

War's tide had turned and Nazi battles of retreat drew near Raseiniai where we lived. Soon, our homes would become a battleground. Time to depart was approaching faster every day. Father set me on his bicycle and we rode to a nearby farm to see about matters of our coming departure.

First to reach our ears were rumbling sounds from beyond the forested hills we were approaching. Soon they changed to the threatening sound of cannon. Plumes of black smoke rose in the distance. As we drew near, the noise grew louder. It hurt my ears. We dismounted atop a hill overlooking a forested plain across the Dubysa River, the same river where friends and I spent the warm summer days. It was not the same today.

There, in groups of three, five, eight and more, were tanks. Some gray and mottled in green camouflage, some all dark green with red stars on their sides, they moved about in blinding clouds of dust and smoke. Their gunfire felled trees as if a scythe had passed the forest. Trees cracked and splintered, ripped out by the roots, their branches flung crackling into the air. The forest burned. Grass was scorched black and smoking. The ground shook and vomited its soil up in the acrid air. Great clouds of dirty smoke erupted from the soil, hiding the carnage for only moments. Artillery shells whistled overhead. Enormous craters appeared where there had been trees. The river surface rippled with the shock. There were voices there, too, but insignificant — lost in the hellish din of battle. But also there were men. Soldiers — German and Russian alike — leaping in flames from burning and exploding tanks. Running for cover through the smoke to no avail, they died like candle flames caught in the wind.

Progressively more fearful as we watched, I cowered silently, holding my father's hand and knowing I was safe as long as that hand was within reach. No, his intent never was to scare me. His hand made that very clear. It would always be there, there to reassure and to protect me. And it would be there to protect all of us in the weeks, and months, and years to come. My head aswim in the unearthly noise, the horror of it all not yet quite clear in a child's mind, but clear enough why father said we had to leave. We would go away until all this is ended, he told me, until they came to claim their dead, to bury them and put everything back the way it was. And only then would we return home again.

But we would not return, and nothing would ever be the way it was.

We left the scene as soon as father thought it safe, but long before the battle ended. He said I must remember what I saw for we would never again see anything so fearsome.

I do remember. But he was mistaken. We would all live to see much worse.

Savages

Retreating to my room in fear, I heard loud voices speaking a language I did not know. Two Russian commissars were moving in. Regina, my live-in nanny while mother worked, was thrown out of her apartment and the two interlopers made themselves at home. Not happy with the apartment alone, they invaded the whole house, used all our facilities without asking, and ate our food. They never paid for anything. We were told to keep our distance and made to feel as intruders in our own home.

Father spoke to them in Russian, a language unknown to the rest of our household. I learned some of what was said years later. Without reluctance, both spoke of the good life in Russia, of all the great things there and the happiness of the people as if they lived in paradise. They repeated everything by rote instilled in them by the Soviet regime. When they discovered we had a telephone, father had to explain that anybody who wanted one had one in their homes. They found it hard to believe, and thought it incredible that even farmers had telephones, let alone indoor plumbing with hot water and electric lights. They called it capitalist excess.

Soviet priority was to crush all ideological subversion and prove communism superior. Every method, including murder and extermination, was used to that end. At the same time, everything of value found in Lithuania was seized and transported to their "paradise". Our telephone was taken. So were all my father's tools, even his wheelbarrow. Electric table lamps, a radio, mother's kitchen utensils, shoes. Wholesale looting by Red Army troops swept across the country. Banks were robbed, churches desecrated, art galleries vandalized, and museums stripped.

But for the time being, my concerns were elsewhere. When mother took me to the nearby park and playground, familiar for many months, the sight rendered me speechless. Grass was churned up by vehicle tracks, the ground pitted and scarred.

Trees were broken, their branches stripped of leaves, burned by campfires whose remains were still in evidence. The playground was destroyed and littered with tin cans and broken bottles. Human excrement was in evidence and trash was everywhere. The Red Army artillery brigade, which bivouacked there, had just departed.

Although I was too young to remember much more of the Red Army's first invasion, I heard stories told and retold when the second invasion loomed large and I was older. Those stories took on a new, forbidding tone each time I heard them. They were told by those who did remember. Theirs were stories not merely heard, but witnessed.

Invading Russian troops imposed horrors no one imagined. We lived in disbelief. We also lived in hope. But the reality of our plight pressed painfully on children even of my tender age. Stories were kept from us by parents concerned for our peace, but many were heard nevertheless.

* * *

The first woman was dragged outside. The family of the neighboring farm was brought at gunpoint to watch the punishment. She was thrown into the farm's shallow well. Armed guards stood watch as she died.

The other woman lived longer. She was raped first, repeatedly. Then, stripped naked, chased into a field of winter wheat and used as hunting target. No one dared interrupt the gunfire. The guards were Russian, a Red Army infantry platoon. It was said the women sent food to armed men in the forest. The farm was burned to the ground before nightfall.

The next day the men were found. They had been taken away before the women met their fate. Tied to trees with barbed wire, they died of bayonet wounds after losing their genitals to knives. One of the men was Tomas, who sold us ham at the Raseiniai farmer's market and heard my story about the greased pig. One of the women was his wife Vanda. Their sharecropper Aldona, who showed me string tricks, escaped unharmed but disappeared. No one knows what happened to her.

There were others we knew well. Some were friends, some neighbors. If some were family, we didn't know. They disappeared

42

without trace. Two returned twenty years later. They had been in a Siberian concentration camp. One died there.

The farm incident was not atypical. All farms suspected of helping supply the resistance were burned to the ground, cattle slaughtered, fields destroyed and people murdered. Rape and torture were condoned by Red Army leadership and repeated many times over. Alexander Solzhenitsyn wrote that the rape and killing of women was regarded as combat distinction in the Red Army. Josef Stalin's dictum of government, *"people fear death; they fear painful death more"*, was being upheld.

Captured partisans and their supporters were dealt with harshly and savagely by the Russians. Being arrested by the NKVD meant torture in basements of the large public buildings, converted for that very purpose when they were claimed by the Red Army. Such makeshift prisons were scenes of the most horrific interrogation methods ever devised. Missing fingers and nails pierced by hot wire were not uncommon. Eyes gouged out of their sockets and screws driven into victims' heads were atrocities systematically administered in prison interrogation rooms. At least one victim is known to have had a meat hook thrust through the soft tissue under his chin, then hoisted by the hook off the floor and left hanging until he died. *(GRRCL)*[*]

Bodies of prisoners murdered in this manner were dumped in the most popular public places, sometimes impaled on wrought iron fences or hoisted up a flagpole. These displays were meant to horrify onlookers and serve as deterrent to joining or helping the resistance.

There was also a more sinister purpose to these displays. Because all partisans operated under code names and carried no identification, they couldn't be tied to friends or members of their family. Their dumped corpses were watched by NKVD agents. Whoever reacted emotionally to the sight were immediately arrested and interrogated on the assumption they knew the dead. Many of them were tortured to extract information about the dead partisans' associates. One of uncle Mike's neighbors, whom we had known for years, came home after four days of captivity with every finger joint in both his hands systematically crushed with vise grips.

If these tactics discouraged resistance in many, they had the opposite affect on many more. But the Russians never let their guard down wherever Lithuanian partisans were known to be active. Their concern was well founded because armed resistance already had the support of the people, who provided it at great risk to themselves. Many supplied food, information, and new recruits. The dense forests served as necessary shelter in underground bunkers constructed to be virtually undetectable. Lithuanian partisans believed strongly in their cause. They only lacked one critical element to succeed — outside backing and the supply of arms and equipment. This they soon expected from the West. That it never came was a bitter disappointment of the entire nation. Support of the French Maquis by Britain paved the way to the success of D-Day, but similar support of Baltic partisans against Soviet oppression was politically incorrect. Russia was one of the Allies.

The men and women at the farm were only four of the thousands of resisters who met similar fate at the hands of the Russians. Many were non-combatants. Only some who fled survived. Some chose to return after another 15 years — certain, by then, the danger had passed. They were mistaken.

I ended up in the United States, as far from Russian terror as one could go in the 1950s, and my safety was still not assured.

Wind

The screen flickers with images of fierce tribesmen loosing spears at a man tied to a stake. Their long black hair, adorned by traditional gilded fan headdress of the stylized South American native, whips about their somber faces in the strong breeze blowing across the arid plain. Dark, stormy eyes reflect their merciless demeanor as they continue their gruesome task. This is a Hollywood "historical" epic — contrived story of Spain's conquistadors in their newly discovered land — entertainment.

I get up and leave the dark theater.

The sun outside is blinding. I cannot afford sunglasses. What small change I had was needed for the movie ticket. But that is important. With Hollywood's help, learning English is much faster. And learning English is important now that I am in America.

But Hollywood is not my only teacher. Three times a week I attend an English class for foreign language speakers, given in a public high school on the other end of town. The city bus which takes me there does not pass near where I work. I must transfer to another at the movie theater. Sometimes the bus takes a half hour or more to arrive. And sometimes the bitter winter wind is much too cutting to endure needlessly. That's when the time in the theater is well spent. The feature is continuously restarted with a pause only long enough to rewind the film. It does not matter at what point I walk in.

After a year, my English is passable. Another year, and it's comfortable. Hollywood helps. Soon I feel ready to tackle a job with language skills prerequisite.

It is not so easy for my father. He works as cabinetmaker now — a skilled craftsman in the carpentry trade — skill acquired out of necessity in another war, of another time. Although he likes to work with wood and does it well, it is not what he was trained for. His life is no simpler now than it has ever been. Childhood spent on a farm and boyhood under the press of Czarist rule hardened his resolve. Military training, forced on him at his maturing age, taught discipline, self reliance, determination, and a will to resist with integrity.

Later, in his own country's service, free from Russian oppression, he earned recognition and respect of his peers through patriotic work devoted to the defense of our homeland. This did not prepare him for the "American Dream". His fluency in five languages did not include English, and there was no time to learn. But my adult life had just begun, and I could afford the time to enjoy the luxury of learning. Nevertheless, he is my hero, one of the few who stand untarnished in my heart.

My transfer bus comes. I sit by the open window and breathe the cool afternoon air. My trip homeward is filled with thoughts of soldiers convinced of their just cause to resist and subdue Spanish invaders who robbed them of their gold. Did Hollywood get it wrong?

Knowing right from wrong is not always easy. What may be wrong for one may be the chosen good for another. But I know my heroes. And I know their erstwhile cause, their motives, and their sworn allegiance. And I know they were not wrong.

Hero

He was the man of steel. He stood, head held high, in front of the splendid formation of his troops. Chin out in regal bearing, and strong, in a face evocative of classic Greek gods. His countenance spoke of energy and power held on a leash until the need to use it was at hand. His sword was bared, held upturned at his side *per pale* along his right shoulder, the bill of his peaked officer's hat drawn low to shade his eyes, the medals on his chest glinting proudly in the morning sun.

It was the culmination of a November parade to celebrate Armed Forces Day. My father, too, was on the same parade ground before the thousands gathered there. But this day did not belong to him. It was my godfather's. It was his troops that thousands came to honor, his achievements to praise. Today, he was my hero.

He was an officer who lived through the same firestorms which my father had survived. Ahead in years and rank only by fraction, he had endured, along with father, the roller coaster ride through upheavals no less daunting than a world war, a foreign revolution driven by misguided ideology, and the rebirth of their own country. They reveled in her success now, rightly proud of their part in her resurrection. Together they had faced adversity and stood side by side through hardship no boy could imagine. But today they were my heroes.

There now, godfather stood at the head of his men. Proud. Strong. Invincible. That he was chosen as role model for me soon after I was born did not surprise me when I made that deduction years later. There was a reason he was my godfather.

"What will you be when you grow up?" as people are wont to ask boys of my impressionable age, was a question I always had a ready answer to. "A soldier, like my father," I would say. "That's what I will be." It made no difference who my role model was. Father was always there.

Although, eventually, soldiering I did go, I went not because I was role model driven or because it was my aspiration, but because mandatory draft of the country where I chose to make my home, and in whose forces I served, required it. It was an honorable obligation which I welcomed and which my father and godfather approved with pride.

During Red Army's first occupation, godfather was imprisoned by the NKVD. Like many officers detained by the Russians, his high position and his rank targeted him for the most cruel tortures. We did not expect to see him again. We did not expect him to survive.

I never knew him well. He was a figure to be admired at a distance. His role model never took root in me. Nevertheless, he was my hero. Forged from stories about him and national recognition earned for his work, my perception of godfather was based in awe. When he was arrested, I was crushed. Perhaps he was not invincible after all.

Our military and political leaders were first. Their homes were ransacked, the people rounded up. All across the country, at exactly 2 a.m., on June 15, thousands were dragged from their beds. Women, children, elders. 32,000 in a single night. They were herded into railroad cattle cars without food, water or sanitation. They were our doctors, lawyers, academics, clergymen, teachers, scientists — the educated intelligentsia, the nation's leaders and inspiration, the very core of our national soul. Many died before reaching their destinations in Siberia. Most others died there. Few returned.

Systematic ethnocide had begun. It was repeated long after the war ended — in 1946, 1948, 1949, 1951 and 1953, a full eight years beyond the peace accords. 300,000 more were lost to the boundless wastes of the Siberian wilderness. Lithuania was to be repopulated by Russian immigrants, the illiterate mob. It was an example of the Russian concept of government, one of Byzantine power over disarmed and speechless masses reduced to subservience.

Even in defeat, the Russians were to be feared. Terrorism of demonic proportion was practiced routinely right up to the last day before German troops entered the country. The Rainiai massacre is only one example of practices carried out across all the Baltic States.

Evidence of the Katyn massacre in Poland is well known, but that of Rainiai remains obscure and bears repeating. Unlike their work at Katyn, the Russians did not stop with execution by gunfire at Rainiai. As prelude to Russian retreat, on the night of 24/25 June 1941, the entire prison population of political detainees held near Telšiai was loaded onto trucks and moved to the nearby forest for reasons no civilized mind could imagine.

Four days after the Red Army's departure and Nazi incursion into Lithuania, the forest of Rainiai was searched for the prison survivors. None were found. Their bodies were exhumed from the four lightly covered mass graves dug in the forest floor. Authorities prepared a report of the findings. They included clear evidence where the victims were tied to trees still showing their blood on bark frayed by struggles to break their bounds. Most bodies still had rags stuffed in their mouths and tied in with rope to stifle their screams. Among other evidence of unspeakable acts of torture was proof of bayonet wounds in the arms and legs, gouged out eyeballs, crushed genitals, ears and tongues cut off, evisceration, nails driven into the skull, and skin flayed off the back and set afire. Mutilation was so extreme, that only a third of the bodies could be identified. *(GRRLC)* *

International Military Tribunal at the Nuremberg trials did not include investigation of these massacres or any other war crimes committed by the Russians. The Big Four divided prosecution of the trials in the following manner: Americans were responsible for investigation of conspiracy to wage war, the British took on treaty violations and crimes on the high seas, the French were tasked with investigation of crimes committed in Western Europe, and the Soviets with crimes committed in Eastern Europe. Needless to say, the Russians were never brought to trial. British and American efforts to conceal and withhold evidence of Russian guilt and avoid the embarrassment of their wartime ally being tried alongside the Nazis were satisfied.

After years of blaming the Germans for the crime, Russia denied their responsibility for Katyn until 1990. No such admission is forthcoming for Rainiai and countless other horrors in the Baltics.

Rainiai was only one of many reasons to flee. Yet, reluctance to leave home, to leave the life we had, and everything we knew, was strong and lasting. Three years would pass before leaving home was no longer up for discussion. And then we fled.

Twenty years later, I received a letter. My godfather, too, survived. We were all in America then. In the envelope was a photograph. An old photo of an old man. The man's face was twisted to a swollen jaw. The scored, leathery skin was drawn tight over gaunt cheekbones pointing to cracked and swollen lips. The short-cropped hair was missing patches down to a forehead creased in welts not yet healed. An ugly stubble covered his face, a face too scarred to be cleanly shaven. The sunken eyes stared haughtily out of their hollow sockets into the camera, their immense weariness penetrating the bleak façade and transfixing the observer.

In his letter my godfather mentioned the photo saying only that he sent it to me so I would always remember who our enemies are. I looked at the picture a long time. It was a photograph of my godfather as he appeared when released from the Russian prison by the arrival of new invaders from Germany. He was 48.

I still look at that picture from time to time. And in spite of its bleak visage, his aristocratic bearing, commanding gaze, and strong, graceful posture is embedded in my memory for all time.

And he is still my hero.

And I know who our enemies are.

* * *

Eleven years after I received that letter, father went to visit his widow. She gave him the hand written journal of my godfather's captivity. She told him it was intended that my father have it. Although no one indicated that it be published, I include an excerpt here as personal testament to Russian savagery endured by people subjected to the Soviet regime.

My translation cannot convey the horror with which I first read the original:

> ... I was thrown into a 3 x 3 meter windowless cell. From the high ceiling hung a single bare light bulb. The cell had cement walls and a pitted cement floor with a small drain hole in the center. There was no furniture of

any kind. The hole in the floor was obviously too small to function as a facility for the calls of nature. I was certain interrogation under torture would begin soon.

I was mistaken.

No one came to the cell and nothing happened. After many hours of leaning against the damp wall and trying to get someone's attention to bring me water, my weariness compelled me to lie down on the cement floor. It was not restful. Pacing the three strides across the cell only increased my thirst, but the walls were so damp, I could lick their moisture with my tongue.

After three or four days, I lost track of time. There were no windows and no activity outside my door. It was impossible to separate night from day. The light in the ceiling was always on. I had not had any food or water since my arrival and began to feel weak. But I did not want to give in to laziness. Pacing back and forth like a caged animal was not very constructive, but gave me some relief from boredom.

When I heard the bolt on the outside of the door slide open, I knew torture would begin. Three armed guards entered the cell. Two of them seized me by the armpits and manhandled me down the hallway. The third one followed, prodding me with a club.

The room to which I was taken was large. It, too, had cement walls and a pitted floor. At the far end, behind a small desk, sat a man in NKVD uniform with major's marks on the shoulder boards. Behind him stood two others in civilian clothes. The three guards remained in the room. The major told me to sit down on the chair in the center of the room. He spoke Russian. I told him I didn't understand. He continued in Russian. I understood him perfectly, of course, but I demanded an interpreter. One of the men behind him spoke Lithuanian. I sat down and asked for water. My request was granted. There was a glass of water already on the desk, probably there for this very purpose.

Interrogation began with endless praise of the communist system and the Soviet quality of life. It was *repeated as if by rote. This went on for some time. Then I was accused of willfully working against the Soviet system. The major asked me to name persons who worked with me. Where were they hiding? Which ones were partisans? Where were the officers under my command? When told that I didn't know, he stood up and pounded the desk with his fist, indicating the file folder on the desk and telling me all the information was there and that I was lying.*

I told him that as a prisoner of war, I was to be treated according to the Geneva Convention and owed him no more than my name and rank. He said I was a bandit and a criminal, and the Geneva Convention did not apply, as Russia never signed it. He also told me to cooperate voluntarily or methods would be used to force cooperation. It was abundantly clear that whatever I did or did not tell him would have no affect on my fate as long as I was in the hands of the NKVD.

When I said I had nothing to tell him, one of the guards behind me reacted to his nod and struck my shoulder with the club. The shock of pain immobilized my arm when I tried to block the next blow. It was then I realized my wrists were still shackled as they had been since my arrival 4 or 5 days ago. I idly wondered how I managed to relieve myself in the cell with hands shackled and nothing to clean myself with.

Blows with the club were followed by kicks to my shins. Then I was picked up by my armpits and marched out of the room. When returned to the cell, the stench of my own waste took my breath away. Apparently, cleaning the cell was not in NKVD's plans.

Later, what must have been the following day, a metal bowl was pushed in through the small floor level opening under the door. It contained an odorless, grey, syrupy substance. It took a few puzzled moments to realize it was meant to be food. I dipped my fingers into it. The consistency was that of thick glue and the taste was reminiscent of potato broth.

By my estimation, I had spent about 8 or 9 days in the cell. During that time, deprivation of sleep was enacted by periodic clanging and loud bell ringing just outside the door, interspersed at odd intervals by the light in the ceiling flashing on and off. I was tempted to break it with the metal bowl, but then there would be glass on the floor in the dark. Lack of food was making me very weak, but the bowl was returned the next day, after I had pushed it back out. It's contents was usually the same, but one day there was a slice of rye bread floating in the watery broth.

The same three guards took me to the same room. There was a different man behind the desk, also in NKVD uniform, but no marks of rank. I was told to sit on the floor. There was no chair. The questions were the same. I was accused of banditry and subversion. When I objected, pointing out that I was an officer of the Lithuanian armed forces at war and must be treated as a POW, I was kicked and beaten with rubber truncheons until I lost consciousness.

I came to when water was poured on my face. Dragged bodily out of the room, for my legs would not support me, I was taken down the hall and shoved through another door. The small room smelled of tar. Two men dressed in overalls stood in the middle of the floor where a large drain was centered under a meat hook dangling from the ceiling. It was laced through my shackles and I was hoisted up to just short of reaching the floor with my toes. The pain in my shoulders was extreme. One of the men put a canvas bag over my head and face blinding me.

Suddenly there was sharp pain in my toes; so sharp, that it took a moment to realize they were hit with something very hard and unyielding. A few seconds' respite and the blow to my toes was repeated, again and again. I stubbornly thought that if I didn't satisfy them by crying out, they would stop. They did.

Then, the bag was ripped off my head and a flood of cold water hit my face. I couldn't draw a breath. I couldn't see.

When I opened my eyes the two men were facing me, each with a bucket in hand. They appeared to be in a fog. When they lowered me to the floor and released the hook, I passed out.

When I came to, a third man was in the room. He wore a doctor's smock, was bending over me, and held a hypodermic needle. He backed away, leaving me on the floor. Apparently, whatever was in the hypodermic vial had already been injected. I felt relief coursing through my body. There was no pain. When I was picked up again, I could even put weight on my feet. I couldn't remember how I hurt my toes or where I lost my shoes.

Returned to the interrogator, I was too weak and confused to answer questions. He said he was tired of playing games, and the next time things would get serious. Before throwing me back into the cell, the guards beat me in the hallway until I couldn't move. Back in the cell, I vomited on the floor which was still covered in blood and excrement. I was sure death was near. When the drug wore off, the pain prevented any thought of rest. I was so weak I could no longer stand.

Some days later, the same major asked the same questions, adding that he could personally enact my release if I cooperated. When I repeated my previous statements, he accused me of inciting armed opposition to Red Army occupation forces. When I pointed out the contradiction of these claims, which established my POW status farther, he said he had information regarding the arming of partisans, whom he called bandits, and my involvement in that enterprise as criminal activity against the state. This gave me a clue to the extent of his knowledge, and armed me with ability of filtering my replies to what he expected to hear. That I could mislead him in this manner in the future renewed my strength.

Similar interrogations continued over many weeks, usually 3 or 4 days apart. Additional accusations were disclosed as material for them was collected. Conditions of my imprisonment did not change. But after one interrogation session, I was in for a surprise. When returned to my cell, I found the floor had been hosed off. It explained the purpose of the small drain hole. Although the accumulated bodily wastes had been removed, the stench was as strong as ever. The hosing left water everywhere. The cell was now as damp as a swamp. It meant I would not be able to stay dry if I laid down on the floor.

Breathing was progressively more difficult without pain and coughing. I lost a great deal of weight. Malnourishment rendered me too weak to pace the three strides it took to cross the room. I still wore the same slacks and ripped shirt in which I arrived at this hellhole. They were in tatters. I had not had enough water to wash and any kind of sanitation was not possible. My beard was beginning to itch from infestation of lice. There was no heat in the cell and my spasmodic shivering was more and more frequent as time passed.

I eventually lost track of the number of interrogations over the remainder of my captivity. They continued with variations, always with additional disclosures of my crimes against the Soviet state. But I grew better armed by perception of the limits of their knowledge the longer they held me captive and consider myself fortunate that I could not help them.

My godfather, Colonel Pranas Saladžius, Supreme Commander of Šaulių Sąjunga (Lithuania's national guard) endured three months of NKVD torture before commencing a life sentence in a hard labor camp. When released by the arrival of Nazi Germany's troops, his health was ruined. He did not live long enough to regain it.

I later read my father's account of his own captivity and imprisonment in Omsk by the *Cheka* (predecessor of NKVD) during the Revolution. Russian methods of incarceration and interrogation had not changed. His account was exactly the same as my godfather's 24 years later.

Wind

The dew filled air changes density as I ride through it in the dawn's already tired light. I feel it readily on my hands and face in the cooling breeze a motorcycle at speed generates. The cool air gives way to a warm pocket here and there. They are less frequent when I'm in the shade of tall pines bordering the road. The strong pine scent takes over then. But that doesn't last. Out in the sun again, I feel the heat rising as the morning wears on with dawn's demise on the horizon.

The sweet aroma of honeysuckle overpowers all else the wind can offer. I inhale its intoxicating air. I do it now, for in another moment it is gone — swept away by the pungent rush of fertilized fields.

My ride is ever changing. I feel I'm part of the world I'm in. I ride not through it, as an observer, but within its light, its densities, its moods. I belong here, in this wind my swift wheeled horse creates. But I must be vigilant. My spirited wheeled horse does not forgive mistakes not of its making.

I have no destination. Not yet. Just heading north until I see a likely patch of paradise. Perhaps paradise is not north of here. Perhaps I'm going the wrong way. But then, perhaps I'm not. Maybe the Eden that I seek is not worth finding.

It doesn't matter. Sooner or later I'll find it, whether it's worth it or not. When I do, I'll stop. Spend some time. If paradise is not what it's cracked up to be, I will go on. For I'm prepared.

My saddlebags are filled with cheese and wine, and bread my erstwhile love had baked to see me through paradise that may have fallen short of its reputation. The tent is folded and strapped onto the pillion, its poles extending under my left knee. I have a small camp stove and a foam pad to sleep on. If Eden does not provide, I can fend for myself.

I have seen the coast, Key West to Newfoundland, this way. It's taken longer than the bread maker could cope with. I lost her long before my paradise was found. In fact, I never found it. My search was in the wrong place, for paradise was never of this world.

Departure

Camping was a favorite diversion as I toured the East Coast of the U.S. by motorcycle. It later endeared itself to my wife who excelled at provisioning for and planning camping trips in the early years of our marriage. Thanks to her efforts and superb culinary talent we always traveled in relative comfort so far as camping can be comfortable at all.

A tent pitched under a large blue tarpaulin to farther protect us from the elements was a welcome idea. Our *blue sky*, we called it, rain or shine. Small innovations in cooking over bonfire, roasting corn and potatoes in the hot coals, and breakfast over an alcohol stove — even *Sterno* (canned cotton soaked in petroleum jelly) — were not new to me, and certainly not novel to the farm honed woman I married.

We enjoyed the Finger Lakes this way one year, Niagara or Nova Scotia the next, or Carolina's Outer Banks, Nags Head, Atlantic seacoast, the New England mountains, Acadia's islands, and countless points south and west of my newfound home in America. But leaving home for an extended period wasn't a welcome diversion in my childhood years, nor was camping in the wilds. It was a condition of survival forced on us by war.

* * *

Before decision was finally made to leave, disturbing events around our home in Raseiniai were more and more frequent. While under German occupation, in the summer of 1943, two German officers were killed without provocation, it was said. They had just left the restaurant where they had dined, when two shots rang out just outside my father's office window in the city. A young Lithuanian soldier, who had been conscripted into the home guard by German authorities, apparently sought revenge for whatever wrong he or his family may have suffered at the hands of the invaders. He hid in wait across the street behind a picket fence and killed them both, a single shot each. Then, a third shot was heard.

He was found dead behind the picket fence.

To avoid prosecution, or perhaps to prevent German reprisal against the community, his third shot was through his own heart. Nevertheless, apprehension and fear of reprisal swept over us, fueled by precedent in similar circumstances elsewhere, when innocent residents were summarily executed for any show of resistance to German authority. The commandant, in this case, did nothing beyond the usual investigation. To avoid further bloodshed, funeral of the two German dead was attended by a representative number of residents from the community.

Warnings were posted everywhere that any opposition to the German Army or infraction of rules set down by the military command were punishable by firing squad. Nevertheless, hopes were high that Lithuania's provisional government would be recognized and independence returned. But the new occupiers of our country were no better than the Russians. And we knew that the enemy of our enemy was not always our friend. The later hope was that when war ended — it couldn't last too much longer — independence would be restored. *"After all, Germany is a civilized nation. We'll have our government back."* How naïve we were...

Feeding ourselves was becoming more and more difficult. Coupon controlled limits to which we were bound provided rations insufficient to feed our family of four. Even if they hadn't been reduced as time went by, food stores could no longer satisfy even those reduced rations. It was especially hard on city dwellers like us. We grew our own fruits and vegetables, kept poultry and a goat. These were bartered for work and furniture we could do without. Father built a smoke house at our home, for when the pigs at uncle Jonas' farm were slaughtered the meat could be preserved longer.

This way eggs, milk, and meat could supplement what little we received for food coupons and was just enough to keep hunger at bay. But bread, grain, and flour were unavailable or reserved for German military. It meant a lengthy trip to a farm owned by relatives and many ingenious ways to hide the goods received there. German inspectors were diligent in their searches of every home in the community, because their troops were only marginally better fed than we.

On one occasion we overlooked a loaf of bread in plain sight on the kitchen table when the inspector walked in. Quick thinking on my father's part saved the day. He offered the loaf to the inspector with unspoken understanding that nothing would be said. Nothing was. We knew such favors would not be repeated.

One morning, on Saturday, the Jewish Sabbath, we saw men from the synagogue next door, who in better times brought us fresh bagels, being marched off under armed guard to work on the construction of a landing strip begun by the Red Army three years earlier. They were kicked and prodded with rifle butts, cursed and beaten if they didn't move fast enough. We were appalled by the inhumanity of the German guards. It was heartbreaking to watch helplessly, but there was nothing we could do to help them.

This continued daily. There was no time for the men to prepare food in quantity enough to feed everyone at the synagogue. Father began prearranged climbs over the wall at night to donate what little we could. Harking back to my earlier adventure at trying to find out what was behind the stone wall, he climbed it now on a ladder kept hidden in the hedge when not in use. Overt contribution of food to the synagogue would have raised suspicion of how we had enough to do such a thing. Way beyond that was that helping the Jews was an automatic death sentence if caught by Nazi authorities. The synagogue was under constant guard and scaling the wall in daylight was akin to suicide.

Then, one day, the men did not return.

Anti-Semitism was a phenomenon we could not imagine before the German occupation. Nazi barbarism knew no bounds. Working with the Nazi exterminators of Raseiniai's Jews was a local murderer serving a life sentence for killing his own mother and boiling her butchered remains in a kettle to hide the evidence. He was released from prison for the very task of extermination. When the Red Army returned, the entire community was accused of collaboration with the Nazi regime to exterminate the Jews. We were threatened with deportation and worse. Everyone expected imminent arrest.

The whole idea was inconceivable to us. Vilnius, our capital city, was known as "Little Jerusalem" (one district still bears the name Jeruzalė). Businesses owned by Jews thrived there for generations. They were the descendents of artisans invited by Lithuania's rulers in the 14th century. They stayed 600 years because they were in a country which embraced immigrants of all creeds. In 1939 our government guaranteed safe conduct to Jews who fled from Poland and Austria to escape Nazi persecution. How could all this be so misconstrued?

Anna and Bella Levin, the Jewish sisters whom we knew very well, had a watch and jewelry store in Raseiniai. When they first established their business, they rented the apartment in our house, shared mother's kitchen, and were generally treated as part of the family. When they later bought their own house, they gave us several watches and gold rings as parting gift. We stayed in close touch with them after they moved out. The Nazis seized their house and their entire store inventory was sent to Germany. Anna and Bella disappeared without trace.

These events, and many others like them, were still not enough to compel people to leave their homes. When word came of the German defeat at Stalingrad and then Hitler's final disaster at Kursk, talk of departure took on a new urgency. By mid-summer of 1944 reconnaissance battles at Lithuania's eastern borders had begun. Russian aircraft were seen flying west over the city. Tank battles drew nearer every day. Russian paratroopers were in Biržai, robbing my uncles' farms a mere 300 kilometers northeast of Raseiniai. German retreat began in earnest. There was no more time.

Russian bombs fell on our city even as final preparations for departure neared completion. Although the attack missed our neighborhood by only a mile, we never found out who the people were that perished in the bombing. There was no time. War was no longer remote, no longer an abstraction.

Bomb craters swallowed houses. Burned, gutted, and black with soot, buildings shed a grey dust carried by the wind. Rooms disgorged their contents as if disemboweled. Dead horses lay in the street. We already knew Germany was beaten and in shambles worse than our own towns. But we chose the bombed and burning

Germany to our west over the Red Army hurtling toward us from the east.

A small group of neighbors and acquaintances made plans to travel together. Strength in numbers was thought to be an advantage. It was later discovered the opposite proved to be true. But at the time, it seemed like a good idea.

Options were limited. The only available means to move westward was walking, on horseback or horse-drawn wagon. If clothing, bedding, food, and shelter for an extended time were to be brought along, walking was out of the question. Horseback travel for a family of four meant three or four horses would be needed. That, too, was unrealistic. That left travel by wagon.

Father wanted to visit the nearby farm, where we often bought produce, and talk about our departure plans. He hoped the farmers had ideas we had not thought of. It was a beautiful, sunny day and he took me along for the outing. I rode pillion behind him on his bicycle. After we had been on the road a while, and just before we reached the farm, he suddenly called for my attention.

"Hold on tight!" he shouted.

I hugged his waist as hard as I could as the bicycle went teetering down the ravine into the drainage ditch bordering the road. We fell off and he pushed the bike into the cattail patch without rising.

"Stay down," he whispered and rolled over me. "Keep quiet."

I heard noises in the nearby woods — sounds of people running. Then the roar of motorcycles approached our hideout. The running stopped. Machine gun fire burst out of the woods. It was so close, my teeth chattered. I wanted to dig myself deeper into the ditch.

We lay without moving or making a sound for a long time. We heard voices in a language I did not understand. Then were attempts to restart the now silent motorcycle. In time, it started and there was no more noise and no more voices. Father looked over the edge of the ditch. Then he stood up to reclaim our hidden bicycle. I stood up too, dirty and shaken, wondering what had just happened.

When we climbed out of the ditch we saw a motorcycle and sidecar turned over on the road, one of its wheels bent and broken.

There were four dead bodies near the wreck. They were German soldiers. What I didn't see, and only heard, was an ambush of two German sidecar outfits, one of which was restarted and taken away by the attackers. We could still see them in the distance. They were heading for the farm. The language which I didn't understand was Russian. Father said they were probably advance reconnaissance troops dropped by parachute.

We mounted the bicycle and started back.

Father and uncle Mike, my mother's younger brother, began canvassing other farms for horse and wagon. The search continued several days as the war front approached. No longer distant, artillery fire could be heard daily. We packed what minimum was sure to be needed for survival while we waited for my father and uncle to return. They returned each day without a horse and wagon. Most were lost to the retreating Germans. The ready means to escape the Russians was taken from us. Another way needed to be found.

Luckily, closer investigation within the group revealed a member who was a widower, traveling alone in a double-hitch wagon. The small wagon was open, but had very high sides. A willow bow frame for a canvas roof was added for weather protection. He agreed to take our family and belongings if we could get another horse — he had only one. A chestnut mare with a white star on the forehead was procured from the friendly farmers who supplied us with bread and grain earlier. We could now join the group and prepare for departure.

To pay for all this the wagon was loaded with our chickens and geese, a generous neighbor's pig, our goat, clothing we would no longer need, and the rest of our furniture. This was taken back to the farmers who gave up their horse to help a group of city slickers they hardly knew. They insisted our small contribution was worth more than their horse and grain, and gave us smoked sausages and hams, several loaves of rye bread, flour and cheese. They also insisted the pig be slaughtered. The meat was salted down and sealed in large glass vats. Hay carried for horses was to be used for bedding.

On someone's advice, mother retrieved a set of 12-place silver dinnerware, and sewed into the linings of our overcoats. Moving gems, silver, and gold across borders was illegal.

By now, the group had grown. There were 8 wagons, 14 horses, and 33 people — a wagon train. Friends, neighbors, and family gathered to bid their goodbyes. There was always the hope we would return soon, but this could also be the last time we would see each other. We etched gestures and voices indelibly in our minds.

After an early breakfast, our last at home, on July 11th, 1944, our band rolled southwest on the road to East Prussia like a gypsy caravan, and our seven-year camping trip began.

Left behind, on a five acre lot at #8 Ligoninės gatvė (Hospital street), was our fully furnished four bedroom wood frame house with a one bedroom apartment, a barn and three additional outbuildings, flower and berry gardens, and orchards of apple, pear and cherry (property worth well over $500,000 today). Valuables were buried in the ground under the floor of the sauna hut where I once hid from the devil. They included the family silver, mother's jewelry, rare gold coins, and father's military decorations and their documents. This was done to protect these treasures when war reached our home. We were certain we would return when it ended.

All our worldly possessions, to be taken along and loaded on the wagon behind our seats, were packed in three large trunks and six suitcases, including the one I received as a gift from the Gypsy with the Golden Smile. Remaining space was filled with food for us and hay for the horses.

Left behind were also our friends, our schools, our families, our way of life itself. With pain in our hearts, we were off to a new life — unknown, untested, dangerous and uncertain. The magnitude of the war convinced my father that we would not return soon. Some of our party disagreed and thought the war wouldn't last much longer and we would return in a few weeks. Everyone felt certain the Russians would leave once the war ended. Uncle Mike and his family were among those, as were most of our relatives, and chose to remain at home on familiar ground, and bear up under whatever hardship may befall them. Everyone agreed that things would get worse before they got better.

My parents' decision was not made by choice. Fleeing the threat of death, or worse, for the unknown, casting themselves away from everything they had known, trusting that what they found would be better. What courage did it take to do that?

My father's strong military background, and a personal history of fighting against the Bolsheviks and the Soviet regime left us no other option. Our commitment was irreversible. If we stayed and waited for the Russians to return, none of us would live to see the war end. Father would not expose us to more danger by returning to his work against the invaders. His choice was clear.

Mobilization into the Red Army during its first occupation was sure to be repeated. This was implemented by the arrest of young men to be sent to the front unarmed and without any military training, to be led by superiors whose language they did not know. They were expected to learn "on the job" and arm themselves with weapons taken from soldiers who fell in battle. Many Lithuanian youths were caught hiding from Russian recruitment and executed on the spot. Those who deserted and escaped joined the fledgling armed resistance already active in some parts of the country.

Meager at first, armed resistance grew rapidly in response to the savagery of the Red Army and the NKVD. Displaced members of the disbanded Lithuanian Armed Forces spawned "Forest Brother" formations of military, police, and fire fighting personnel who retreated into the dense forests to oppose the Russian oppressors. Organization of these units was based on the army model of independent Lithuania. The men wore army uniforms and fought as a legitimate partisan force led by surviving members of the army's professional officer corps. But after the purges of two foreign invasions their numbers were limited — most officers were of lower rank.

Partisan ranks were filled by young men from colleges and universities (even high schools) no longer functioning, and by farm boys whose families were losing their homes, and then their land to collectivization without compensation. Training was carried out in haste and under fire, but in a very short time armed resistance became so well organized, with such an efficient communications system, that it fielded 30,000 troops, and could double that number in a matter of hours by mobilizing the "reserves" — those living and working within the general population. This was possible because the civilian support base was well over 100,000 strong.

With radio, mail and telephone communications being controlled by the enemy, messengers were used as liaison and the supply means for the fighting units in the field. This role was filled by women and girls of high school age. They supplied fighting units with food, provided liaison between command posts and procured forged documents. The underground press was maintained without pause to inform the people, disrupt enemy political aims and unmask propaganda. Its distribution fell largely to the messenger network as well. Women were also part of armed resistance because if their men — husbands, friends or relatives — were in it, their own lives were in danger whether they took part in it or not.

Average age of all these people was twenty-two, and their life expectancy was about three years. More than 23,000 suffered torture and execution in addition to an equal number lost in action. Many more were deported to the Siberian wilderness for supporting the armed underground. We know now, of course, that this civilian collaboration, which provided the partisans with food, shelter, clothing, communication and moral support, was directly responsible for the longevity and effectiveness of Lithuania's underground resistance. No other country under Soviet domination lasted as long with all its instruments of independence intact until the time was right to reclaim it.

When we consider the size and might of the enemy, that armed resistance in Lithuania lasted more than ten years is astounding. It was one of the longest lasting guerilla wars of the 20th century. It continued without pause until 1956. The last partisan commander was executed by the Russians in 1957. The last resistance fighter killed in action fell in 1965, and the last one to come out of hiding did so in 1986. The underground press established by the partisans was still functioning in 1990 when independence was restored.

East Prussia

Our tearful farewells did not end with departure from Raseiniai. In Jurbarkas, where we planned to cross the Nemunas River and the Lithuanian border into East Prussia, lived mother's one time best friend and classmate and other friends of long standing. Odd that we were pleased border crossings had been delayed by German authorities. It meant a few more days in our native land and time to visit in Jurbarkas.

To celebrate mother's reunion with her friend, a sumptuous supper was prepared. It was to be the last meal for us at a dining room table for the next fifteen months. It was also to be the last time I would taste *kisielius*, the traditional Lithuanian cranberry, pear juice and potato flour, Jello-like desert — an all-time favorite.

Our stay in Jurbarkas felt like a social visit. Our entire group was of like mind, but we stayed only two days. Any longer than this was unsafe. Russian aircraft flew over with growing frequency and bombings drew nearer by the day. With deep regret we knew the time had come. Reluctant in the extreme, our group resolved to take the final step away from home and onto foreign soil, not knowing what awaited us there.

The bridge across Nemunas River was a choke point. The road was a mass of vehicles and people stretching for miles. In addition to a retreating German Panzer regiment, so many waited to cross, it would be days before we reached the bridge, never mind the border beyond.

Thanks to my father's initiative, it was arranged for our group to cross well downstream of the bridge, by fishing boats lashed side by side in pairs, each with a wagon tied down to wide boards laid on the deck. With so many wagons, and only four boats available for the venture, the fishermen would need many crossings to get us all to the other side.

I sat on the river bank for hours, fascinated by the work to build these two outlandish contraptions. Everyone helped. Even I was asked to run an errand or get some tool from one of our wagons which the fishermen didn't have. This complex assembly took time to set up and it was sunset before the first such makeshift ferry was loaded with its cargo of a single wagon. Before it could be loaded, a ramp had to be built. This, too, was a major undertaking and continued well into the fast approaching, foggy dusk.

The fishermen refused the attempt in daylight, claiming it would be discovered to their peril. The Nemunas River was not on the state border at this point, so it was difficult to understand their concern.

By the time the first precarious contrivance made away from the river bank, it was already dark. More time was needed to load and unload the wagons than it took the boats to cross the river. I made several trips across not because it was necessary, but because of my fascination how it all worked. And I could only see a small part of the operation during a single crossing. I was scolded soundly when discovered.

Although the sun was rising before the last wagon crossed, the pearly morning mist did not dissolve until well after breakfast. Everyone made it safely across before full daylight. Horses were swum across first to make the disembarking easier, as the left bank was considerably steeper and would take more than manpower to move the wagons off the river. The fishermen were paid with food and home made liquor. They were so pleased, they offered similar services to others still on the north bank, but had no takers.

Crossing the border at Sudargas took considerably more time than anticipated. Our wagon train joined the long line and waited two full days to reach the control point and proceed into East Prussia. Beyond this long delay, the border crossing was uneventful. Lithuanian passports and permission documents to enter Germany were the only proof of legality required. Everyone in the group had them. Weapons were not permitted to cross the border. Father hated to part with it, but had to surrender his Lithuanian Army issue, American made, Browning revolver.

German authorities needlessly coached us how to behave in East Prussia. The region was home to many Lithuanian families and carried Lithuanian place names. East Prussia (Rytprusiai) wasn't quite the foreign land to us that Germany proper would be. Nevertheless, the crossing marked the end of the familiar and the beginning of the unknown, the first gate closed behind us, the first bridge burned.

* * *

Our first night on foreign soil was spent in an evergreen forest. It was free of undergrowth and we drove the wagons well into its interior, away from the road. Supper was prepared over a communal fire built of dry wood found on the forest floor. Bedding was spread over a thick layer of pine needles under our wagon. We would soon grow accustomed to accommodations of this kind.

I had not slept in the open since father took me to a Boy Scout camp and we stayed several days as guests of my godmother's friend who administered the camp, and was instrumental in my joining the Lithuanian Boy Scouts shortly thereafter. Father was pleased that I took an interest in scouting but, of course, all that came to an end when the Red Army crossed our borders.

The night in the open now brought memories of the Gypsy with the Golden Smile. I wondered what had happened at home since we left, how long it would be before I saw her again.

I was awakened by a mournful sound. Wolves howled their eerie song as I lay awake, listening. I found it soothing — the wolf's howl — and once heard, never forgotten. I had no fear of wolves, as many children my age had. They were told stories of wolf pack attacks and legends of abductions of babies from their beds to be raised by wolves in the wilderness. I was told that wolves were the most intelligent creatures on earth, next to man, and lived in clan families based on a social structure not unlike our own. The stories I heard were once confirmed by wolves which visited my uncle's farm.

One bitter cold winter's night a yelping and whining was heard at the door. My aunt opened it to a blast of snow and freezing air and a bedraggled wolf cub stumbled in. She thought it had been orphaned and kept it in the house, as she was wont to do with any stray cat or dog. The cub was weak and cold, and soon fell asleep by the wood stove. Before dawn showed its first light, a hideous howling chorus commenced all around the house. The wolf pack had come to claim its errant youngster. The door was opened and the cub released. The howling ceased instantly. The peaceful, white silence of winter returned.

* * *

Several kilometers southeast of the border, our column of eight wagons was slowly making its way through our second day on foreign soil. We moved in silence, our abandoned homes heavy on our minds.

The plane came in low over the trees. We had all seen aircraft before, but this was not normal. The plane was too low, its banked turn aimed to line up with our column.

"Jump!" someone shouted. "Run!"

Mother was already under the wagon. Father grabbed me round the waist and we tumbled headlong into the roadside ditch. The dirt around us suddenly erupted into the air, hit by bullets from the plane. I didn't hear the machine gun chatter — only the roaring plane. Bullets plowed up the ground within inches of my face. I felt my father's weight over me, saw mother trying to hide her retching once the plane was out of sight.

After the single pass, the pilot did not return.

No one was hurt and damage was slight, but one horse had to be put down because of injuries. The animal had fallen, still hitched to the wagon it had been pulling. Half under the front wheels, the beast thrashed about and bellowed a howl I didn't know horses could make. It frightened me more than the Russian plane.

Although it was illegal to carry a weapon, one of our party had a pistol, which he hadn't relinquished at the border, and shot the animal dead before unhitching it from the wagon. The group's horse allotment had to be rearranged. As knowledge of hunger was still in our future, no attempt was made to harvest horsemeat. We did not suspect it was to be a staple source of protein in the months to come. For now, we all felt bad about burying the carcass in the ditch by the road. But there was little choice.

Unexpectedly, the tank battle father and I witnessed on the banks of the Dubysa River was vivid beyond words, now that I had lived through the first truly violent experience of my life.

It was my first exposure to open fear in adults who were my protectors — its manifestation obvious even to a child my age — but I was oblivious to the sacrifice they made. My godmother's words had not yet gained their full meaning: "Nothing wrong with being afraid. Fear can keep us from harm," she said when I was ashamed to admit I was afraid of the river after dark, the same river where we spent warm summer days swimming. "No need to be ashamed of being afraid," the Gypsy with the Golden Smile told me. "Fear is nature's way of making us smart."

What reason did the pilot have to attack a defenseless wagon train of refugees? But knowing previous Russian behavior, no one was surprised. It was suggested we travel only in bad weather or only at night. This was viewed as an impractical solution by some even though everyone expected these attacks to continue.

We recovered and moved on.

Wisps of smoke rose in the distance. As we approached the source of the smoke, we saw people digging. The road was littered with upturned carts, a baby carriage, and scattered belongings everywhere. Two horses lay dead in the road, the wagon in ruins. A woman sat in the dirt cradling a crying infant. Another was keening over a dead man laid out in the grass. Her grief alarmed me — so intense, so overwhelming.

The diggers were burying another, a woman.

I stared at the scene with unbelieving eyes. I felt a band tightening around my chest. A burn in my throat. But I couldn't cry. It was too late now.

When the plane attacked us I was frightened. Now, it was more than that. Not pain, not fear, only an overwhelming sense of unreality. There were dead people in the road. It could just as easily have been one of us laying there.

We stopped. Everyone was speechless. Father climbed off the wagon with the other men in our group.

"Stay in the wagon," he told mother and me.

They talked to the stricken and helped bury the dead. We couldn't sit by doing nothing and got off the wagon to gather their things from the road. Prayers were said over the graves and stone markers were pressed into the ground.

We offered to take them with us. No, they said, they couldn't go on. They were going back. Hard as we tried, there was no persuading them otherwise. They were Lithuanians from Matlaukys, a small village near the East Prussian border, where we crossed. They said it was only 40 kilometers back. They were going home.

Our party stayed with them through the night. In the morning, we bid our goodbyes. Their ruined wagon was fashioned into a large two-wheel cart. They refused to take one of the horses from our group to pull it, and said they were three strong men and could push it themselves. We couldn't talk them out of it or into coming with us. The parting was tearful and sad.

The end of this day, however, was to be the start of a brief rest. The air attack notwithstanding, repairs to wagon wheels and shoeing of horses was already overdue. We were on the lookout for a blacksmith shop. One was passed too late in the day to find service, but just beyond was a small farm next to a large estate. We stopped at the farm. A woman met us there and, to our surprise, greeted us in Lithuanian, not German. Her husband, the blacksmith, was not moved to help us until the estate master came to see what was what with a wagon train in his farm. He understood our plight and convinced the blacksmith helping us was in his best interest.

We stayed the night in the barn, sleeping on straw — the first such accommodations of many more to come. The sound of steady rain lulled me to sleep. Before I slept, or perhaps later, disjointed visions came. Airplane. Dirt kicked up in my face. Mother vomiting. Smoke. Baby carriage smashed in the road. Dead man. Woman keening. Father digging.

I awoke late. The sky was grey and full of rain. But it had stopped. It was still windy and cold. We had slept fully clothed. It made it seem even colder on awakening.

Our three days on the farm were productive and beneficial to all concerned. Wheels in need of attention were duly trued and metal bands tightened, axles reset and greased with tallow, all horses shoed. Friction brakes were relined by nailing pieces of tire rubber to the wooden pads. The woman let our cooks use her kitchen and sold us milk, bread and vegetables enough to last the rest of the week.

Each family of our party contributed to a high stack of unrendered bacon and smoked ham as payment for her generosity. The blacksmith was paid in cash. We left the farm with a good feeling about our first interaction with people in East Prussia.

As we moved westward the people were progressively less Lithuanian and more German, as was expected. That did not alter their willingness to help us in return for bartered goods, cash, or farm labor. One night was spent in an abandoned farm. Some people, still somewhat distant from the approaching Red Army, had already moved westward. Like our home in Raseiniai, theirs were abandoned and vacant with everything left as if still in use. It was a sad reminder of our plight.

Our first stop of longer duration was just beyond the town of Altenkirchen. Its namesake, thick walled, stone church was truly old and rich in history of the region. While visiting there, father was approached by a local police official and offered a stay in a nearby estate to help bring in the grain harvest. This was seen as a welcome stroke of luck.

It was a mistake.

On the estate was a large horse farm for breeding Turkish horses. How they managed to evade requisition by the retreating army was a mystery. We knew the German army was not far ahead of us and sometimes stopped to build defenses in the hopes of slowing the Red Army advance. Miles of anti-tank ditches were being dug across the Russians' anticipated route. This was the price we paid for accommodation at the estate. In addition to taking in the harvest, every able bodied man and boy were recruited to digging trenches. There were already more than a hundred doing this work when we arrived.

Anti-tank ditches were three meters wide and two and a half meters deep. The men dug at the bottom to the next man on a step above, who in turn tossed the dirt over the top to the man whose job it was to spread the dirt out flat. This last turned out to be the first job I ever had. And I was never paid.

Russian fighter planes strafed the work zone almost daily. There was no defensive fire from the German troops. But we always had warning and time to take cover in the trench. Two men were lightly wounded the first day, neither from our group.

Another one was hit in the arm two days later. His injuries were more serious and required medical attention.

Aside from this disturbing experience, our stay at the horse farm was without incident. In return for harvest work we enjoyed reasonably good food and the best shelter we've had since crossing the border. We stayed in rooms on the estate and our horses were well cared for. This was a welcome break from camping under wagons, sleeping in barns, defecating in the woods, and cooking over bonfires.

The first day there, however, we got our first surprise. One of the estate's laundresses came to visit before we had time to unpack. She bustled in, filled with an imperious air, as if we were there to obey her every whim.

"I must have your bed sheets," she demanded.

"Our bed linen is clean. We do our own laundry," mother told her.

"No, no. I have to dye them black."

This seemed like an unusual way to hide the dirt, mother thought out loud. Wasn't washing them better?

"It is for *Verdunklung*," the woman explained.

Blackout after dark was enforced in every town and village to prevent them becoming bombing targets. Black bed sheets were hung over windows for that purpose. Sometimes, blankets were used.

"But there is no electricity and we only use candles."

"Have it your own way. I warned you," the laundress said and hurried out the door. "You'll be fined," she added on her way out. It meant we couldn't even burn candles without blacking out the windows, and candles would have to be snuffed out each time the door was opened for fear their light would be seen from the sky.

On Sundays we were free to visit other refugees in neighboring farms, exchange information and make plans for future action. We were cautioned not to wander too far, as mines had been laid on some roads where anti-tank ditches could not be dug. This warning was not taken seriously by the owner of our wagon. He was bicycling to see an acquaintance in Altenkirchen, hit a mine and was killed instantly.

We were allowed to bury him in the estate's family plot. My father made the wooden casket from material donated by the estate.

As he had no relatives known to anyone in our party, distribution of the man's belongings fell to the group leader. At a meeting with everyone present, it was decided my father would keep the horse and wagon and the rest would be distributed among members of the group according to their needs. Father made out an IOU to whoever was to inherit the wagon after the war and entrusted the document to the group leader.

These events thrust me unexpectedly into the second job of my work career. Our two horses were now in my care — a daunting responsibility for one so young and ignorant of horses. My childhood visit to uncle Jonas' farm was on my mind around the clock. I wished there had been more visits and more time with Dana and Vida there. Perhaps I could have learned more about horses. My two country cousins were in my thoughts daily, and how they showed me a girl could be a friend before I was old enough to believe it. Father had sent word to their parents that we were leaving; no way to tell if they ever received it. I wondered whatever became of them when the Russians came. I was not to know for another fifteen years.

For now, I was to learn about horses however best I could. This occupation was meant to keep me away from trench digging and fighter plane attacks. Both horses already knew me well. It made things easier, but I still knew no more than I did at uncle Jonas' farm. There was no lack of sources for this information here at the estate's horse farm. The trouble was that information was available only in German — a language I had yet to learn. So there I was, the second real job I ever had and no way to learn it without learning the language first. A "catch 22" if ever there was. But learn I did, by trial and error.

"*Nein! Nein! Links. Links,*" the foreman urged me to move to the left of our gelding as I prepared to muck the stall. Then he stepped ahead and pushed rudely against the gelding's shoulder with his own. The animal sidestepped and moved over without resistance.

"*So,*" the foreman added. "*Immer links.*"

I understood, but didn't know why it always had to be done from the left. I would learn the reason soon, just as I would learn never to walk behind a horse unannounced. I already knew not to walk directly ahead of one when leading. Staying just off to the side prevented the horse from shoving me with its muzzle. I had also learned to water the drinking trough and muck out the stalls. The manure fork picked up the droppings while the sawdust bedding fell back to the ground with each swing out the door. It was easy. But I had never done it while the horse was in the stall.

Godmother's advice: "When you need help, don't wait for it. Work for it," gained new meaning. I thought of her often and missed her golden smile, the words she spoke to me. They were with me always, and I bemoaned the possibility I would hear them no more.

With help, from people as well as the horses themselves, I slowly acquired a rudimentary knowledge. I worked for it. I knew to be wary of pinned ears or a cocked hind leg. I welcomed a friendly nicker, and took time to calm a fear induced snort. Entering a stall without announcing myself was the first mistake I corrected. The natural instinct to flee was unavailable. Self defense was, and that could spell disaster for me if I wasn't careful.

Getting a horse to side step in the confines of the stall was an impossible task. But I learned a memorable neat trick from a boy twice my age who lost his job herding cattle. He did it with a slingshot and got caught. But he knew a thing or two about horses. He showed me how to turn the animal's head to the right with a lead rope, and slap the side so that the right hind leg stepped in front of the left and hindquarters moved left, or vice versa, for balance. So simple, yet a mystery before I was shown how to do it.

Our gelding was never saddled or ridden, but our mare had been ridden back home, and I was allowed to ride her if I wished. I had no interest in this. Memories of falling off the gift hobby horse father once gave me reminded me not to try it with a real live horse. But the slingshot cattle herder egged me on and dared me. In my view he was an expert horseman, and I just knew I would make a fool of myself. So, one day, when he wasn't around, I stepped up on an upturned bucket to mount the mare with my heart in my throat, and hung on round her neck. Of course, there was no saddle, and if there had been, I wouldn't have known what to do with it. She didn't seem to mind, but stood there quietly until I sat up and got hold of her mane. No sooner I pulled up than she shook me off, and down I went into the dirt. But she didn't move away. Instead, she nuzzled my shoulder as if saying: try again, I don't mind.

Setting the bucket upside down next to her side again, I mounted gingerly and sat up as straight as I dared. She didn't make a move. I wiggled my knees. She took a step and nickered. That was a good sign. I worked up the courage to kick with my heels and she walked. Wow! I was riding.

The next time the expert horseman came to taunt me, I mounted the mare. He was so impressed, he showed me what I did wrong and, in the weeks following, taught me to ride bareback. That was a gift. Soon after that, he was recruited and went away with the army.

For the most part, I learned from my own mistakes. Watching others helped, but did not explain things sufficiently to avoid a mistake when conditions changed. But things improved if I paid attention. Between the German speakers showing me the ropes in hands-on intimacy, and the Lithuanians explaining what I saw, my progress with horse husbandry galloped right along. And I was learning German in the bargain. I took particular pride in telling father what I had learned each day when he returned from the fields or from the trenches. Mother was much relieved when the digging was done and father was free to give me a hand with the horses. But I was always the boss, he the helper. It was my job. And I had never felt so proud.

As summer turned to fall, Russian air attacks intensified. Although there was no more trench digging, the attacks now were by bombers. The nearby city of Tilžė (Tilsit) was bombed nightly. Even at a distance we felt the ground shake and saw fires rivaling the flares dropped from the planes. Search lights reflected from the clouds, setting an eerie glow across the sky. It was frightening everyone in the group and signaled the need to move on. We knew what it meant to be caught working for the Germans: if you worked for Russia's enemy, you worked against Russia, and that was treason.

One day I walked into the room while everyone was focused on the radio broadcast, as they were wont to do whenever one of the few stations still providing uncensored news was transmitting. The broadcast ended just as I entered. All the men of our group were there. So was mother. They were so intent on what they were listening to, my arrival wasn't noticed. When I closed the door behind me the radio was turned off. The room fell heavy with silence. They stared at one another, the look of shock etched in their faces.

Something was wrong. I had to know.

"What happened?" I asked and held my breath.

"The Red Army is in Raseiniai," my farther said.

Our hopes of returning home soon could no longer be sustained. Going back while the Red Army was there was akin to signing our own death warrant. That uncle Mike's and uncle Kostas' families stayed behind was as puzzling to me then as it is clear today. None of them had any connection to government or our armed forces. They were engaged in private enterprise which was not burdened with interests of state. Their personal histories contained no association with political organizations and there was nothing to implicate them as sympathizers during the Nazi occupation just ended. This was the category into which most of Lithuania's population fit at that time. They were totally harmless to the Soviet regime. It could not have been a more erroneous belief.

It was many years later that we learned of action taken by the Soviets against my cousin Arūnas. He was an outstanding athlete and pursued gymnastics to world class level. By the time of the 1968 Olympic Games in Mexico City, his athletic ability was at the top of his field. As Russia no longer had an Olympic team of its own, the Soviet team was assembled from among the best athletes in the countries Russia had invaded. Arūnas made the team.

It will be remembered that Soviet Olympians were to live on board a cruise ship under guard while at the 1984 Olympics in Los Angeles, had Soviet Union not withdrawn from the Games altogether. It was touted as security precaution. Was it, in fact, a safeguard to prevent defection? It will also be remembered that there was just such an attempt by a Soviet athlete at the 1960 Winter Games in Squaw Valley, and again, 16 years later, in Montreal. It begs the question why Arūnas never made it to Mexico in 1968.

While awaiting the plane in Moscow airport, he was taken on some pretense to a room, and detained under lock and key until the plane with the Soviet Olympic team on board was in the air, then released without explanation. Was he already under suspicion to defect to the U.S. via Mexico?

If Soviet suspicions were not groundless, was my cousin's plan to defect hatched at the last minute? If so, the authorities would probably not have known. If not, how long had this idea steeped in his mind and how long had he been preparing? But at the time we were on Altenkirchen's horse farm no such dramatic or suspicious incidents could be tied to my uncles' families in Raseiniai. Their decision to stay behind was not an unreasonable one.

While plans were being made to commence our journey, the men were taken once again, by the local police, to dig trenches. This time, far enough from the estate to have them billeted at the job site rather than the farm with their families. This was the worst possible timing for us. No one knew how long before the men would be free to move on. The front had advanced to the Nemunas River and was at the East Prussian border. We were running out of time.

Imagine our surprise when father returned that same night. It happened that when the conscripted diggers lined up for roll call, and everyone's name was called, my father's was omitted. When told to sound off if not called, father kept silent. After everyone fell asleep he escaped and returned to the estate. On subsequent nights he went back to the digging site and relieved another of our party so he could spend the night and the following day with his family. This continued until the job was finished. I hate to think what would have happened if my father got caught impersonating another.

By then the air attacks and bombings were no longer restricted to Tilžė. Bombs were dropped on villages and farms nearby. Some German as well as Prussian families began leaving their homes to start westward. Everyone on the estate felt threatened. Our departure was already overdue.

Wind

There are times when the urge to revisit old haunts is irresistible. I give in. I do so without regret. Sometimes my reward is disappointment.

It is so today.

I've driven to the remote end of Millers Island Road only to discover what was once *Rumrunner's Pub* is now an abandoned hulk in need of more thorough destruction. It saddens me to see these remains of a once lively gathering place of strangers who became friends while there.

Along with fine food, Mediterranean style, game pieces were provided to do battle on chess boards painted on the tabletops. Food orders taken by the bartender were whisked to the kitchen along an overhead cable on lead-weighted, wheeled alligator clips. Once prepared by the chef, his culinary masterworks were self-serve. No waiters needed here. Off-menu preparations were as common as daily specials. And if something was wanted beyond those, no one was reluctant to ask. Desserts were as likely to come from the family kitchen at home as from commercial sources. There was a camaraderie between patrons and staff uncommon elsewhere. Even the hours varied by demand.

Owned by an attorney for whom law practice had lost its appeal shortly after her attainment of the state's bar, it was a place with its own brand of peculiar charm. The look of an old fashioned ice cream parlor, but with a liqueur license and real food, was not accidental. It was intended. The friendly demeanor of the owner and her staff inspired a relaxed atmosphere. It was one of those rare places where, in spite of its public venue, it felt like home.

My discovery of *Rumrunner's Pub* was like the discovery of many other out of the way places. My method, perhaps not unique, was born of an original idea. Maps held a fascination for me since before my first day in school. I traced paths along their squiggly lines, dreaming of places through which they passed, to which they led, to which I may someday travel. My fertile imagination rendered them exotic, unseen by anyone but me.

I never lost that fascination. I gaze at maps today with similar involvement. It was a simple step to elevate it to a game, to choose a road which the map showed ending into water. It was a ready excuse to straddle my motorcycle and ride with purpose. Whatever I would find at the end of that road was my objective. Many rides later, to the end of many strange roads, I have come to accept some of the things I will never outgrow. I never lost the boy I once was.

It was at the end of one of those roads that I first saw windsurfers. They ghosted along in the light breeze on gossamer wings. The small beach, into which the road ended abruptly, was littered with blankets, sun umbrellas, folding chairs, picnic coolers, sailboards, clothes piles here and there, and a lone artist at his easel freezing the scene on canvas.

Persuaded to try windsurfing, I spent more time learning to right the sailboard before I drowned than I did learning to windsurf. But it was exhilarating. It was new. A day, and then the night, in company of strangers I would never see again.

Around a bonfire on the beach after sundown we consumed the contents of the picnic coolers. My contribution was wine and cheese — always carried on these rides — and stories of other dead end roads.

Maps, Horses and Trains

I drew mock battle maps when in the field for advanced combat training with the U.S. Army. Taken to task by my commanding officer for misspelling *mashine* gun, I made it a point to study and edit my work more diligently in the future.

I should have known better.

Our lives once depended on the reading of maps. It was my father's responsibility as we fled westward. To move at speed matched exactly to that of the advancing Red Army behind us, and yet not so far ahead as to fall into the hands of retreating Germans, was a balancing act unforgiving of error. And we did this for weeks and months at a time. The breaks came only when the battle front halted or the Red Army stopped to be re-supplied.

Father's uncanny skill in collecting information and applying it effectively to our situation at any given time appeared routine to the pre-teen child I was then. Now, the whole process never ceases to amaze me.

It was done in the open, usually without covert action. Trusting anyone along our route was dangerous. Attracting attention by failure to blend in could be disastrous. But a man on a bicycle, riding to find food for his family was as commonplace as the rubble through which we traveled. As we plodded along by horse and wagon, father was well ahead, often fifteen kilometers or more.

Canvassing farms along the way yielded fresh produce, but information was limited to local news. Knowledge farther afield could be gained at goods distribution depots, telegraph bureaus, post offices, railroad stations, and local administration agencies, but at progressively greater risk.

Theatrical talent, I never knew father possessed, was sometimes needed to assume fictitious identities and contrived reasons for being wherever the sought information was to be found. That he managed it so well, so often, for so long, is a remarkable thing. That we survived without coming to grief was a miracle.

Based on information secured by these methods, conclusions could be drawn only on the immediate future — days, sometimes hours ahead — no more. Then the information gathering process resumed. More often than not, it never stopped. Thanks to his military background and experience, his interpretation of the facts and rumors heard was seldom in error.

One day he returned from a scouting trip in an especially good humor. We expected good news. As it was, only my fascination with maps was rewarded. Purely by chance, father discovered the location of an abandoned Wermacht headquarters. He went to investigate. There, after a thorough search of the premises, he found German military maps somehow overlooked by looters. This was a boon to our later travels. Many years later, those maps brought a hefty sum of money from a collector in the U.S.

On one occasion, it was learned that a rear unit of German troops lagged behind with the purpose of collecting what few horses remained in the farms. They were needed to speed the retreat.

Difference of opinion regarding route to be taken had shrunk our caravan to 4 wagons, 6 horses, 3 bicycles, and 12 people. We shared our wagon with a young woman orphaned early in the war. She had been traveling with a couple who decided against continuing to Mecklenburg and went their own way. Alla was a welcome addition, and had her own bicycle. Her knowledge of a language no one in our party spoke came in handy on several occasions when nothing else would do. She was Ukrainian. The group also included a family of four in the second wagon, another family of three in the next, and an elderly bachelor alone bringing up the rear.

The dilemma we faced was serious.

If we turned back, the Red Army would meet us in a few days. If we pressed on, we would lose our horses along with most of what we still owned. In either case, control of our own destiny would be short changed if not snuffed out altogether.

Father decided to leave our group temporarily, at least until this problem was solved. How he managed to find a farm which supplied food to German troops no one knows. The important thing was that horses were needed to transport the farm's goods and would not be requisitioned by the army. The farmer was an asthmatic man in his late sixties, lame from a wound suffered in the previous war. Like that of all farmers in Germany, his labor force and horses were serving the army. Most farms had no horses to pull the plow. If this were still spring, plowing fields would have fallen to us. But late summer work also needed extra hands.

He agreed to put us up posing as farm hands, provided our meager possessions could be hidden and our wagon burned. Perhaps, in spite of his current work, the farmer was not a Nazi sympathizer to take such risk. But, in truth, like most German farmers during the war years, he was probably forced to comply with military administration directives as to his stored harvest and current crops. He needed the extra hands and horses, in return for which the risk was worth taking.

People in East Prussia were strongly opposed to Hitler's policies and saw them as harmful to Germany. Perhaps that is why the Prussians proved more willing to help refugees than Germans we encountered farther west.

We were housed in a barn with our horses. Our trunks were buried in a potato field, and our wagon was dismantled into its individual parts which we scattered about the farm grounds (father refused to have the wagon burned). I helped take the wagon apart and worried how we would ever put it back together again. There were so many different parts and we had to hide them everywhere. How would we ever remember where they all were?

Wandering behind the barn, I heard coughing and wheezing near a small shed covered with tarpaulin. I approached it cautiously to have a look. The old farmer had a gas mask filter in his hand and was pouring blood through its fibers into a bucket on the ground. I stopped and stared, afraid to make a move and be discovered. Then I changed my mind and took off running. I don't know if he saw me.

Breathlessly, I told father what I had just seen. He laughed. "That wasn't blood," he said. "Did it smell like gasoline?"

"I don't know. I didn't smell anything."

"Well, I'm sure it was gasoline."

He explained that people used the dense filters to remove red dye in gasoline marked for military use, then added green dye to mark it for agricultural use. The farmer was breaking the law which governed rationing.

"You did the right thing by telling me, though," my father reassured me. Of course, I didn't know it was valuable information to hold over that farmer's head should the need arise when the German army troops arrived.

The German army unit stopped there the next day. They loaded their trucks with farm products and departed with no questions asked. At the farmer's request we stayed another four days. In return for labor we were fed and sheltered in comfort, far surpassing the months spent under nature's blanket of stars when we were lucky, and under her web of storms when not.

This was a harbinger of our later survival, after the war's end. In the meantime, it was learned that Mecklenburg's farms were the largest in Germany and in need of laborers and horses. Mecklenburg was Germany's breadbasket. But agreement among us could not be reached. It was feared that being so close to an army in fighting withdrawal would subject us to hazards already endured in East Prussia. Chief among those was the likelihood of men being recruited into labor battalions and separated from families, who knows for how long. According to new directives of local administration all refugees' horses and wagons were to be seized or left behind with the farmers. Families were to be transported westward and men sent to dig trenches for the troops. Enforcement of these directives spelled certain disaster for us.

By dint of word received at a railroad terminal, we stumbled on another option. Mecklenburg's needs were so pressing that trains en route westward were harboring refugees who had horses.

Without delay, father saw to bribing the station master with smoked pork rind and half a ham, still remaining from food earned at the farm, and securing two railroad boxcars — one for our horses, another for the wagons. These rail cars were on a spur with no siding. To load wagons and horses a ramp needed to be built. At 4 o'clock that afternoon, the cars were to be coupled to a train heading west. We had three hours to get the job done.

Half hour later our wagons arrived at the railroad station. I was driving while mother secured our belongings for the trip. Father and the other men were already there, where they hammered together a ramp made of wood procured from a derelict rail car which they dismantled. This, too, required a food bribe to the dispatcher who had authority to release the material.

The station was teeming with humanity — people trying to find room on trains heading west. Many were East Prussians prepared to leave their homes to escape the Red Army. Although somewhat removed from Russia's earlier onslaught, they knew enough from passing refugees who preceded us to avoid being caught at all costs. Those were no idle fears. According to a communiqué to Stalin, on the heels of Russian front line troops between January and April 1945, nine NKVD regiments had "removed" over 50,000 enemy "elements" in East Prussia.

Most of the crowd was in the station building. A few ventured onto sidings, hoping to stowaway in rail cars which weren't being watched. One group was a Jewish family who feared the Russians more than they feared the Nazis in the west. We were amazed when the man inquired if we had room for his family of four. They would get transit passes, he said, and the only luggage they had was what they carried.

By now we knew what Hitler's policies were concerning Jews, and we had seen what happened to our neighbors at the synagogue in Raseiniai. It surprised everyone that his family wanted to travel west. My father could not convince him otherwise, and we could not refuse him. We would make room for them while they went to see about the transit documents. The man assured us they would be back long before the 4 o'clock departure.

Shortly after 2 PM the ramp was mounted and rope winches were rigged with block and tackle to pull the wagons aboard. They had to be unloaded first to reduce weight. All my mother's efforts at securing things in our wagon for the train trip had been for naught.

To test my knowledge of geometry, I was tasked with measuring the interior of the boxcar and help determine how to best fit all four wagons within. I took this responsibility more seriously than it deserved. My arguments were lame in the face of the urgency time imposed on us. But some of my suggestions were taken, and never was a boy so proud to have contributed importantly to the combined efforts of our group.

The women were tasked with finding hay for the horses in the other freight car. Alla, the enterprising young Ukrainian woman who had been with the group since it shrunk to four wagons, contracted a nearby farmer to deliver the hay.

It was now well past 3 o'clock. We had just finished loading. The train was approaching the spur to pick up our two boxcars. The hay had not arrived. I stood between horses, calming them after all the commotion they had been through. The door was only half open and my view was limited to the approaching train. Suddenly the door screeched in its tracks as it crashed open. It startled the horses. I lost my footing and fell to the straw covered floor.

Being kicked by a horse hurt less than the German curses directed at me by an irate man with a pitchfork. His hay wagon was alongside and he wasn't expecting six horses and a child in his way. Nevertheless, paying me no heed, he pitched the hay were it fell. It was not enough I was kicked by a horse whom I tried to help with best intentions, I was now being buried in hay!

Not to be outdone, I held my tongue over the pain, both physical and mental, and struggled to move the hay where I judged it should be. The horses calmed without my further intervention, apparently appeased by food served with such vigor.

The next shock came when the train reached my boxcar. Impact of coupling was so great, even the horses tumbled against the walls. I fell again. Although this time the animals had learned to avoid me.

The elderly bachelor from our group climbed into the car to make sure horses were tied and ready for the trip. He took me off and we proceeded to the wagon car, where the rest were making last preparations for the trip ahead. Making ourselves comfortable in and around the four wagons crowded into the confines of a railroad boxcar seems daunting now. But then, we had all been used to far greater discomfort than that, and we took it in stride.

All of us looked anxiously for the Jewish family to return. Space was allotted for all four in the already crowded boxcar. We set up a table made from straw bales and the tailgate from one of the wagons. Then we waited.

Our railcars were checked by railroad officials who demanded to see our transit permits and passports. We asked about the people we expected. They knew nothing. It was 4 o'clock. We waited.

At half past four, they still hadn't come. If they changed their minds, it was probably just in time. Armed guards in brown uniforms (*Sturmabteilung*) — Brownshirts we called them — wearing black and red swastika armbands, marched up and down the line looking for something in each rail car. They, too, wanted to see our papers, searched all four wagons, and ransacked our belongings. One of them boldly helped himself to some dried plums we still had from my father's orchard in Raseiniai. We had no idea what they were after. It was all very frightening.

I saw a woman from the neighboring train walk off some distance, for modesty's sake, to relieve herself. The train started to move before she was finished. When she realized what was happening, she rose and ran. A small boy was reaching out of the train window, crying: "Mama! Mama!" She stumbled over the rails and fell. When she got to her feet, the train was moving too fast for her to catch up. She called her child's name over and over again, in tears. The Brownshirts came and escorted her back to the platform.

It was another of those times when the bitter burn in my throat told me I should cry, and I couldn't.

In time, our train jerked into life and we were on our way to another unknown.

Babel

That the old Hippodrome Theater in Baltimore was restored in 2004 to its former glory is testament to it historic worth. Meaningful to me is its part in my first step to doing what I learned to enjoy. Writing. And doing so in a language I did not learn until my 19th year. It happened by an accident of good fortune, as so many worthwhile things did in my life.

Starting times of movies shown at the old Hippodrome Theater were listed on the ticket booth window, but I seldom paid them much heed. It didn't matter. As soon as the feature film ended, it would be rewound and restarted, the intermission pause lasting only long enough to complete the rewind. If I liked the show, I could stay and watch it all over again. It hardly mattered at what point in the story I walked in. There were no subtitles and my English was limited to the few words and phrases needed only for the most basic daily tasks. This was still a learning process, a work in progress.

English language classes for recent immigrants were held across town from my sponsor's home where I was staying. It meant an hour's commute every Monday, Wednesday and Friday. The group was small, but included students of several nationalities in the same class, and learning smatterings of their language as well as English was an unexpected bonus.

The other four days of the week I worked night shift, hand sorting and assembling a major daily newspaper for a minimal wage. After food, clothing and the language classes, I made certain there was enough left for theater admission to the Hippodrome. My generous sponsor provided accommodations gratis, at least until I found a better paying job. But at age 18, my priority was language. And that is where the Hippodrome made a meaningful contribution.

My commute included a transfer from the streetcar which ran between school and down-town, to a bus from there to my sponsor's home. As luck would have it, the transfer point was right in front of the Hippodrome. Rather than taking the next afternoon bus, I habitually paid the 50-cent admission and enjoyed whatever was playing there at the time. With rare exception, what played there were westerns. Tom Mix, Roy Rogers, Lone Ranger and Tonto, Red Ryder, Hopalong Cassidy, The Cisco Kid, and Lash LaRue. And, of course, there were serials — shorts before the feature presentation. These included Batman, Zorro, Superman and others of their ilk. As episodes changed only once every two weeks or so, I could follow their stories too.

Features or shorts, they all worked the same way to advance my English. The action on the screen, combined with what was learned in class, helped tie the words and phrases together into sentences. The actors demonstrated pronunciation and inflection of speech which supplemented classroom work.

Within months, my fractured English grew to a useful whole, owing much to the Hippodrome and the Hollywood western. So much so, in fact, that I left the English language class before completion. A better paying job while completing my high school education was the latest priority change. Thanks to the Hippodrome, the change was not as difficult as it first seemed.

I've seen enough westerns to last a lifetime. The puzzling thing is how I failed to acquire a mid-western drawl. I'm told my English now does not betray a foreign tongue but to the sharpest ear — another puzzling thing. If I have a knack for languages, I also have it for forgetting them when in disuse. That's what happened to my limited grasp of French, Hungarian, Ukrainian and German. My Lithuanian is strong only because I use it every day. Where interest in language came from, I cannot say. Perhaps necessity was catalyst. There was a time when the great ornate theaters and concert halls of Europe fell to rubble with the rest of man's proud works. Magnificent places like the Hippodrome, with their columned façades, wall-size reliefs, carved gargoyles, ornamental friezes, frescoes, and gilded balcony surrounds under buttressed, vaulted ceilings, all succumbed to the heartless destruction of war. It was a time of flight across Europe to escape the devastation. It was a time of learning new languages on the run, as needed, and then discarded just as swiftly when another was to take its place. The learning process was not enhanced by classrooms or the luxury of a Hippodrome.

We lived in close proximity with speakers of French, Polish, Hungarian, German, Estonian, Latvian, Ukrainian and Dutch. Listening and posturing with vigorous animation and much arm waving was the basic method of communication. There was seldom time for note taking. If a foreign speaker did write something down, it was a gift. Thinking in one language while speaking in another at the same time became the norm. Translating in our heads as we spoke was second nature. It stayed with me for all time and I still find thinking and speaking in the same language a rare surprise.

Making mistakes while learning English could turn misunderstandings to embarrassment. Making a mistake when I was learning German could cost us our lives. But although we were trying to learn German out of necessity, we loathed to speak it.

There were times, too, when it was better not to know the language. When explanations could lead to trouble, interpreters could not be trusted, as one memorable occasion proved. Fortunately, this one proved in our favor.

Staying in the gap between retreating Nazi forces and the Red Army, as we moved westward, was always a risk laden task. When that gap narrowed, it was always safer to favor the fleeing side than be caught by the Russians. We had come dangerously close to German lines where their defenses were being prepared. Able bodied men among the civilians and refugees were conscripted by the hundreds to dig trenches along the coming front. This spelled a serious threat to our survival. Any delay in crossing the Oder River now would surely cast us into Russian hands.

We hid father in a sauerkraut barrel buried in the hay wagon drawn by two horses and proceeded to the checkpoint along the main road. There was no visible avenue of escape.

The customary *"Halt!"* by the Brownshirt guard was followed by *"Papiere!"* (papers). On examining those, and seeing Lithuanian as our nationality, he still addressed us in German. We feigned ignorance. He wanted to know what was in the wagon under the hay. Mother pretended no knowledge of German and told him, in Lithuanian, that we were on the way to a farm on the river, another kilometer downstream, where we were staying and helping with chores, the gist of which was true. She kept repeating this information until the guard lost patience and went looking for a German speaker among the line of refugees behind us. He returned shortly, followed by a grizzled old man who greeted us in our native tongue. What he said to the Brownshirt next, in German, paled our resolve.

"Search the hay," he suggested. "Sometimes they hide there."

We saw other men being marched off under armed guard and loaded onto army trucks for transport to the trenches. We expected father would be joining them soon. Then, we would have to wait until the trenches were finished, perhaps a week. And then the Red Army would be here.

There was no time to consider alternatives. The Brownshirt was already poking the hay with a short pole. We held our breath.

"I can do that," said the grizzled old man and took the pole to start poking in earnest. As he went by me he said "Don't worry, I won't hurt him," and winked. The Brownshirt wanted to know what he said. The man turned around.

"I told him to steady the horses while I poke the hay," he said in German. The Brownshirt seemed satisfied.

Then the pole hit solid wood. "What's that?" The guard demanded. He moved some hay out of the way to expose the barrel. We held our breath. Was there panic in my mother's eyes?

"Just a kraut barrel there," the old man said. "Full."

He returned the pole to the Brownshirt, and as he passed he winked again. The guard returned the documents and waved us on.

Sauerkraut barrels on hay wagons were not uncommon around farms that time of year, and he must have thought no more of it. Mother looked frightened, but I could barely suppress a smile. I never learned my father's view.

Beyond language, additional education came my way informally from father presenting a problem of science, math, or logic each morning and expecting a solution from me at the end of the day. The results would be discussed over supper when mother could participate. Her support of my solutions carried much weight, as she was the only consultant available to help me work the problem through the day.

This style of education followed me throughout the war years, whether I attended a formal school or not. Solving a posed problem, be it a practical or a theoretical one, was a daily task. Perhaps it was the catalyst for later engineering studies when I reached college age. Reading a subject and reporting on material covered was never my strong point in school. I always looked for the hidden problem and tried to find new ways to the solution. Even when there was only one solution, other people's methods of arriving at it held little interest for me. I wanted to find my own path, in my own way. It was a trial and error sort of learning and took longer than necessary. Perhaps I was just a slow learner. Sometimes overcomplicating a simple process became my stumbling block — a trait I remained wary of throughout my later career in engineering.

For now, the daily problem solving exercises were real eye openers and supper table sessions taught me the art of discussion. They were also a lot of fun. School, such as I left in Raseiniai, would not come my way for another three years. In the meantime, like most children of the war years, I became somewhat of an autodidact. I wish I could personally thank all the wonderful, caring people, of three different nationalities, who contributed so hugely to that process.

Wind

Hiking the Appalachian Trail is a diversion, a pause from the daily ritual of work, now that I have a job in the U.S. But I must guard against pushing myself too far and ruining my enjoyment of this beautiful walk. There is an open meadow. And so, I stop. I rest.

The meadow is my carpet. It cushions my head as I lay on my back observing the full, white billows of cumulonimbus clouds. They drift slowly above me, no destination in mind. But their course is not random. Wind directs their every move or dissipates them into extinction. As their shape changes ever so slowly in a light breeze, or more urgently in a stronger blow, I see forms of beasts, both mythical and real, change shape at the rate wind commands. Fleeting images of man made things appear and dissolve into vapor, as most man made things must. Fleeting glimpses of people I have known, and lost, drift by.

The sky above me is the same sky the Gypsy with the Golden Smile shared with me so many years ago. I see it now just as I saw it then, the child's imagination not yet lost. But there's a change. For now I wonder — did she still live? She would be older now than father was when I lost him. How did she battle the indignities of age? Had she let her spirit grow old? But no. I cannot believe that. She would still see the same ghostly forms in those clouds above me now. She would still point to the one like piglets with their curly tails. Yes, she would still point and give me her golden smile.

The clouds are ever changing. Recurring more and more often are vague forms of steam, steam from train engines, not beasts. I see wheels slowly turning in the lacy white mist. I see smoke rising from the engine's great stack. Sometimes the smoke is dark, foreboding. But it soon dissipates and the train itself melts away into the blue of the summer sky.

I wonder if the Gypsy with the Golden Smile is watching...

So sure was I that nothing ends. Time changed that. It changed me. I like to think it made me wiser. I've learned that all things come to an end. I grasp those worth having with less hesitation now before wind disperses them into extinction.

The blue sky retreats. Clouds change hue from frothy white to leaden grey. They grow dark and angry. It rains.

The Railroad

The train approached Tilžė (Tilsit) on October 10th. We were within sight of the city when the train stopped. The reason was soon apparent. Soviet bombers were droning in the eastern sky. Thinking the train may be bombed, everyone got off and ran into the forest. But the bombers continued on to Tilžė. Fires and explosions soon followed as we emerged from the forest. Bombs were falling on the city as we watched. This was the second bombing attack Tilžė suffered within a week's time. We were sure the train would not continue the journey. We prepared for the laborious task of unloading without a rail siding.

A German Reichsbahn constable came to tell us to stop. The train would continue, he said, and would go on as far into Tilžė as possible. The bombing continued. Everyone was apprehensive about what awaited us in the city. Planned stopover was to be brief — only long enough to pick up five more cars loaded with cattle — but no one expected the train to get near enough. Fires burned everywhere. The city was filled with smoke.

An unexploded bomb detonated just behind the building our train was passing. I felt the shock and was struck deaf as the brick walls collapsed into their own enormous cloud of dust. Bricks flew in the air and landed on the roofs of buildings still standing. Some reached the train and slammed onto our railcar. Wood splinters rained down on our heads. A blast of fear like a winter wind chilled my spine.

We gazed at the scene in silence. Slowly, my hearing returned but my head was still filled with the noise just past. The train slowed to walking pace. Perhaps a man was sent ahead to check for damaged rails before the engine wheels reached them. Perhaps the train waited for the bombing to stop.

Then, the train stopped. Again.

Bombs were still falling on the far end of the city, but the planes droned on soon after, and the bombing stopped. The noise around us changed. Sirens wailed their mournful song and bells tolled. The train jerked into motion. Soon, Tilžė's railroad terminal was in sight. It, too, was filled with smoke and debris was everywhere.

We watched the remains of the once proud Prussian trade center go by the open boxcar door as we approached the station. Mountains of rubble now stood in its place. Asphalt was creased and piled up in grotesque, convoluted waves where it had solidified after melting in the superheated air and flowed like lava through the streets. The stench of burned wood and carrion from the previous bombing was strong. People's arms, maybe legs, could be seen among the debris of one house. It was impossible to tell if they were still attached to the bodies.

Heavy, insulated pipes ran along the rails, then away at twisted angles, steam leaking from their joints. With exception of a solitary figure here and there, the streets were deserted. Strewn about were bed frames, broken bicycles, smashed baby carriages, and burned plants still in their pots on the sidewalk. Hat boxes were rolling in the wind. The stench of natural gas, like rotten eggs, filled the air.

I saw a woman sitting on the curb. Her suitcase served as pillow for her sleeping child. Men stood in small groups, watching over small fires they tended to burn the remains of small animals killed in the bombings. Rats scuttled about in the gutters. Buildings burned all around us. Images drifted past my confused eyes with no clear demarcation between fantasy and reality.

A fine grey ash chalked everything. Its bitter taste was on my tongue. The city was dominated by a single color. Ruins were grey, houses were grey, the trees were grey. Even the people were grey.

Rubble of brick, concrete, and stone covered the ground without interruption — crushed bricks, furniture and broken glass piled two stories high. Streets were littered with debris, burned out cars, and dead horses. The stench followed us through the city. Soldiers were rolling the carcasses into bomb craters which peppered what had once been tree lined boulevards and wide avenues through residential neighborhoods that once housed the elite. Tall chimneys, like charred broken fingers pointing accusingly to the heavens, were all that remained of their burned out homes.

I was sure that was what was left of ours in Raseiniai. We wondered if our friends, and others we had loved who stayed behind, survived. Seeing Tilžė in such sweeping ruin sowed seeds of doubt that anyone could survive such consummate destruction in Raseiniai. Tilžė burned for three days after the bombing.

But for the few unfortunates we saw earlier, the city was deserted. Miraculously, while the train station was badly damaged, the rails and platforms survived the bombing. That's where all the people were. The ruins of the train station were alive with masses of them looking for a way to escape either the Nazis or the Red Army tide from the east. They were hemmed in. Not yet in panic, but with desperate determination etched in their faces, they fought to gain access to authorities in charge of transit permits.

Unlike the station we started from the day before, Tilžė's was a large, noisy and confusing place. Everyone was in a hurry. Little help could be expected in finding trains to take them away from the perceived Armageddon. We thanked our luck for not having to go through the bureaucratic boondoggle these people faced after the hell of the bombing they had already been through.

I had no idea then what that meant, but death from bombing is gruesome, never mind the sheer terror preceding it. Those killed outright at point of impact were the lucky ones. The rest were crushed, blinded, deafened, asphyxiated, or burned alive. I was a very lucky child to have never been under direct bombing. Five thousand children died in Hamburg in a single night of bombing.

Hooking on the cattle cars took hours to complete. Our progress, in general, was painfully slow. The railroad was busy with military trains moving westward. They had priority. Our train waited its turn at every station. When it moved, it was at snail's pace. We spent more time stopped in terminals than we did on the move. An entire day sometimes passed while we waited for our turn to leave the station. At one stopover, German soldiers tried to beat off people getting on a neighboring train through the windows. When droves of them perched on railcar roofs, the soldiers gave up. The train pulled out with people clinging to the rooftops in the choking smoke.

Once, we happened to be in a station at supper time. We were given a thick vegetable soup, or stew, and rye bread smeared with lard. It was the fare distributed to the military traveling by rail. This was a godsend, as cooking on the train was difficult if not impossible. Hot food was a rare treat the whole way to Mecklenburg some two weeks on.

Russian air attacks were now more frequent. They targeted anything that moved by rail and made no distinction between retreating German army trains and civilian transports. Our train was hit several times, but wasn't stopped by the attacks. We huddled in the boxcar under our wagon, hoping to put enough wood between us and the flying bullets to absorb their kinetic energy if not to deflect or stop them.

During one early morning attack I felt my leg suddenly burn as if by branding iron. A bullet nicked my calf just enough to cause much bleeding but no permanent harm. I was more amazed than scared with this nasty surprise. Antiseptic bandages and pressure soon stopped the bleeding. The searing pain persisted for hours. The ceaseless jostling in the train did nothing to help my misery. I grit my teeth and tried not to cry. I succeeded for longer intervals as time went by. Two days later, many bandage changes and gritting teeth behind me, everyone said my leg looked as good as new. There was fear of infection setting in, but Alla had some nurse's training, as did mother. I was in good hands. I was particularly impressed by Alla's knowledge of folk remedies. Things like fennel for fever, ginger root for indigestion, rue for flatulence, dill for stomach disorders, and so on. Based on all that, I had no doubts my full recovery was assured.

Eventually, I found the clickety-clack monotone of the train soothing and returned to watching the countryside through the half open door. We were passing large pine forests and small farms. My short naps soon turned to full fledged sleep.

I was awakened by a change in the movement and rhythm of the train. It had slowed down to a crawl. Loud clanging of the railcar couplings and the screeching of brakes slowly brought us to a complete stop. It was suddenly very quiet. Someone slid the big door fully open and we looked outside. There was another rail line right next to ours. It could not have been more than a minute or two when another train came roaring through alongside, and was passing us. There was a terrific noise as it whooshed by. It passed so close, that if I reached out through the door, I could have touched it. A great blast of wind stormed into our car through the open door with such force, everything loose went flying. The men quickly slid the door shut, but the train had already passed — it went so fast! It was a passenger train and I saw faces streak by in its windows like flashes of blurred light behind the dark glass. It probably had military priority, and our train was ordered to take the side spur and let it go by.

A Reichsbahn official came to talk to us when the door was reopened. He said our two boxcars would be uncoupled and left here to wait for another train to which they would be attached. He gave no explanation; wouldn't even tell us where we were. Father thought we had stopped somewhere near Wartenburg. Alla laughed, saying he made up the name to be funny (*warten* means wait).

The women prepared to light up the stove and start cooking. The railroad man said it would be an hour before the other train came. This was an opportunity to fix some hot food. Mother handed me a knife and set a sack of potatoes in front of me. I knew what had to be done. I peeled about a dozen, carefully tossing the eyes and blue centers out the door and saving the skins to be fried for breakfast. I was so busy, I forgot all about my bullet wound. Alla chopped up a head of cabbage and diced some onion. The result was a big pot of steaming cabbage and potato soup. I thought this was better than the stew thickened with barley which had been our last hot meal back in Tilžė.

By the time everyone finished eating, the hour had passed. No sign of the train. We jumped out of the boxcar to take a walk and look around. We were in the middle of nowhere. In the far distance was a farm — nothing else. Our boxcars stopped directly over a culvert spanning a small stream. What luck! We went to check on the horses in the other freight car while the women filled several buckets with water from the stream.

After another hour we were beginning to wonder what happened to the train. No one was worried yet. We all knew things moved slowly and train schedules were constantly changed to accommodate the military. I helped with mucking out the horses' car, examined both rail cars in some detail trying to figure out how everything worked, and asked a lot of questions.

At dusk, four hours later, the question adults were asking was where was that train. Have we been left here and forgotten? Was the train attacked and destroyed? Did it encounter damaged rails, or stopped for some other reason? How long should we wait? Should we spend the night here before searching for the nearest road?

The last option seemed most reasonable. We prepared for the night, but not everyone slept. The men took turns keeping watch. I slept like a log.

I awoke to the aroma of tea and fried potato skins. The door was open only a wedge. It was raining — a dreary, forlorn sound on the boxcar roof, nothing like the pleasant sound of windless rain in the forest, falling through the trees, the smell of wet earth in the air.

The darkness in the boxcar was broken only by the Primus flame under the tea kettle. Everyone was quietly watching the rain and sipping tea. Then someone noticed me stirring and conversation livened up. Might as well wait for the rain to stop before taking action, they were saying. Father was packing his backpack with bacon rind and home made liquor, the customary bribe currency. Apparently some decision had been made while I slept.

"Well, at least we have a roof over our heads," one man said.

"Are you sure we can get the horses off without a ramp?" someone asked. I, too, wasn't so sure about that. I had only seen horses jump up, not down. But then jumping down is easier, isn't it?

The question was ignored. Moving the wagons off the train was a more pressing matter. Tools were already laid out for removal of the big sliding door. It was to supplement lumber saved from the ramp used when loading. Now, a new one was to be built. Wagons would have to be unloaded again. Mother said she was sure there must be another way. She, too, was ignored. Father thought the wagons may have to be partially disassembled to move them off even with a ramp.

Rain subsided to a drizzle and sun peeked out from between the clouds. When rain stopped, it looked like it was going to be a bright, sunny day. Father took the backpack and set off along the rail-bed toward the farm we saw in the distance. Someone suggested he use the bicycle, but the ground here was much too rough to ride. He walked. We lost sight of him after a while. It was decided to wait for whatever information he brought back before making our move.

An hour later we heard a train whistle. Soon, we could see the rear end of the train slowly backing toward us. Surely, father heard it too, and was heading back. I looked toward the farm. I didn't see him. The train was closing faster than it first appeared. I wasn't the only one concerned that he would be left behind. Mother was urging people to do something. She was distraught. But there was nothing to be done. We could hear the train's wheels clicking over the rails and see its engine's smoke at the far end, only a few railcars away. It was a short train without a caboose. A man was hanging on to the step rail of the last and nearest car, ready to jump and secure the coupling. It was a civilian passenger train no more than six cars long — something we hadn't expected. Those were usually reserved for dignitaries when not serving the Wehrmacht. We never found out what had delayed that train.

Father was still out of sight. Didn't he know what was happening? Mother was pleading with those who spoke better German to ask the train to wait. One man tried; to no avail.

"We'll have to wait for him in Torun," he said. It meant we would have to unload and disembark the train, and no one knew if there would be enough time or that it would even be possible.

The train's next stop was Torun. Maybe father could get there before us. No, they said, it was too far. He could never make it in time. How would he get there? Could we get off at Torun? Continue by road? No one knew. Could he get on another train? Impossible.

"Help me with this wheel," one man said. He stood on the tongue between our two boxcars trying to turn a big hand wheel. He didn't have to ask twice. I had no idea what they were trying to do. I kept looking for my father.

Soon, our freight cars began to move — very slowly at first. That's when I understood. Rails ran slightly downhill toward the farm and away from the approaching train. The men were releasing the brakes and we were rolling down the hill. That's when I saw father. He was running. But he was so far away. He would never make it before that train reached us. I had visions of the woman relieving herself on the rails, and her child calling as their train pulled away.

The man on the train was hollering, gesticulating and pointing. He was now no more than thirty yards away. He was very angry. We rolled slowly down the rails, but his train was gaining rapidly. We were still rolling when it made contact and engaged the coupling with a clang. The railroader jumped off to check it.

"Verfluchter, Ausländernen!" he cursed. This was followed by additional *Donner Wetters* and similar language as he shook his fist at us before returning to his perch. I paid him no heed. I was watching father, still running and still too far away. As soon as the train reversed direction, we were underway again. Everyone shouted at the railroader to stop the train. He paid no attention. Our speed was now faster than my father could run.

He stopped running when it became obvious there was no hope of catching up. He waved. Mother was in hysterics. I cried. Subdued conversation centered on finding a way to reunite us. I was too distraught to follow it. I sat on the floor trying not to weep. We only lost a day. It could have been a lot worse if we had to revert to travel by road the rest of the way to Mecklenburg. But it couldn't be worse now that father was being left behind.

It wasn't long before Alla noticed the sun was no longer on our left. Sure enough, we were heading south. If we had really been stopped near Wartenburg, we must be half way to Warsaw by now. This was not good. Apparently we were not hooked on to the originally intended train to which we were to be attached. Everyone thought we should demand to be uncoupled at the next stop so we could off-load and continue by road. But our day of surprises wasn't over yet.

As we passed another rail line branching off the one we were on, the train slowed. On the other line was a long freight train heading toward us. As our train came to a stop, the freight train's caboose connected to our wagon car with an almighty crash. Everything went topsy-turvy. We heard the horses snort and whinny in alarm in the next boxcar. We were now connected to two trains!

The same angry railroader stomped over to release us from his passenger train. He was muttering to himself as he pulled the pins in the coupling and let the latch fall on its hinges with a bang. I guess he was glad to be rid of the hated *Ausländernen*. And, just like that, we were hooked on to yet another train. This one wasted no time. The men barely had a few moments to check the horses, and off we went, steaming west toward Torun.

We didn't see anybody, but there were people in that caboose. We heard music and women's laughter for miles. Then we saw empty bottles being thrown out the caboose windows.

I missed the only musical entertainment we had since leaving home — father's harmonica. He played it while we traveled by train, and he played it well. It was an effort to hold back tears wondering where he was, worrying for his safety.

* * *

Torun rail terminal was jam packed with trains and mobbed with people trying to get on. Everyone was anxious to get away from the approaching Russians. By now, they had heard enough stories from the Poles and Prussians who had preceded them. Any means to move west were being utilized, and there was nothing faster than trains in spite of their inefficiency. German gendarmes kept order but the crowd looked ready to overcome their authority.

Our train stopped alongside a long platform filled with people. We hastily slid the door shut and latched it. I looked through the small, slatted window which I could reach only by climbing atop the driver's seat of our wagon. A shrill whistle announced the arrival of another train. It slowed along the opposite side of the platform. SS storm troopers armed with machine-pistols jumped off even before the train came to a stop. They lined up shoulder to shoulder along the edge of the platform and looked like they would shoot anyone trying to get on. I froze, waiting for the shooting to start. But no sooner had it stopped, than the military train pulled out again, the storm troopers running to get back on. Father's whereabouts were not to be discovered in Torun. No one was allowed off the train.

Our train's turn was next. Although we were glad to be leaving Torun, our hopes of finding my father were dashed. Our train would not stop again until it reached Stettin, 300 kilometers away. Mother was in tears. She was certain we would never see him again. I stubbornly held on to the opposite view, sure of my father's determination to find us.

The longest stop was in Stettin (now Szczecin in Poland). There was time to get off the train, stretch our legs and look around the city. For reasons unknown, the planned two-hour layover stretched to an entire day. Mother, and several others, went off somewhere to search for information which might help in locating father. He was never out of my thoughts and I wanted to go along. That, however, was not in my mother's plans. I was instructed to stay with the train. There was a chance that he may have gone on to Stettin.

Seeing the situation in Torun, he might have done just that if he had made it that far. We hadn't given up hope. He knew the route of our train and was sure to follow it. A whole day's delay here would only help him.

From what could be seen in the streets nearby, the city was still intact and functioning. There were no bombed out buildings and people seemed to be going about their daily tasks. We returned and walked around the station. I couldn't tell if it was larger than the station in Torun, but it was huge. Busy with military and civilian trains, it was crowded, noisy, dirty, and filled with a choking smoke from the coal fired engines. The hiss and clouds of steam were everywhere. I was careful not to wander too far, as train departures were always unpredictable. I was also anxious about mother getting back in time. Alla kept me company. Without a common language between us, she could offer scant consolation. But I learned a few more words in Ukrainian.

We noticed the floor of a cattle car on our train had broken through. A cow's forelegs protruded through the jagged hole. They were bloody from being dragged over the railroad ties. Alla brought this to the attention of a railroad official.

"Men are dying at the front, and you're worried about a cow?" was his reply. Nothing was done. At the end of the day, father's whereabouts were still unknown. The train pulled out before sundown.

We didn't get far. The train stopped again, reason unknown as usual. We waited and looked up the tracks ahead to see what was going on. Nothing. It was already getting dark. Just as we thought to get off and take a walk, the train jerked into motion. A few minutes later, it stopped again. There was another train stopped on our track. We pulled up close behind it. This time we did get off and walked over the short distance to have a closer look.

A large group of people were busy around the wheel carriages of that train. Projector lights were hung under the rail cars. They were removing the axle housings on one of the boxcars. The smell of smoke and oil was strong. It looked like they had just put out a fire. The work looked difficult.

We asked what happened. The man who replied did so in a very agitated tone of voice. He spoke too fast for me to understand. But the curses he used were familiar — always the first words learned in a new tongue.

It seems the bearing boxes were filled with sand. Once explained, his ire became clear. Bearing boxes, the size of a bread box, contained axle lubricant grease. There was one on every wheel carriage. Not unlike a bread box, each had a lid to protect the grease inside. These lids were not locked and could be easily opened. Apparently someone filled the bearing box with sand which mixed with axle grease and eventually destroyed the axle, setting the wooden undercarriage on fire, and putting the whole train in jeopardy.

We were not surprised. Sabotage by the underground was common, and this had all the marks of one which succeeded. It had already stopped all other trains running on our track. The Reichsbahn may not have liked this development, but we knew the longer we were delayed, the more likely my father would get ahead of the train and find us. There was no side track or spur where the damaged boxcar could be pushed out of the way. That meant it would be hours before the two trains could get under way.

This was an opportunity to cook a hot meal and to collect firewood. The latter was my task. The wood was to be used for a small fire, built inside our rail car, to dry laundry while underway later. Our clothes would smell of smoke, but they would be clean.

While we waited for the freight car to be repaired, which took the entire night, Alla showed me how to plant radishes in a box kept in our wagon. They later became my favorite spice in all kinds of food.

The trains came back to life after dawn, and we were on our way once more. We hoped the delay was long enough to give father a good head start. Someone in the group said we owed the local partisans our thanks.

Wild Boar and Fancy Dinner

On crossing the Oder River we were in Mecklenburg province. The station in Waren was a sharp contrast to Stettin. Ours was the only train. Not much was going on and the place looked like it was cleaned regularly. Pulled up to a siding, we were given 36 hours to vacate the train.

It was learned that a local hotel was hosting a meeting of farm inspectors. These officials of the Reich were charged with the administration of Mecklenburg's farms. Once we learned the size of these farms we understood the need. They were the biggest farms we had ever seen. The men in our group attended the meeting, made our presence known and offered our resources. When they returned, father was with them!

We were overwhelmed with emotion. Tears of joy flooded our faces. Our reunion was shared by everyone within earshot. Nothing, but nothing, could have made me happier at that moment. If mother was shamed by her loss of all hope, I was proud I had kept faith, always certain father would find us.

We listened to his story in awe. At the farm we saw in the distance, to which he had set off on foot from where our rail cars were stopped, he learned that the Wehrmacht was moving produce and other goods from area farms westward. This was to supply the German troops retreating to the Oder River. Father waited on a hill overlooking the main road leading west. He watched the sparse traffic through binoculars which he always carried on reconnaissance. It was on the morning after out train had left him behind that he saw a small military convoy. He knew, from information gained at the farm, that supply convoys usually stopped in the village behind this hill to water the horses. But this was a truck convoy. He ran down to the village in case it stopped anyway.

The convoy did not stop. But the narrow, winding street between the buildings forced such slow speed that father was

113

able to board the last truck in line without being seen. The convoy stopped in the next town on some business at its post office. Father got off the truck, again unseen, and approached one of the German officers. He knew nothing good would come from being discovered as a stowaway. He bribed the officer with home made liquor he carried in the backpack — an item commonly used as currency. The Wehrmacht officer agreed to take him as far west as the convoy was going. This turned out to be well south of Stettin, our train's destination after Torun. This officer advised him to steer clear of Torun.

By the time he would reach Stettin, however, our train would probably have already departed. He decided to continue on to Waren, our ultimate destination in Mecklenburg. But the supply convoy was not going to cross the Oder. Twelve kilometers from the river, it turned farther south. Father thanked the officer for the ride and set off towards the river on foot. There, he joined a group of refugees from Poland, also planning to cross the bridge near Gartz. They had work permits and authorities were not too diligent in checking everyone's papers at the usually jammed and chaotic river crossings. Taking the chance, father blended in with the group until it reached the west bank. After another 40-kilometer walk, he reached Waren the day before our train got in. He knew we would be there sooner or later. He also knew about the meeting at the hotel and expected someone from our group to attend.

* * *

Shortly after the farm inspectors meeting one of them instructed us to disembark the train and proceed to a specified location for assignment to a farm. Our group was split up among the farms in the province and assembled in the future only on Sundays. Two families went their own way and continued westward. We never reestablished contact with them.

Our assigned farm was part of a 10,000-acre estate which included numerous farms and a wild game preserve used by wealthy hunters before the war. It was called Blücherhoff and was owned by an invalided veteran of World War I. As in all Germany, the only able bodied men were foreign refugees. We made up the work force. Among us were many Poles and Ukrainians. We were the only Lithuanians.

Our one room accommodations were Spartan but comfortable. We lived in barracks specifically built to house hired help. All buildings were brick, were heated, and each had a small kitchen. Roadways were cobble-stoned and yards were fenced. Father was employed with our two horses to work the fields of sugar beets and potatoes. His day began at six and, with meal breaks at eight and two, continued until seven. My day began at the eight o'clock breakfast with a Lithuanian tutor from another farm who taught me the basic middle school subjects: math, science, geography, history, and language. There were no others of school age at the farm, so I enjoyed exclusive use of this education. To help improve my German, his tutoring was delivered in German as often as it was in Lithuanian.

By now we knew American and Allied forces had landed in France. New hope sparked in our hearts. Our objective now was to reach Allied lines before the Russians caught up with us. To that end, plans were made to proceed westward as soon as possible, and my education came to an end. The inspector paid father for the seven weeks' work. We prepared to leave Blücherhoff and go on to the next unknown.

Before we left, the land owner asked us for one last favor. His game preserve was tasked by the government to hunt game for food. Requirements and limits were imposed on every estate and it was the owner's obligation to fulfill them every year. Hunters from surrounding estates took part and celebrated at hunt's end.

A small army of beaters was needed to drive the game. Having been treated well throughout our stay, father felt we owed him another day before departure.

Hundreds lined up with horns, drums, whistles, cymbals fashioned from farm implements, rattles of all kinds, and even sticks to beat on empty galvanized pails and metal milk cans. On signal, we advanced in a curving line abreast across the forest, making as much noise as we could. Ahead of this colossal din, all creatures great and small ran terrified into the pre-planned clearing where the hunters waited. To avoid being shot by stray bullets, we were instructed to lie down in gullies just before we got there and signal was given to open fire. The noise we made was so loud the shots were never heard.

Only wild boar were taken. Rules of the hunt allowed each hunter only one shot, and if the boar was not fatally wounded, the hunter was obliged to track the animal down and deliver the coup de grace by hand. We saw a man circle an infuriated boar, which had lost the use of its hind legs, looking for an opportunity to strike with knife and hammer. Many minutes passed before that opportunity presented itself. It was painful to watch. I could never do that to an animal, I thought. I must have been right. I never hunted.

The hunt yielded some two dozen wild boar, several to be roasted on spits and consumed in a feast at day's end. Next day, we were given a copious helping of game meat and wild boar sausage for our trip and left Blücherhoff with more than enough food to last the few days it would take to reach our next destination.

* * *

We now traveled alone. It proved to be safer as we attracted less attention from authorities and did not present a tempting target for Russian aircraft which still crossed the skies overhead with regularity. Worse were instances of roads choked by refugees being cleared by *Luftwaffe* planes for the retreating German army. Those killed were left in roadside ditches, all of them barefoot, their shoes removed by survivors. We happened across such a scene without survivors. That's where I gained a pair of shoes to replace the ones my growing feet had been painfully crowding. Mother constantly darned and enlarged my socks as needed, but I was outgrowing shoes faster than larger pairs could be found. So, this was a happy occasion, even in the face of all those lives lost.

Father's reconnaissance rides now had another objective. He canvassed all farms of significant size for work and accommodation. Some were already filled to capacity by refugees who preceded us. After four days of slow progress we pulled our wagon into a large courtyard surrounded by a newly painted fence. The courtyard was paved in brick and everything was scrubbed clean.

Vollrathsruhe was a huge spread near Waren — 8,000 acres someone said. It had its own rail terminal and, typical of

Mecklenburg's large estates, a number of small farms within its realm. We were greeted at the office by the government inspector/administrator and issued ration coupons for our daily needs, food stamps for which we could buy food in Warren, wage and work permits, and documents allowing movement in areas guarded by the army. This was becoming normal as we moved farther west. Restrictions increased as the threat of colliding fronts loomed and food shortages became routine. We were expected to produce some document or another, everywhere we went, to indicate permission and reasons for being where we were.

Before assigning us to a farm the inspector invited us to his home for dinner. He said he wanted to welcome us to his estate which he owned as well as administered. This was a huge surprise on many counts, so unexpected father was not sure he should accept the invitation. It was only after he learned that several professional posts on the estate were filled by refugees who were also invited, that he felt it appropriate to attend.

We dressed in the best clothes we had. Mother wore her only dress and patent leather shoes, saved deep in one of our trunks for just such an occasion. Father brought out his suit jacket, not worn since we left Jurbarkas. Mother said it smelled of mothballs.

At the manor house we met Dr. Danuta Bergman. She was the estate physician from Latvia, and a war refugee like we. She was very pleased to be addressed in her own language, in which my father was fluent. Caretaker of the estate stables was a retired Lithuanian cavalry officer, also a refugee. There were children my age at the table and one girl of ten or eleven was in charge of setting the table for dinner. She was just finishing her task when we arrived.

There were deep rugs on the flagged dining room floor. The room was large, its walls hung with tapestries as if this was some fairy tale castle, and a huge fireplace at one end. I had never seen one so big. I could have walked into it, had it not been lighted.

The tablecloth was of bleached white linen with an embroidered runner extending the full length of the table, large enough to seat twenty or more. Lace fringed napkins were folded alongside china ringed in gold, and silverware sparkled in the candlelight from two candelabras, three candles each. At each end of the table, set on a velvet doily, was a large white soup tureen, one shaped like a swan, the other like nesting pelicans. Serving dishes steamed at table center, wafting their aroma to fill the room and awaken our collective palate.

One wall was hung with a huge tapestry of a hunting scene and portraits of what may have been the ancestors of our host and previous masters of the estate. It was all very regal but lacked the pretense and demonstrative opulence of the nouveau riche. This was a household which had not yet been touched by war. But everyone knew those days were numbered. We were here to enjoy this respite while we could. It must have evoked fond memories of home in my parents' hearts.

With all of us seated and about to be served, the man of the house called to the girl who set the table and told her to bring a step ladder. She rose without hesitation and returned with a small stepladder. The man told her to climb it. She did as she was told, but with a worried look in her eye. The man told her to look down on the table. Our host was a staunch disciplinarian with his own family as he was with hired help. But we later learned he was always generous and fair in his treatment of people who worked for him.

"*Was hast du vergessen?*" he asked the girl. What have you forgotten?

She quickly jumped down, rushed the ladder from the room and returned with the single fork she had overlooked. She sat back down, her face burning in crimson hue. I was acutely embarrassed for her and hid my eyes throughout the meal, concentrating on my table manners which mother had drilled into me before we arrived.

I remembered to keep the knife in my right hand, the fork in my left, and never cut more than one bite at a time or switch hands. (Many years later I had to modify this to the exact opposite, to comply with proper etiquette in America). Soup was always served last and it carried the simplest requirements of propriety. All I had to do was use the spoon without slurping.

Sour beet root soup was not to my liking, but the thick cabbage stew with sour cream was not bad. Potatoes, boiled in their skins, and flavored heavily with leek was the best dish on the table.

I even dared to ask for seconds. There was also a loaf of white bread, a special treat we hadn't seen since we left home. There was no meat. After having been used to a grey pea soup, groats, dried peas and turnips, this was a veritable feast.

For dessert, we were served poppy seed cakes topped with a honey glaze. They were exactly like the ones my mother used to make at home. Other foods on that marvelous table are now beyond my recollection, but the vague smell of flowers from the pale green tea made from linden tree blossoms is as vivid in my nostrils today as it was then.

Conversation around the table centered on the Russian advance westward. Our hosts were concerned. Are the Russians already at the German border? Are they really so terrible that you have left everything to escape them? Is it true they rob and rape the people indiscriminately? They were afraid they would soon become refugees like us. This was now a growing concern among the German population in general. No one believed the Nazi propaganda. Everyone knew the war was lost.

Although my understanding of the conversation was limited, I grasped more of it than I thought I could. I suppose being exposed to German speakers more often than people who spoke other languages had its effect. It advanced my command of it rapidly, and I would soon speak it well enough to deal with all my daily needs.

This whole affair affected us in no small way. Although we were treated reasonably well by most German people along our route, there were more than a few bad experiences. We looked on this one as the most unusual of all. The food this family shared with us was not all that much better than food available to us by more ordinary means, but it was served in old world grandeur. Sharing their table with complete strangers from a foreign land, who suddenly appeared on their doorstep and may have been moved to take criminal advantage of their generosity; as happens so often in war; was a unique experience for us, and never forgotten.

Example of the other extreme came our way some weeks prior. At one stopover farm, on a blustery, ugly, rainy night, we were put up in a vile smelling cattle shed and expected to share the straw with the animals while their sewage flowed along the cement swale at our feet. It was the only occasion I remember when father lost his temper with our host before the barn was opened for our use. Sleeping in barns in foul weather and fair was always expected and appreciated. Some were better than others, but they were what the farmers had to offer. If the available accommodations were really that bad, we slept in our wagon even through the worst storms.

Vollrathsruhe was apparently better than that. Father was shown to a large woodworking shop with tools and finished lumber, where he was allowed to cut and nail together whatever furniture we needed for our stay in Hallalit, the estate's farm where we would work. He was instructed to use only the smallest, fine tooth, high speed saw. It made the work slow and painstaking. The sawdust it produced was very fine, like flour. It hung in the air making it hard to breathe. When it settled to the cleanly swept floor, it had to be collected into a dust pan and deposited in a small bin made for that purpose. It was typical of German preoccupation with cleanliness and order.

We loaded our wagon with a double bed, a table with two benches, some shelving, and a smaller bed for me — all made by my father's own hand in the course of a single day in spite of the inefficient saw he used. The only help came from my holding one end of a board while he cut the other. In return, he used what scrap wood remained to make a wooden scooter for me. I was thrilled. With one foot on the low platform between the wheels and holding on to the handlebar, I propelled myself along by pushing off the ground with my other foot. A far cry from his bicycle, but this was my own transport vehicle which moved faster than I could walk.

Before seeing us off, the field foreman saw to it that we were fed. He told us we'd be on our own in Hallalit. There was no one there to cook for us, he said, as if we expected servants. We shared the table with four Polish girls who took care of domestic chores on the estate. It was a pleasant interlude, as mother was fluent in Polish and two of the girls were veritable chatterboxes. They served us a thick potato soup with onions and bread smeared with thick layers of lard. Lard had been a staple at our table for quite some time. We hadn't seen butter for ten months and this was familiar fare, except the bread was white, the same as the inspector served at his manor house, and with the same gritty softness and dusty taste we had never encountered before. We asked the girls about it.

"Oh, it's the sawdust," they said.

"Sawdust?"

"Yes. We mix it with the flour. White flour is scarce. This makes more bread," they explained.

Now we knew what the fine tooth saw in the woodshop was for.

We were met in Hallalit by a cheerful Lithuanian teacher who already worked there. His wife was a Red Cross nurse and their daughter Nijolė was my age. She became my playmate within minutes and remained so throughout our stay in Mecklenburg. We got along so well, in fact, that we surprised our parents with a pre-rehearsed skit to celebrate Lithuanian Independence Day on February 16th.

We worked on our little skit in secret. It consisted of a poetry reading and a folk dance, and it took all our energy and free time away from the tutoring program her father conducted for the two of us while we lived in Hallalit.

Now that he had two students, her father was motivated to write his own textbooks (there were no others) for us to study. These were hand written and bound with needle and thread into tiny, cigarette pack size books which we could carry in our pockets and read wherever we went. I safeguarded his little geography textbook and count it among my treasured possessions today. It is the only one which he typed. It was done on a typewriter found abandoned in a German gun emplacement bunker.

His family is yet another among scores of acquaintances and friends of whose future whereabouts, even survival, I never learned. Each parting with people we met along the way was a time of sadness and regret that we may never see them again. I thought of them late at night when sleep wouldn't come. Coping with this did not get easier with time. Nightly images sometimes interrupted my sleep, those nightmare demons that time failed to exorcise: Vida making a straw whistle. Vida grappling the greased pig, suddenly bloody. Vida falling from gunshots in a field of sunflowers. Arūnas spitting beeswax farther than I. The Vollrathsruhe girl falling from the stepladder to reach the forgotten fork.

When father thought I was cold for tossing and turning in my sleep, probably fueled by those mixed dreams, he always gave up his blanket for me. I knew he would dream my nightmares for me if he could.

Shortly after the war ended, father saw Dr. Danuta Bergman in Hamburg. She told him that Vollrathsruhe's owner/administrator, who feted us at dinner in his home, was murdered by the Russians with his entire family. Dr. Bergman escaped and remained in Germany's British Zone of occupation after resettlement. Like my father and many of her generation, she did not live to see her country free and independent again. Danuta Bergman died before Latvia regained her independence in 1991.

My parents, Eugenija and Motiejus Karaša, 1935

Our house in Kaunas, my first home; destroyed during the war.

General Staff of Šaulių Sąjunga (Lithuanian National Guard). Motiejus
Karaša seated 2nd from left.

Outing with mother at one of the many museums in Kaunas before I
learned to walk.

Winter outing with friends. My father, in uniform, talking to my mother-to-be, seated in the sleigh.

Uncle Jonas' "shuttle service"

My godfather, Supreme Commander of the Lithuanian National Guard (Šauliu Sąjunga), Pranas Saladžius; Armed Forces Day 1939. Behind him, in the tribunal: Women's National Guard director, Emilija Putvienė (deported to Siberia), Latvia's Aizsargi commander, General Kārlis Prauls (executed by the Russians in Riga), Estonia's Kaitselinda commander, General Johannes Orasmaa (died in Siberian slave labor camp)

This is the only image I have of my
godmother, the "Gypsy with Golden
Smile" (on the left), 1944

Our house in Raseiniai, undergoing major renovation.
It burned to the ground after the war, along with all other buildings on the
property

Uncle Mike with his bees

Antanas Gantautas, "Ponas Uoga",
after the war

Preparing for the night, East Prussia 1944.
Father's reconnaissance bike strapped
to the back of the wagon

Celebrating Independence Day,
Hallalit, 16 February 1945

Father sporting the French beret which
helped save us from repatriation, Hamburg 1947

Remains of the house we left moments before it was shelled to
destruction, Tobringen 1945
(photo taken after rubble was cleaned up and everything
salvageable removed)

My first formal school in a foreign land. On the left are two of
my most memorable teachers, Henrikas Stasas and Magdelena
Kudirkienė, 1945

Henrikas Stasas, founder of the school, at a formal
dinner in the U.S. with his youngest daughter, 1965

Mother and I with our "home" in the background, Wietze 1945

On our way to the Boy Scout Jamboree,
France 1947

The Stasas sisters "at tea", Gross Hesepe
1945.
Ingrida (on the right), now Honorary Consul
of Lithuania

Homeroom class in Gross Hesepe, 1946.
Note the hand knit outfits made by parents,
friends and neighbors in the camp.
(Author 2nd from left, back row)

133

My cousin Arūnas, Olympic athlete (1968),
before his alleged defection attempt was thwarted

Stančikaitė-Abraitienė in her studio after the war

Lithuanian high school and elementary school, with faculty, immediately after they were established, Diepholz 1948

Lithuanian DP Camp administration building in Diepholz. Note German Adler and Nazi swastika imprint over the entrance after their removal. Our high school was housed in abandoned Wehrmacht barracks just like this building

My cousin Narimantas Karaša, Munich 1947. He was instrumental in securing the means for us to emigrate to the U.S.

Lined up in our Sunday best, we await selection to flag raising honor guard duty, Diepholz 1948

Sunday discussion circle under my window, where I learned
the news by eavesdropping, Diepholz 1950

Violeta, all grown up

My country cousins, Olė and Vida, after the war.
Both stayed on the family farm until evicted by collectivization

My city cousins, Gintautas and Arūnas, after the war.
Gintautas went on to renown as a stone sculptor

Author – U.S. Immigration photo, 1953

Author (center) – U.S. Army
advanced combat training, 1959

Wind

The sea is calm, but the cold is such that ice fog forms over the water. Like smoke, it drifts with swells and follows their undulating motion. The sea is calm, silent — the arctic sun's light still blocked in the cold air of dawn. The shimmering, silver ice fog hangs low to the water, savoring its chill. Above it are giant peaks bordering the glacier we are passing to starboard, their ghostly outlines just discernable in the early morning haze. The silence is deceptive. It does not portend the dangers these mountains hide.

I stand on the bridge wing of my ship, dwarfed by the immense size of the icebergs that surround us. Our passage takes us up the Davis Strait into more and more frigid waters, even though it is still mid-summer here. Ice breakers find work farther north, and that is where we are going.

Suddenly, a crack!

Sharp and clean like a leather whip on wet marble. But louder. A shard of ice, half the size of the Empire State Building, breaks away from the glacier in a great spray of freezing steam. It slides, first slowly as if trying to find its way, then faster and faster, to bury itself in the icy ocean. It pauses just before submerging and disappears in the fog. It rises then, back up out of the depths, with equal violence to more than half its height. Suspended there momentarily, unwilling to relinquish its place among the other peaks, it succumbs nevertheless, to join the giant ice flows on a sea no longer calm, no longer silent.

The wave it gives birth to comes rolling at the ship, growing in speed and size as it nears. The disturbance briefly shatters the ice fog and I can see it coming. There is also wind, fanned by the giant's motion and the sea's reply. I brace to the rail, feet planted firmly to the deck. I wait for the ship to roll.

Exactly on cue, the starboard side dips ever so slightly downward, then the ship rises with the huge wave and rolls the other way as the swell passes under the keel. I look for it on the port side, but the ice fog claims it again and the calm sea returns.

I had been standing here some time, marveling at the spectacle as we pass glaciers on our way north. But this is the grandest break-off I had ever seen.

I enjoy the icy cold of winter many times, in many ways. If I am on skis, winter is more personal, more intimate. Blowing across snow the wind is bitter. If I face it directly, it takes my breath away. But if I forge ahead, let my skis follow the snow down the mountain and make my own wind, I breathe deeper with the excitement of my run. I am revitalized. I soar.

Winter is crisp, its air fresh and pure, clean and bright beneath the endless mountain sky. I can be happy here, in this cold and fatally beautiful world. But I must not stay. Friends await at my run's end. We ski together less often now than we did in younger days. But it is still as much a social venture as it is a sport. *Apres-ski* can be a party as it always was. Stowe welcomes us with its old world charm — old world by American standards. But I have not returned to ski the Alps in years and when I did, the temptation to turn northeast and add another thousand miles tugged ever so faintly like a homing instinct not yet lost in the land whose streets are paved in gold.

I have not returned to my country of birth. Consciously so. Memories of home are strong. The memories are good. They cannot be improved. Earlier on I did not want to see the wounds my homeland suffered. Now I do not want to see the change. It is as foreign as the Alps without their beauty. I keep the memories I have, for memories of home must not be tarnished. And mine are bright and clean as winter snow.

I stop to rest a moment and enjoy the view. The slender firs shed snowflakes in the wind like a fine mist. Birches hide the ice on their white skin, but it glitters its presence on bare branches moving in the sunny wind. Whirling devils of fine snow, like miniature tornadoes, are lifted by the ground breeze and urged uphill to rapid self destruction in the open white desert of snow. It glistens in their wake like stardust. There is no sound. An eerie stillness follows the whirling snow devils to their gentle deaths.

If I stand here long enough, I too will meet a slow death.
I turn my skis downhill. Time to go.

Point of No Return

We are in the bean field picking Kentucky Wonders and Longrunner beans. The field is on a pick-your-own farm near my new home in America. My wife and I frequent the farm for this purpose often during the season. Spring yields the tender greens. Later, squash and zucchini fill our baskets. Beets and carrots are a more demanding crop — we have to coax them out of the ground first. Early fall is time for spinach and kale. Peppers and cucumbers are easy, and corn is always plentiful in season. Then, once the peach orchards, cherry trees, and blueberry bushes have been picked clean, apple season starts.

We do this not because we are too poor to buy fruit and produce at the store. We do it because we get the cream of the crop at a much lower price, and because old habits die hard. My wife of thirty-eight years grew up on a farm and knows the value of hard work and the benefits of fresh harvest. My own health survived the war thanks to providing for ourselves in like manner at every opportunity.

While on East Prussia's and Germany's estates, father and I were in the bramble-thick fields picking wild blackberries as often as we were in cultivated orchards for apples and pears even as Russian aircraft zoomed overhead. As we no longer traveled with a group and presented no threat to picking an orchard clean, we were almost always allowed to pick the fall fruit crop along our route. Except when we helped at harvest time, we always paid the owners for the favor. It was later denied to us, as to all refugees, thanks to those few who abused the generosity of these good people.

Fending for ourselves was becoming second nature. We found ways to feed ourselves which would not have been conceived, let alone considered, at home. But now it seemed the most natural thing to do.

One afternoon we were on a drainage-ditch-bordered road, passing through low, marshy ground. Father stopped the wagon.

"Get the baskets," he said.

By the time I returned from the rear of the wagon with our picking baskets, mother and he were already busy in the roadside ditch. I had no idea what they were doing.

Father handed me an 8-inch long green shoot of something he had picked and was eating another one just like it. Not to be outdone, I chomped down on it and discovered a tasty, refreshing treat. It was the young spring shoot of cattail. The ditches were full of cattails, but I didn't recognize them without their trademark brushes at the top. This discovery had me pulling shoots up out of the muddy ground in no time.

Later in spring we picked off the bloom spikes to be cooked as any other vegetable. Wherever we saw cattails, we always stopped. The yellow pollen was the most difficult to harvest without waste, and the quantity needed for use was enormous. But I didn't mind the effort. It made great tasting, golden pancakes when used as flour. Although mother never did, other women ground cattail roots into flour to make biscuits and white bread, when white bread was a rarity. But she had me pulling up milkweed. Its bitter taste, even when boiled for hours, has stayed with me to this day. Watercress, picked from small streams, was better.

While at a large farm in early summer, we noticed a group of women bicycling out in the same direction on frequent mornings with baskets tied behind their saddles. They returned at mid-day, their baskets filled. We followed them one day, father and I, and ended up the center of attention. We were the only men there, and bore the brunt of the women's angry, reproachful stares. They had led us to a huge field of wild strawberries, and were reluctant to share their find with strangers. But we returned with a big basket full of strawberries nevertheless. It was a surprise my mother talked about for years to come. She was used to queuing up for small helpings of produce at local markets whenever available. And those helpings were always small. Our basket filled with strawberries was a veritable bounty.

When not immersed in my studies, I helped making pickles and pickled onions, food I would rather not have eaten. But, for lack of food in general, anything palatable was welcome. Chopping cabbages for soup was better. I could do that without holding my nose and cabbage soup wasn't all that bad.

But the soup I took with reservation was bone soup; at least it began as bone soup. When lucky enough to have chicken, we gnawed the bones clean — father even sucked the marrow out — before tossing them in the pot for broth. Then, as days went by, other leavings, such as apple cores, peapods, potato skins, and husks of barley variously flavored the soup, so it never tasted the same twice. We called it day soup then. But this only worked in winter when it was cold enough to keep. Apple skins were never used in day soup. I remember vividly how father fed me slices of peeled apple, and ate the skins himself.

At summer's end, we picked up acorns off the ground under certain kinds of oak trees. Shelling them took hours and boiling them even longer. But if not boiled to leach out the tannin, they were inedible. It was my job to keep the fire going under the next pot of boiling water when water in the previous one turned a dark brown. We changed the water many times over the three or more hours it took to make the acorns palatable. They had a sweet, nutty flavor when roasted. Ground up in mortar and pestle, we ate them as grits.

The triangular fruit nuts from beech trees were better. They required no boiling. Shelling them was easier, and they could be eaten raw. Bleached in the sun or roasted, they tasted pretty good.

As we drew closer to the Elbe River, summer was long gone and early fall harvest was behind us. Our foraging for food changed to searching the forest for mushrooms. This was a major adventure for me, complete with path finding by compass and risk to life and limb.

Foraging in fields was one thing, but in the forest it was easy to get lost. The small compass my godfather gave me as birthday gift had been in my pocket since we left home. It was a memento of my hero and I wouldn't part with it. It was a toy no longer. Now, my father showed me how to use it and charged me with the responsibility of guiding us back after our baskets were filled with fresh mushrooms. This was a deliberate plan, of course, and probably a good thing. I didn't know a true boletus from a fly agaric, and were it up to me to choose which ones to pick and which to leave behind, it would have been up to father to sort them out later. Our baskets would take all day to fill.

Nevertheless, I learned to tell the poisonous ones from the rest in short order and, after a week or so, I picked as well as father. Mushrooms became a staple food and mother managed to turn out varied dinners enough to share with our benefactors whether cooked in their kitchens or outside over open fire. Among those was a favorite of mine: mushrooms and bacon boiled with leeks.

As weapons were illegal, hunting game for food was not an option. Trapping small animals was also unwise. It required staying in one place for extended periods of time — something we could not afford to do if we were to stay out of Russians' hands. It was only by accident that father caught a cornered rabbit once. That called for a celebration! It was the only meat we had eaten since the wild boar hunt in Blücherhoff.

Winter was laced with days when food was scarce. Less was available in village stores. Cities were worse. But rationed food stamps were now being issued more widely by the government. Father made an effort to get them whenever we were entitled to them. Rumors of food arriving in stores sent women banging on their doors.

One day father and I were in line with other food stamp holders at the local bakery. The line had been long, but now only two men, a boy some years younger than I, and the woman behind him were the only people ahead of us.

Suddenly, there was a scuffle. The baker announced the last loaf available and the two men were fighting over it in loud, accusing voices, their breath fogging in the cold. The little boy started crying. The woman behind him looked on for only a moment — her eyes stormy with anger. She stepped forward, picked up the big bread knife off the counter, and cut the loaf in half. She took one half and handed the other to the boy. He clutched it to his breast and ran off as quickly as he could. She stood there another moment, daring the men to object. There was complete silence as she walked away.

Although German radio was filled with hysterical speeches by Adolf Hitler, it was obvious the German people knew the war was lost. Gangs of children scuttled like rats over the wreckage picking up anything useful. Starved dogs with ribs showing, coats eaten away by mange, roamed the streets and turned feral with rabies. We threw bricks at them.

People were out in the streets clearing debris, rubble, and bomb damage wherever they could. Father and I joined them often. Long, human chains, mostly of women (German men were in hospitals or POW camps) were shifting debris with buckets too small for the task. Mountains of bricks were being cleaned and stored in preparation for rebuilding. Sometimes reusable wood, which escaped the fires, could be found. When we found it, we hid it under rubble. After dark, we came back to claim it.

My job was recycling cigarette butts into new cigarettes. As currency, they were perfect — small, easily carried, and non-perishable. Exchange rate was ten marks per cigarette. A whole pack was a major bribe. Cigarette paper was hard to find. Sometimes it required a bribe. Cigarettes were not smoked, but passed like money from hand to hand, often at profit.

To keep material from falling into enemy hands, the army was emptying its warehouses and giving away goods for free to anyone interested. If father took advantage of this, he never mentioned it and he held firm the importance of being self-sufficient as long as possible. When approached by a *Nationalsozialistische Frauenschaft* (national women's organization to care for refugees) worker, who offered free accommodations in dormitories, father declined. It meant living in a city, crowded in close proximity to disease and discontent, where he did not want to take us.

One small estate was the supplier of lumber to a sawmill in Karstädt. Help was needed in taking cut wood out of the forest. The ground now frozen, logs could be dragged over the snow by horses. With the two horses from the estate, and our gelding and mare, father was now a lumberjack.

I was occasionally allowed to accompany him to the forest and help with light tasks. A heavier one was hitching the horses to logs up to twenty feet in length and two feet in diameter. It took all four beasts, hitched side by side, to move the biggest logs. Even then, a sled like shape had to be chopped with an axe into the leading end of a large log to prevent it digging into the snow when dragged. It was a job I was never allowed to tackle. In fact,

I was never allowed to touch an axe. But I was pleased to run the occasional errand and help with the horses.

We lived in the large, airy woodshed building's small sawmill. The sawmill was like a shed within a shed, designed to contain the sawdust when logs were cut into lumber. Scent of freshly tooled, seasoned wood cast a pleasant breath to the air. Now, the sawdust served as bedding. It was surprisingly warm and comfortable under heavy blankets and down quilts which the estate provided. We still had our own sheets and pillows. There was a small cast iron wood stove which could also be used for cooking.

It took a lot of convincing to persuade the owners to let us use it and not set the woodshed on fire. But once they understood we were not crude, careless people, the stove's addition to our daily needs turned our accommodations into the most comfortable ones we had that winter. We were extremely fortunate to have it. That year was the coldest European winter in decades. Not the occasional freezing temperatures we whine about, or the theoretical understanding of cold which southerners have. This was subzero cold, even at mid-day. Arctic cold. If-I-fall-asleep-I'll-freeze-to-death cold. And, if not for that little cast iron stove, we probably would have.

Misfortune cut our stay short once again. Father returned from the forest with a heavy limp. While hitching the horses to a large log, they pulled it over his foot. Compression into the soft snow saved his leg. No bones were broken. He went back to work the next day. But pain and swelling cut his day short and the estate owners had to be notified. They were not pleased, but summoned a doctor to look at my father's leg. He administered medication and recommended staying off his foot for at least a week. This, the estate would not condone and refused to house and feed us with nothing in return. We even had to pay the doctor's bill.

This time preparation for departure fell to mother and me. No one on the estate offered to help and father was not paid for his three weeks' work. We left the next day.

* * *

Butchering became another skill father learned virtually overnight. Sheep were kept on a farm without hands to tend them.

He was at the right place at the right time and his services were secured to help with slaughtering after the last shearing before winter. We did not benefit from the sheep's wool, but we ate well for at least two days. With no ice or refrigeration, mother couldn't manage to stretch the lamb any longer.

Without wool clothing, of which we didn't pack enough with the assumption of a speedy return home when the war ended in weeks, not years, keeping warm was an ongoing challenge. We sometimes wore two coats, one over the other. It was difficult to move unless one coat was a few sizes larger. I wasn't big enough to wear an adult size yet. So, when it got really cold, I was immobilized — mother made me wear two coats of similar size. But, except for the cold, that was alright — no chores were assigned to me then.

We learned long ago that paper is a great insulator. We used it in our socks, and laid in sheets of newsprint under our sweaters. Its only disadvantage was that it didn't last long. First it shredded with use, then turned into powder if worn too long. But paper was easy to come by. It fell from the skies!

I had just come out of the forest with a basket of edible fungi and mushrooms when it started to snow. It was a strange snow, falling slowly in convoluted, jerky loops and twists I'd never seen snowflakes make. When it reached the ground wind scattered it like white leaves in autumn.

Aircraft had just flown low overhead. The "snow" was paper leaflets dropped by the Allies to prepare the inhabitants for imminent arrival of ground forces. They were printed in German and fell by the millions over populated areas of the countryside.

Allied aircraft now flew from the northwest, heading for Berlin, more and more frequently. They did not threaten and never opened fire on the villages and farms where we stayed. The leaflets they dropped assured the local population would be treated with respect and encouraged German soldiers to surrender, guaranteeing fair treatment of POWs and adherence to the Geneva Convention.

This was the greatest news for us in more than four years. But more important now was the paper. We stuffed our socks with American leaflets. When packed between two pairs, they were more comfortable than newspaper and kept our feet warm even without shoes. It was the first gift to us from America. Who could suspect what bounty of gifts would come our way from the same source in the future?

How imminent was the arrival of the Allies was anyone's guess. We knew from bitter experience not to trust rumor, the German media, or Soviet propaganda on the airwaves. Radio broadcasts kept us glued to the set in the evenings as father searched the dial for news in a language at least one of us understood. Most accurate were BBC broadcasts and *Voice of America*, but no one around knew English. Political surveys discussed by a professor Salis from Switzerland were sometimes given in translation, and *Radio Free Europe* was broadcast in several languages we all knew.

Russian advance gained ground at unprecedented rate. The Red Army had crossed the Oder north of Frankfurt and moved westward toward Berlin with scant opposition. The speed of this advance impressed General Eisenhower to urge American forces toward Berlin sooner than was originally planned. It was best for us to stay north, nearer the Baltic coast and away from the fighting.

I understood that the Germans were now fighting against the Russians, but I didn't understand what it meant. I thought maybe they would kill each other to the last man, and then we could go home. But now, there was no turning back. We had reached the point of no return. Our dash to cross the Elbe River was going to be a race against time.

* * *

Winter ended without much snow, at least not what we were used to at home. Sledding and snowball fights, forts built by snowman building methods, dives into drifts higher than our heads, all were welcome diversions even for the adults. They may not have enjoyed shoveling snow out of our house, but I thought it was great fun. The foyer was constructed like an oversize shower stall, with tiled walls and a drain in the floor. When snowstorms buried the house up to the roof, shovels kept in the heated foyer were used to tunnel our way out the door by tossing shovelfuls of snow onto the floor to melt and run down the drain. The doors always opened inward.

Our March 20th departure began normally enough, insofar as anything was normal at the time, but within days we were forced to continue on foot to reduce weight in the wagon. At mid-day we halted to rest the mare, refill her muzzle bag, and cook dinner over an open fire. Resting the mare was important, because we had been reduced to one horse. This necessity came about in a protracted series of misadventures. The first of these was more puzzling than troubling for me.

In the distance, wisps of smoke rose in the hazy air. Lined up along the road were several large, round-roofed, wooden wagons decorated with carvings and bright ribbons. They had windows on their sides just like the ones found on a house. I had never seen anything like them. Their horses were unhitched, grazing by the roadside. Behind the wagons, a sizable group of people sat and squatted on the ground around a small fire. Pots and pans were steaming with food.

"Ignore them. Maybe they'll leave us alone," my father warned.

At first I couldn't imagine why they would bother us. But as we drew near, I noticed the children were dressed in rags, the men were unshaven, and the women dirty, their hair wild in the morning breeze. They looked at us with fierce eyes, gesticulated and shouted something in a language we did not know, as if wanting us to stop. When we didn't, the children ran out onto the road behind us cackling and jeering and throwing stones.

Father slapped the reins to hurry our horses out of range. I looked back at our pursuers. Most were younger than I. The oldest among them, a girl, stopped and stuck out her tongue. I turned away, embarrassed for my staring.

"Who are they?" I asked.

"Gypsies. *Rom*," father said.

"Are they bad?"

"They beg, cheat, and steal."

"Is that because they're poor?"

"No. That's just the way they are. They're not poor."

So much for my romantic image of Gypsies. And what of my godmother? She could never be like that. She could never have been like that. I must be wrong about her. Next time I see her, I'll

153

have to tell her about Gypsies, but never that I ever thought she was one. That would destroy me.

I wondered if she ever came home, if she had left at all. I wondered if she still had her golden smile. I thought about her with a heavy heart. Would I ever see her again?

* * *

We stopped for the night near Mayenburg, on a farm owned by a grizzled old man. I was taken aback by his strange appearance and his unorthodox manner. Short of stature, but wide and doubly bent, he shuffled as he walked and shook his head incessantly, which was topped by a huge halo of white hair like a dandelion tuft. He spoke Brazilian Portuguese and kept a caged parrot which repeated everything he said. The incessant chatter of the two made it difficult to get a word in edgewise. It was anybody's guess which of them would reply if father ever did get to say something. It also took some time to learn the man did understand German after all.

The old man lived alone and had no interest in maintaining the farm. He said the war was lost, we would all be dead soon, and nothing mattered. He showed us the barn where we could leave our wagon and tie up the horses. There was hay and rye for feed, and we were welcome to take any amount we needed when we left. He put us up in the largest room in his house. It was the best room he had, but the mattresses were lumpy and uncomfortable. Winnowed and baled cornstalks were used for ticking. As always, we provided our own linen, which he let my mother wash in his basin as laundering in rivers was too cold. The wet laundry would freeze before it dried.

After a breakfast of potato pancakes in the old man's kitchen, mother bought a small sack of those potatoes at a particularly high price in return for the man's generosity. We normally always had potatoes, but now that we were leaving Mecklenburg's huge estates behind, fewer opportunities were available to help dig and peel this great source of sustenance in return for taking however many we could eat. There also was no time to stop and work. Our flight now was on the verge of desperation to stay ahead of the Russians, in the narrow gap behind the retreating

154

Nazi forces. Our survival depended on timing. And there was no time left.

On checking the horses before departure, father found trouble in the barn. The horses were tethered on long leads to reach the hay. Our large, strong gelding managed to break his bounds and get into a grain sack of rye. He gorged himself before father discovered this disaster. We hoped for the best, but feared the worst. Once wetted in large quantity, rye expands faster than it can be digested and can cause serious, even fatal, damage.

I took to walking the gelding about the grounds in the hopes of working the grain through his system before serious harm. We were good friends, that horse and I. When spending nights in East Prussian barns, he was always awake early, and made it a point to wake me by nudging gently with his muzzle before I overslept and missed something important. Although mother forbade it, there was a time, on a cold night, when I wished we could lay touching in the hay to keep warm. It was rebellious on my part, but I thought safer than sleeping with fire heated stones. It endeared me to the animal with whose care I was charged in East Prussia and made my task easier by half.

Now, I walked him all morning with stops to rest but not feed. Water, too, was harmful to take. The poor beast was suffering. And I knew there was little else we could do.

By mid afternoon, we hitched both horses to the wagon and set off for Mellen. Before we reached it the gelding refused to pull and thrashed about making farther progress impossible. There was a veterinarian in Mellen. For the price of silverware (worth more than money), which mother had sewn into her clothing before leaving home, the doctor came to see the horse. He tried his best to help, but nothing could be done. The gelding lay on his side and beat his head on the ground in pain until the doctor put him down with drugs.

He advised us to see a game warden before burying the carcass. He said there was canned horse meat available for carcass contribution to the food plant in Mellen. Father took his advice, loaded the carcass on the wagon and took it to Mellen. He returned with a generous supply of canned horse meat, which I later found quite palatable.

Such was our parting with an animal that had served us without tiring half way across Europe.

The wagon had to be rigged for single hitch. The mare was not nearly as strong as the gelding. We sold what few things we still had that we could do without. Among them was the heaviest trunk and most of its contents. I only knew it contained items needed when settlement of longer duration was established. That possibility now seemed remote. As money was worthless, and we could only trade for so much food, the trunk and its contents were left with the veterinarian who helped us. Mother kept her silver.

With lightened wagon, we still felt the small mare was overburdened with us on board. We walked.

Along the way, we met a man named Bruehl, an East Prussian who fled shortly after the Russians surged into his homeland. He had been an orderly in a Königsberg hospital and escaped when it was commandeered by the Russians. He told us they broke every window in the hospital, throwing equipment and furniture out. What food was not eaten, was squandered the first day. The sick were thrown out of their beds to make room for women who were robbed, stripped naked, and raped. Their screams could be heard throughout the building. A forty-year old nurse who resisted was pinned to a door with a bayonet through her stomach.

He was lucky to get out alive.

His was the first of many stories we heard in the weeks and months to come. East Prussians were leaving their homes by the hundreds of thousands to escape the Russians. We encountered them more and more often, and their stories were the same whether they came from Königsberg, Tilsit, Gumbinnen, Elbing or Danzig. As if the existing devastation wasn't enough, Russians set fires in the ruins of Königsberg and Danzig. The cities burned for days. The looting was on a grand scale. Russians robbed banks, art galleries, museums, and churches in every community they overran. Everything of value went east.

Countless thousands of East Prussians were shipped to Russia for slave labor. Most of them died there. One post-war survey showed 1600 Prussian girls returned to Germany in a cattle train in 1948. More than half died on the trip. Their average age was 19.7 years. 48% had been raped, 20% more than ten times, and

4% over one hundred times. *(Giles MacDonogh - After the Reich, 2007)**.

If Red Army troops were viewed as liberators by the most naïve, they were feared by the women. It was abundantly clear what would happen to them. Very few welcomed liberation from the east; the rest had no time to wait for liberation to come from the west and fled. In February, when the fall of Elbing isolated East Prussia from Germany, refugees fled across the ice of the frozen Frisches Haff. Russian warships of the Baltic Fleet opened fire on them. Horses, wagons, and people perished in the breaking ice by the thousands.

On their first border crossing into East Prussia, Russian troops killed nearly a hundred women in a single day. Most had been raped, of whom one was eighty-four, and another, a twelve-year old child. One village girl was raped by an entire tank squadron from eight in the evening until nine the next day. She was sixteen. In Nemmersdorf, East Prussian women were crucified on barn doors. Whenever alcohol was to be found, Russian troops conducted endless orgies of depravity and destruction.

Red Army command viewed rape as a healthy expression of hatred and therefore good for morale. It was encouraged everywhere. An estimated three million German and East Prussian women were raped by Russian troops. These were almost always gang rapes. Before the western Allies reached Berlin, crude abortions, suicides and murders were commonplace. Americans first saw Russians as "...big, jolly, balalaika-playing fellows who drank vodka and liked to wrestle." Before long, however, Americans announced they would shoot to kill any Russian raping a woman in Berlin. After that, looting and raping ceased.

In Gumbinnen, where the Russians met no German military resistance at all, air raid shelters were torched with flame throwers. They were filled with women and children trying to hide.

In Danzig, the Red Army pillaged, burned, raped, and murdered indiscriminately. Boys who tried to defend their mothers were killed on the spot. Churches were defiled and set afire. At the Sisters of Mercy Hospital nurses and nuns were raped over the bodies of unconscious patients in operating theaters together with the women in the maternity ward. Anyone who intervened was gunned down. *(Giles MacDonogh - After the Reich, 2007)*.*

All armies in the front lines of war commit rape to some degree, but nowhere is it condoned by the military command as it was in the Red Army of World War Two. In anticipation of their fate, tens of thousands of women in Russian occupied countries committed suicide to escape rape and murder.

We now knew what must have happened in our homes in Lithuania. Although these were just stories then, they were all confirmed by countless witnesses in later years. Tony Judt, Giles MacDonogh, Alan Palmer and other eminent historians recorded these events and support their findings by incontestable proof.

Elbe River

Father said it was time to stop and shoe the mare, as he said he should have done when we passed the Gypsies. They are known to be good with horses and probably had a farrier among them. He said so in jest — I knew he could shoe horses himself. Horses were no longer scary, and I found myself looking forward to helping father with the mare. My experiences with them in East Prussia were good memories.

Mother lit the Primus stove to prepare the mid-day meal while we worked. She also aired our bedding on a rope strung between trees.

"Put some oats in the muzzle bag," father said as he unhitched the mare from the wagon. I did as instructed and hung it by its strap over the horse's head. It would keep the beast occupied and calm while its shoes were changed.

I held the lead rope while father removed the old shoes, trimmed and brushed each hoof clean, then nailed the new shoes on after careful fitting and adjusting to fit the hoof. That last part put the mare to a restless tossing of the head, although perhaps she was just trying to reach the rest of the oats in the bottom of the muzzle bag. Firmly held between my father's knees, the hoof was soon re-shoed, and the head tossing stopped. Father checked the hind legs, but only the forelegs needed work. I was impressed by my father's skill. I knew that shoeing horses was a specialty reserved for farriers, not learned by many.

Before father explained it, I wondered why the Germans didn't use Gypsies with those skills. Racially undesirable, they called them — *Rassenverfolgte* — as they called the Jews, and set out to exterminate them. Gypsy tradition of compassion for the hunted and their efforts to help the Jews worked against them. They transported black market goods and stole food ration cards from distribution centers and they, themselves, were hunted.

159

But their small groups, elusively scattering and regrouping in incessant mobility, saved many. Still, half a million perished in the Nazi concentration camps.

On the way to the next community with its own Bürgermeister, with whom all foreigners were to register and secure work if planning to stay, we were about to enter Lenzen, the last small town on our planned route before the Elbe River.

Recent allied air strikes were in evidence all along our route. Mile after mile, abandoned and burned vehicles littered the road. Tanks, wagons, trucks, and guns lay toppled into roadside ditches as far as the eye could see.

Approaching us was a long, strung out column of people slowly moving in the opposite direction. They were flanked on each side by a line of armed guards in German uniforms. At a distance, we could not tell who these people were, but we had our suspicions. There were rumors that Hitler intended to exterminate the Jews. Although we found it too preposterous to believe, evidence had been mounting for months. We knew that German Jews were still being rounded up and sent to labor camps. We didn't know these camps were also used for extermination of so-called undesirables which included Gypsies and foreigners without proper papers or suspected of sympathizing with the Allies. Among them were thousands of refugees from Poland, the Ukraine, and the Baltics, Jews and Gentiles alike.

As the column drew near, our apprehension grew. What if they find something out of order in our presence here? Will we end up in that column?

The German guards wore Wehrmacht uniforms, not SS. Perhaps they were not escorting civilians — normal duty for the SS. But we couldn't be sure. Our apprehension turned to alarm when a guard with lieutenant's rank insignia approached our wagon. Father ignored him and continued.

"*Halt!*" the lieutenant commanded. Father tugged on the reins and stopped the mare before the guard reached for the bridle.

"*Guten Tag!*" The guard was being polite — always a cause for concern with German military. "*Papiere, bitte,*" the man demanded.

My parents produced their Lithuanian passports and work permits received from the last Bürgermeister we visited. The man gave them a cursory glance and asked where we were going. Father told him we were on the way to Lenzen, then west across the Elbe. The man looked me over. "*Ihre Sohn?*" he asked. Father nodded.

Satisfied, at last, he motioned us on without asking to see my birth certificate.

His captives were Russian soldiers, prisoners of war in bedraggled uniforms — a thousand or more — many without shoes. The shoes the lucky ones wore had no shoelaces. They were removed to hobble any attempt to run. Their generally poor condition and weary steps testified to bad treatment by the enemy. Few gave us a second glance as they passed, and in the eyes of those who did was a world-weariness beyond their age. Most could not have been much older than twenty. How resigned they were to their fate was anybody's guess, but we knew Russian soldiers in German hands were in an untenable position. If they tried to escape and failed, they would be shot. If they were returned to Russia through prisoner exchange at war's end, they would be executed by their own side. Capture or surrender to the enemy was viewed as treason in the Soviet armed forces, and treason was punishable by death. We were soon to witness Russian POW awareness of these Soviet policies who were prepared to do anything to prevent their return to Russia at war's end.

We later learned that POWs were put on a barge in the port of Lübeck and towed out to sea. There, the barge was sunk. Had we known this at the time, we should not have been surprised by one prisoner's action. He ducked behind our wagon and climbed up its side to hide. It was a desperate move and immediately put us in jeopardy. Father stopped the wagon. He could not have done otherwise. The young Russian jumped and ran.

"*Halt!*" one of the guards shouted at him. The man kept running. He was barefoot.

Father clucked the mare to continue. I looked back over my shoulder just as a shot rang out. The man was still running. Several more shots failed to stop him right away, but then he tumbled headlong onto the road shoulder. A guard walked over to him, looked down briefly and kicked the body into the drainage ditch bordering the road. The long column of men continued as if nothing had happened.

The acid burn in my throat said I should cry, but couldn't — the reflex to an unexpected horror — never mind the fallen man was as much our enemy as he was the guard's who killed him.

His death was of no consequence to his own superiors, whose general disregard for human life was legend. We knew the Russian practice of marching troops over minefields to clear them was standard procedure, even if it did shock General Eisenhower when so informed by Marshal Zhukov when they met in Berlin. Years after the war ended, we learned of yet another example of the low value of life in Russian eyes.

I would like to think it was nothing less than a desperate move to fill out the dwindling aircraft pilot ranks that girls with flying experience; even high-schoolers in aero clubs; were recruited to air combat duty. But it was an ongoing program begun early in the war before any such desperate measures were called for. They were given rudimentary training and grouped in all-female air regiments to fly short range tactical bombing missions in antiquated, World War One vintage, bi-plane trainers. These light, fabric covered contrivances were unarmed and barely reached a speed of 100 mph in an age when jet fighters were just over the scientific horizon.

The girls — as young as seventeen — were expected to approach their target at night, cut their engines to avoid detection, and glide silently to the drop zone. Then drop the bombs, restart engines, and try to survive the anti-aircraft barrage and the Luftwaffe night fighters. Only Japanese *kamikaze* pilots were more likely to die completing their mission, and they knew exactly what awaited them. The Russian teenagers were there for the glory of Mother Russia, drilled into them by propaganda and, in their naiveté, had every expectation of survival. Germans called them *Nachtzauberinen* (Night Witches), a name still applied to them in literature today.

* * *

The small road we followed ended into the muddy waters of Elbe River. There was no bridge. The main road bridge was a quarter mile upstream, but it was not for us to use. Through the lenses of my father's binoculars, I saw endless lines if military vehicles of all kinds slowly rolling across the bridge. Armored transporters, armed personnel carriers, trucks and staff cars followed the occasional tank still under its own power, or a self-propelled gun on tank tracks. A combat engineer unit, with its array of fantastic looking machinery, trundled along leading horse-drawn artillery and solid masses of infantry, pulling their heavy weapons on hand trolleys behind them. There were ammunition vans, field ambulances transporting the wounded, and flatbed supply trailers teeming with men too weary to walk.

The German Army in defeat was a sad sight, and they were moving now to the western front where the Allies had already liberated France and inexorably advanced into Germany.

We found ourselves between two battlefronts. Crossing the Elbe was our only option to avoid the Red Army, which was already fighting in Berlin. But doing so we risked being caught in the combat zone now taking shape between German forces entrenched west of the river and the Allies advancing eastward against them.

Maps clearly showed ferry service across the Elbe near our present position. Perhaps we were on the wrong road, father said. There was another secondary road downstream and he decided to find it. While we waited on the riverbank, father pedaled away on his bicycle, map in hand.

Half hour later a double-hitch wagon approached, apparently looking for the same ferry. It stopped behind ours and two men got off. I immediately recognized the teacher from Hallalit. It meant Nijolė, my Independence Day celebration partner, was here. I couldn't contain myself, and raced to greet him. He held me round my shoulders and said yes, she was here, asleep in the wagon with her mother.

When told father went looking for the ferry, they said we could cross the river upstream, over the bridge used by the army if we left our wagons behind and walked. Only pedestrian civilians were allowed to use the bridge. This, of course, was not a tenable option. They decided to wait for my father's return and join us for the road ahead. So, now our group consisted of two wagons, three horses, three men, two women, a boy, and a girl.

163

While waiting, I told my impromptu teacher how much I had learned from the little textbooks he gave me before we left Hallalit. He was pleased and said that my education could continue now that we were all together again. We took turns watching the busy bridge and talked about what was expected on the other side of the Elbe.

Sudden hectic activity on the bridge attracted our attention. I raised the binoculars to my eyes again. Soldiers were running off the bridge in both directions. An officer atop an armored halftrack was waving his arms in the air, saying something. Several soldiers looked like they were loading their weapons. I was about to hand the binoculars over to my teacher when we heard aircraft overhead. Before we had a chance to look up, there were huge explosions all around the bridge. Bombs!

The bombers were too high to hit, but rifle and machine gun fire from the bridge erupted even before the bombs fell. I saw four airplanes. And they dropped four bombs. The river erupted with gouts of water like giant geysers shooting up in the air. We could hear the water splash back down just as the dull blasts died and the firing stopped. It was all so fast, so sudden. And then quiet. Nothing moved. All four bombs missed the bridge.

"What are they doing?" my teacher said as he looked through the binoculars.

I saw crowds of people and soldiers running down both banks into the river. Some were jumping in the water and wading around in a most agitated manner.

"Get the buckets," he said handing back the binoculars. "Hurry up!"

I wanted to get a better look, but he made it clear there was no time. I set the binoculars on the ground and ran to the back of our wagon for the bucket.

"Come on!" he urged us down the bank into the river, and all six of us plunged into the cold water, a bucket or pot in hand.

The river was filled with dead fish, floating downstream from the bridge. We waded in as far as possible and scooped up as many as we could. I wasn't tall enough to wade in very far, so my catch was meager. I only got two. Nijolė did better, even though she was shorter than I. She scooped up four! But others nearly filled their buckets.

We were dripping wet and very happy when father returned. He heard the bombing and hoped the target was the bridge and not our wagon, he said. But he had great news. The next road was serviced by a cable barge ferry. All we had to do was get there before sundown. The barge did not operate after dark. Another surprise was that my father and the second man were old acquaintances. He was a professor of agronomy in Kaunas, the city where I was born. But this meeting was not the pleasant event it should have been. He told us that while he was away lecturing in Finland, the professor's family had been herded with thousands of other unfortunates into railroad cattle cars without food, water, or sanitation, and deported to Siberia — the Soviet hell, the eternal damnation — with death the only escape.

His wife was already in poor health and did not survive that journey of horrors. The only letter he received from his two sons told of the slave labor camp where they worked 18 hours a day and lived in a mud-daubed hut without heat, in the frozen wilderness, behind barbed wire. He was convinced they couldn't survive there. But if by some miracle they did, he wanted to be back in Kaunas where he felt he would be in a better position to help them when war ended and the Russians left. We know now the Russians stayed 49 years.

But for that single letter, no word was ever heard about his sons' fate. Nevertheless, at war's end the professor returned with the few others who made the same choice and, like the rest, was never heard from again.

We reached the cable barge well before sunset. There was a large bell suspended under a wooden yoke. I was detailed with ringing it to attract the ferryman's attention on the opposite side of the river. We saw him come out of the house on the riverbank and start a huge engine on the barge. It was a smoky, coal fired contraption which made steam and took a long time to create enough to turn the screw which powered the barge across the river.

The sun was setting by the time we rolled the wagons onto its heavily timbered deck. There was a screw at each end of the vessel and, with no need to turn around, it reversed across the river again guided by a cable, which ran shore to shore through

165

a row of metal rings along its side. The coal smoke was choking and it was impossible to get away from it in the cramped quarters of the barge. I laid down on its deck to stay as low as possible and crawled under our wagon.

Although uncomfortable and risky, the crossing was trouble free. We pushed the wagons while the horses pulled them up the steep incline of the left bank and we were done. The fee for service was exorbitant, my father thought. The other men agreed, but paid what we were asked. The German mark was already worthless east of the Elbe. Father gave the ferryman some fish. We couldn't have eaten them all anyway.

Just beyond the first bend in the road we saw a small bonfire surrounded by people near a wagon pulled off the road into a clearing. We drove there to investigate. The people turned out to be a family from Pomerania and a young couple from East Prussia. We joined them. Even though it was already very late, we built a bigger fire. Father gave me a knife and I learned how to scale fish. Then we had a great fish fry and celebrated our good fortune. The Pomeranians and Prussians hadn't had fish since they left their homes. They were very happy to see us. We later kept their company for farther travel the next day.

I stood by the fire a long time, drying myself off and listening to Nijolė's chatter about all the things she did since I had seen her last. It was great to see her again, and we were still friends.

The line of vehicles trundled across the bridge in the distance all night. We stayed up listening to them and I didn't want to go to sleep. Nijolė and her mother climbed into their wagon, but I was wide awake and, sitting in the dark, was forgotten by the adults around the fire. Their conversation was mostly beyond my grasp, but I learned a lot of new things I hardly imagined. I also learned that sleep deprives us of knowledge. But I slept in the wagon all the next day as we rolled westward.

Not wishing to lose any more time, we did not stop in Lenzen before crossing the river. Now that we were on the left bank, it was advisable to register with authorities in the nearest town. The Bürgermeister of Gartow received us as a group. We were 14 foreigners, from three different countries, fleeing a fourth, and afraid to be hemmed in by the two in battle which was now thought to be imminent. It is small wonder the town official was bewildered. He was very brusque with us and specifically forbade us to go near a small compound where Russian POWs were being held. Because we were too large a group to be housed together, he recommended the large lumber mill right on the river bank. It would be temporary he said, then we would have to move on. There was no work available for us here.

At the mill, we were in for a treat. The building we were shown to was the size of an airport hangar. We rolled both wagons under its roof, unhitched the horses to their feed in muzzle bags, and made ourselves comfortable on the wide, mattress covered benches put there for our use. As usual, we were treated better by the rank and file German inhabitants than by their authorities.

Next day, as we prepared for departure, we were visited by some 20 or 30 young people — employees of the lumber mill. They were Hungarians and East Prussians who got here the same way we did. They brought rye bread, sausages, sauerkraut, cake, and wine. Main course was stewed turnips and horse meat. We had not seen such bounty since leaving home. It was Easter Sunday and we celebrated in style. The Hungarian women sang and the other three nationalities present joined in as best we could. Easter went by without church service, but it was celebrated with dignity and good will. We departed morally refreshed and filled with hope all would be well in the coming weeks.

* * *

The Red Army had taken Berlin and was approaching the right bank of the Elbe. The Allies were now virtually unopposed in their drive eastward across Germany. This was not the time to make a wrong decision. Our group agreed that moving farther west now would expose us to German pockets of resistance likely to break out in combat with advance British units known to be in the area. The Elbe River was a buffer between us and the Red Army. We hoped the Russians would advance no farther with the Western Allies being so close. Radio Free Europe broadcast jubilant news of their progress on a daily basis. The BBC carried enough detail information to persuade listeners that Nazi Germany was beaten and war was coming to an end. We didn't view this as propaganda and decided to stay in nearby Tobringen until the front stabilized, or hostilities ceased.

Gartow's POW compound was being vacated as we left town. The Russian captives were being marched to the river and embarked in small boats to be taken across and returned to the Red Army on the other side. Many jumped overboard and were swimming back. We watched in silence. Everyone in our group understood the meaning of this act without comment. The POWs were supervised by Gartow's civic police, not the military. No move was made to stop the swimmers.

On our arrival in Tobringen, we were met by a Hilfstelle worker. She split us up into two groups, a wagon each, and sent us to the largest homes in town. Ours was owned by a haughty widow who looked on us as intruders. Perhaps she was justified in her view, but she lived alone in a large house, half of which was not in use. She should have been inconvenienced less by our presence than many other townspeople. Our room was spacious, with a high ceiling, two large windows overlooking the street, and a gabled balcony rail between them. Father and the other men worked at a farm four kilometers from the house. Spring planting was in full swing.

One day, a woman from a nearby farm came running for help. Her only cow had fallen into a bomb crater. The professor from Kaunas, father and I set out to her pasture with our mare and towing bridle. The pit in the crater was filled with mud. The cow was stuck up to its udder and unable to move. We dug a slope with shovels. The woman had canvas belts which we looped around the cow and, hitched to the mare, pushed and pulled the wretched animal out of the mud. The woman gave us ten eggs for our trouble, a delicacy we hadn't seen in months.

It took hours to wash the mud off ourselves and our clothes, and dry them enough to be worn again. We splashed around in the river, using only its waters to do the job. We had long forgotten the luxury of soap.

People in town already lived in an alien new landscape of churned up streets, burned out buildings and charred homes with interiors open to the sky. But the next day we heard gunfire from the west. Artillery shelling was closing at alarming speed. Our worst fears were being realized. There was time to prepare for an attack from the air — approaching planes could be heard in advance. Artillery shells gave no warning before they fell. In fear of our lives, we ran to the slit trenches left behind by the German army. How ironic to be fleeing from the Russians and be killed now by the Western Allies with whom we sought salvation.

We were in the middle of a combat zone.

Several buildings exploded on direct hits. Great mountains of dirt and stone flew up in the air and rained down all around us. The noise was infernal. The ground shook underfoot. A smoke storm rushed over our heads. Dust clouds rose and settled over us as we cowered in the trenches. The pain of concussion in my ears reverberated in my head. I was struck deaf by the shock waves, but heard my heart roar, pulse loud like a jackhammer. I held on to father's protective arm for support and reassurance. Small arms fire continued as the artillery shells fell. I couldn't move my feet because I didn't know where they were. They were dulled numb. The acrid smoke stung my eyes and thick clouds of dust made breathing difficult. I was choking and certain that death was near.

As suddenly as it began, all firing stopped. We waited before rising cautiously from the churned up earth and peeked over the edge of the trench. No one was hurt. Only dead chickens littered the street. People were already hurrying to pick up the bloody birds and carry them off in wicker baskets.

There was a tickle on my arm. I stopped myself from slapping at it just in time. A ladybug had landed near my elbow. It wandered up my arm as if nothing happened. My cough frightened it into flight.

I coughed incessantly with tears in my eyes and wondered why I was still alive. Or was I? I wanted to know what it meant to die, to no longer be among the living, to be something else, somewhere else. Did father know? That night, at supper, I would ask him.

Two British tanks rolled out of the smoke. They stopped within yards of us and rotated their turrets aiming at a windmill nearby. Seconds later the windmill disintegrated under cannon fire. I felt the ground heave up under me and lost my balance. I fell back into the trench. Then all was quiet. The sudden silence was eerie even as the noise still rang in my ears. Strong smell of cordite was in the air. The tanks went their way.

We didn't understand what just happened. German troops had already retreated from the vicinity. Was this Cervantes' Don Quixote battling windmills? Our first glimpse of Allied forces in action did not impress us. We hoped this would change soon.

But for the moment, the smell of cordite crowded my senses. Its distinctive, sharp odor was unmistakable and unforgettable. It was to follow me always — another stark reminder of war to add to the alarmingly growing number in my mind. How will I ever explain it to myself? Can someone else do that? But can anyone who wasn't there imagine how it was?

That question about death went unanswered. Unanswered, as far as I could gather. Father's explanation was brief and perplexing. Mother was upset by my curiosity. She called it morbid. It looked like an argument, a sad one. My question caught my parents unprepared. It was embarrassing. I understood very little of what was said. One thing was clear: no matter what, knowing what to do when death was near was the important thing, whether I lived or died. Contempt for fear was in my father's tone. Fear, he said, served little purpose. And he would know, wouldn't he? His words held secret meaning, but I went away knowing I did not fear death. I feared helplessness.

* * *

The next day was quiet. No artillery. No tanks. Father returned to work and I to my studies. Concerns about our future were still beyond my appreciation, but I already knew how rare and valuable were those who took the time to teach me. Hard for me to believe as it was that I would ever use what I learned of math, physics, and history, I strived to do well if only to please father and reward the kind people who taught me.

Robbed of formal school education and opportunity to interact with peers my age, I spent more and more time in long conversations with adults and in eavesdropping. Previously, I only enjoyed such talks when the Gypsy with the Golden Smile took time to indulge me in my questions. Now, I was learning to look at life with adult eyes. I learned that hundreds of thousands of women were gang raped routinely by troops of the Red Army as it moved across Europe. Thousands were murdered indiscriminately. Much of what I heard was beyond my comprehension, but based on what I had already seen, I found it believable. Hard truth though it was; as I learned later; it confused me, and created an endless list of new questions which I would ask for years to come.

Concerns of education and unanswered questions would have to wait. More pressing matters were at hand, and the adults who kept me company had other things on their minds.

Work needed by farmers was still at the top of that list. It was still the most reliable way to put food on the table. Now, the planting of potatoes was the last to be done, then our help would no longer be required. Although the men were not paid, room and board was adequate. This would cease once spring planting was finished. What would we do then?

Wind

When there is no rain, I don't mind the automobiles I dodge on my bicycle, and I don't mind the long commute. Soon I'm on country roads and away from rush hour traffic. Bicycling is my only means to get to work. Although I am in America now, whose streets are paved in gold — so we were told — I cannot afford a car and there is no public transportation where I need to go.

Daniels is a small place in Maryland, a mere hamlet with a railroad terminal which dates back to the 1820s. It was born of a mill town in a horseshoe bight of the Patapsco River. My work takes me there daily, where I enjoy my first full time job since graduating from high school. My work is pleasant and I earn enough to someday own a car. For now, the bike serves well. Much as I hate to depend on others when winter comes, I have to find a ride. But now, the self-made wind cools my brow when I ride home in the heat of late afternoon. Over an hour each way keeps me fit and healthy. In bad weather, I suffer colds and sundry other discomforts. But I've gained a reputation at work now and cannot change my habits even if I wished.

A favor extended to me by the good people of Daniels is permission to keep my bike safe and clean in the one lane bowling alley under the post office. The small building is next to the old railroad terminal, converted now to a manufacturing plant where I work. We make weather protection curtains for NASA launch pad towers at Cape Canaveral, and we make other things that either use, or protect against, the force of wind. We also use artificial wind to keep air buildings inflated while we test their mettle against the elements. The elements test me sometimes, when I must ride in rain and cross wind. It is unpleasant, but it is what I must do.

The history of Daniels is etched in its soil, and the tranquility of the place fails to hide one tragic aspect of the old mill town.

Overgrown with weeds and scrubby bush is a forgotten graveyard. Its gravestones lean this way and that, some lay resting on the unkempt ground. My lunchtime walk permits a few minutes to read their inscriptions. Buried here are children, all within the same two years, and all of very young age, some mere infants. No war was ever fought on Daniels' ground, and no adults are buried here. Was it an epidemic that took them to the their deaths so early in life? Or was it some disaster?

The elements of Mother Nature are to blame for the eventual demise of Daniels. Hurricane Agnes swept across the river's bight in 1972 and washed away the last of the old buildings. The little graveyard probably did not survive. Wind took the brush and trees downriver and little remains of Daniels now. But such wind compares poorly with winds my parents saw me through. Theirs were the winds that brought me here, and here I chose to stay. America is my home now, and it is hard for me to imagine someplace better.

Americans

The Red Army reached the Elbe River and stopped. It was up to the Allies to do the same from the opposite direction and squeeze the Nazi army out of existence.

We were jolted awake by the roar of engines and a horrendous rattle. We jumped from our beds just as the sun rose over the rooftops, and ran to the windows overlooking the street. There was a loud clatter of rolling treads and the air was filled with the raw smell of diesel fuel. Tanks were lining up just under our windows. Fear was the first reaction. But stars on these tanks were not red. The stars were white!

German residents were hanging up flags made from white bed sheets and pillow cases to signify surrender, as if there was need for such pointless display. The Americans were neither shunned nor welcomed. No disrespect was shown but for one exception.

An American officer walked up the stairs of our neighbor's house and tore down a filthy sheet made into a flag and hung out the window. The woman occupant who shouted at him, cursing Americans in general, was pointedly ignored.

We were overwhelmed with joy and relief to see Tobringen in Allied hands. We were free from pursuit by the Red Army and we had survived. The war would go on a while longer, but for us the worst was over, or so we believed. We were mistaken.

It was May 2, 1945, the day after German radio announced that Hitler was dead and Berlin surrendered to the Red Army. But this did not mean the war had ended. Germany surrendered six days later, and a different kind of war began.

* * *

Reason for mistrust of anyone in uniform was confirmed once more in Tobringen. Father saw an American soldier stop a civilian on the street, threaten the frightened man, who then took off his wristwatch and handed it to the soldier before hurrying away. We

175

were therefore apprehensive when four Americans came to the house. One, a sergeant, asked if we had a bicycle and wanted to see it. His German was poor but understandable. When shown father's bike, the sergeant explained he needed it. Father pleaded with him not to take it. But he insisted and said it would be returned soon.

As he was leaving, a young pair astride bicycles came round the corner. The Americans stopped them, spoke briefly and took their bicycles. The fourth soldier already had one. All four then got on the bikes and rode away.

The two young people looked bewildered, standing there, in the street, with backpacks on their backs, the man's left trouser leg still clipped tight to his ankle to keep it out of the chain when pedaling. Not knowing who they were, we introduced ourselves in German. When they learned who we were, they replied in Lithuanian. It turns out they were from Varėna, in southern Lithuania. She was eighteen, she said, and orphaned during the Red Army's first invasion, five years earlier, when both her parents were taken to a church, told to pray, and then were shot.

The man was older, perhaps thirty. He told us the Russians took all the books in the small library, piled them up, and set them on fire. When the librarian tried to stop them, she was shot and thrown into an abandoned trench. Then they buried her, still alive. People who tried to save her were killed on the spot.

His father was arrested by the NKVD, and never seen again. His crime was using a handkerchief to blow his nose, which was considered a bourgeois luxury. In Russian eyes, this made him an enemy of the USSR.

When the Red Army entered their home town a second time, they escaped and rode their bicycles the whole 1000 miles to the Elbe with nothing but the backpacks on their backs. They crossed the Elbe River swimming behind their bicycles on a barn door. Now they looked lost without them.

We lost touch after the war and never learned who these two intrepid people were. Their story deserves its own book as thousands of other war stories do. But few will ever be heard. Later in life, it was to be my frustration as a writer.

The American sergeant told them all bicycles would be returned later that day. There was no reason to believe him. Nevertheless, they two and father waited on the street the whole day. At supper time the soldiers returned the bikes.

Our first impression of Americans was neutral. We didn't know what to make of them. Among them was a large group of men with such dark skin their facial features were obscured at a distance. They all looked alike. I had never seen a man like that, and curiosity overcame any apprehension I might have felt. I stood there, staring. One of them noticed. He walked over to me and, reaching in his knee pocket, pulled out a small tin can and handed it to me, smiling. He had the brightest, most contagious smile, and the whitest teeth I had ever seen. He said something in response to my puzzlement, alternately pointing at the can and at his teeth. I had no idea what it meant.

He took the can back, pulled out a small tool attached to his dog tag chain, and opened it. Then handed it back to me. It emitted a strong odor, an unfamiliar aroma. I held it at arm's length. Broadening his white smile, he dipped a pen knife into the can, scooped up a bit of its dark yellow contents and ate it.

That was a clue!

I dipped my finger in and did likewise. The stuff was soft, oily like butter, but firmer, gritty and almost sweet. It was great! Now, my smile matched his. It was my first taste of peanut butter, and I've loved it ever since.

Other encounters with American troops were not always so pleasant. The day after arrival, a large group came to the house. They went room to room, ransacking everything in sight. Cupboards spilled their contents on the counters, pantry emptied out its shelves, and women's dresses were flung out of closets on the floor. When our haughty landlady objected, they evicted her bodily from the house. In the cellar, they found wine, then invited us to join their party when a group of Polish girls who worked in the surrounding farms showed up. They dolled themselves up in the widow's dresses and the party began in earnest. We politely declined the invitation and retreated to our room, but stayed awake all night as the party continued till dawn.

The soldiers found our landlady's piano. One of them could play it well, and entertained us for hours. It brought to mind the Gypsy with the Golden Smile, her crystal- chandelier-lit grand piano, and her cloud of red hair. I couldn't get her image out of my mind for days.

The Americans did some mysterious digging. At the farm where father worked, an American Infantry platoon went round, probing the ground along fencerows with bayonets. They found a huge trunk buried near the spring house. Inside were medals and other valuables the farmer had hidden (the Allies had banned the wearing of medals). Nothing was taken, but a German speaking soldier pointed at the military service ribbons and medals in the trunk.

"You were a good soldier," he told the farmer and tapped him on the shoulder like an old friend. The decorations were for service with the Keiser's army in the First World War.

Another search by an American patrol unearthed a cache of weapons hidden in a casket and buried in a graveyard. How they knew which grave to dig was speculated on for weeks. They arrested two members of the *Volkspolizei* (local police) and took them away for questioning.

None of these events were any help in forming a meaningful opinion of American soldiers. We still didn't know what to make of them. And who could trust the Americans? After all, Roosevelt's government officially recognized Pétain's Vichy France.

* * *

Temporary American headquarters in Tobringen was scheduled to be moved south. Tobringen would be turned over to the Red Army within a week. We packed and left without word. West was the general direction taken, without a plan, into the next unknown.

Just beyond Ülzen, an American Jeep passed us, stopped, and blocked our way. We were not yet alarmed, but concerned that none of us spoke English. An American soldier with captain's bars on his shoulders came to the wagon and spoke to us in fluent Lithuanian. He said his parents were from Kretinga and had emigrated to Chicago before he was born. Lithuanian was the language spoken at home and he grew up bilingual.

He asked why we left our home in Lithuania. We were puzzled that he did not understand our reasons. He also told us to stay south for the next 30 or 40 kilometers, but did not explain why. We knew many roads were "red-balled" — closed to civilian traffic — and thought that was the reason. Before leaving he gave mother and me several chocolate bars and wished us luck. He chewed something the whole time he spoke. I had never seen anyone do that and wondered if it was some sort of illness or affliction.

Minutes later, a short column of trucks, filled with noisy American troops, passed us. They showered our wagon with more chocolate bars and packs of Lucky Strike and Chesterfield cigarettes. I noticed that some of them were also chewing something just like the captain who stopped us. I was puzzled.

Father paid heed to the warning. We took the next road to the left and headed south. After a few hours, near Bergen, we saw a prominent sign posted in Russian and German. It instructed all refugees from Soviet occupied countries to proceed immediately to an internment camp in Fallingbostel, 20 kilometers west of us. This was too close for comfort. Father donned his French beret and reviewed some French words and phrases I had learned earlier in our travels. Then he got our axe and put it on the seat between us.

Sure enough, we were overtaken by a soldier on horseback in a uniform I did not recognize. He reminded us about the sign we saw and urged us to go to Fallingbostel. He spoke Russian. Father pretended not to understand. Mother and I needed no pretense. The man switched to German and asked who we were. French, father said, heading home. On cue, mother and I exchanged the French phrases we had rehearsed. For effect, father turned to scold us, also in French. I noticed his hand resting on the axe handle beside me. It struck me as an incredibly brave move, but I knew that after the Revolution, the First World War, the wounds he suffered in battle, and now this, there was little left to frighten him.

But the soldier believed us and rode on.

This was the closest to Russian captivity and certain death we had come since we left home, and that included shelling by Allied artillery and strafing by Russian planes. We went on in silence for a long while, knowing what a close thing this had been. But we didn't know how lucky we were.

Three or four kilometers farther on the air carried a peculiar odor we had never encountered before. It grew stronger and

179

more sickening. We saw a high barbed wire fence. The gate was guarded by British soldiers. One of them stepped out on the road and began waving us on to hurry up. Although we didn't understand English, it was clear he wanted us to hurry on by. The smell was now so nauseating I was compelled to cover my nose. Father slapped the reins to urge us on. We looked through the barbed wire. Bulldozers were filling a ditch in the distance. There were people sitting on the ground who didn't look human — mere skin over skeletal frames. They wore rags and striped pajamas. Some were naked.

They were inmates of the infamous Bergen-Belsen concentration camp where 90,000 Romanian and Czech resistance fighters, French students, Ukrainian farmers, Gypsies, Poles and other political prisoners were held, half of them women. Among them were also 18,000 Jews. Only 40,000 were still alive when liberated by the British Army. Hundreds were dying every day and 28,000 died after the liberation. *(Abzug - Inside the Vicious Heart, 1985)*.

How dehumanized these liberated prisoners had become was later demonstrated to the British Second Army commander, General Dempsey, who saw one *'standing stark naked, washing herself with some issue soap in water from a tank in which the remains of a child floated.' (Shepherd - After Daybreak)*.

We hurried away without looking back. There is no need to repeat the long litany of the Holocaust. Countless others, more qualified that I, have already filled volumes. Western Allies saw the remains of Nazi horrors when they entered Germany. No such discoveries of Russian atrocities were made in Lithuania, Latvia, and Estonia because the Allies never got there. And the Russians were already expert at covering it up.

Near Winsen, father's advance scouting by bicycle revealed an assembly point for POWs liberated from German camps. We found night accommodations in two very large barns with real beds and food provided by the U.S. Army. There were several hundred released British, French, and Danish soldiers on their way back to their own countries or their units which were still in the field. From them we learned about the situation farther west and the areas to avoid.

We stayed only the night, still uncertain of American hospitality. At supper we were served canned beef, white bread and butter, oranges, canned tuna and other foods we had not seen since we left East Prussia. The white bread was a very strange, foam-like, pre-sliced, loaf (discovered years later to be standard fare in the U.S.) It was surprisingly edible. This was the first butter we had had since we left home. Cooking with lard had become so commonplace, we could no longer appreciate the taste of butter.

The soldiers made much over me, probably because they had not seen children for some time, and I was a novelty. One of them gave me a short, olive colored metal tube. This was as much a mystery as was the canned peanut butter. He put it to his eye, and rotated it slowly, then gave it to me indicating that I do the same. I peered into the small opening at one end and rotated the tube as he had done. Nothing happened. I didn't know what to expect but, surely, he must have meant there was something more to it. When he realized my puzzlement, he turned me towards the sun.

Wow! A kaleidoscope! The tube was filled with multi-colored glass chips at one end and, when rotated, they fell in random patterns within the mirrors inside and made the most spectacular patterns I had ever seen. This kaleidoscope now resides on my bookshelf — a memento of fleeting pleasure, while surrounded by the chaos and destruction of war.

We struck out in the morning across the Niedersachsen plain armed with new knowledge how to protect ourselves now that we were behind the front lines and our world had changed.

Wind

The sapling is an inviting prop. I lean against its lissome trunk before the pack is off my back and helmet off my head — a brief rest before I take the ground for a longer one.

We are at A.P. Hill, training ground for the U.S. Army in the Carolinas. The twenty-mile march with full combat gear on our backs has ended and we wait for the deuce-and-a-halves to pick us up and truck us back to post. We are worn out. Twenty miles without rest can be a man breaker to those not hardened by the two month training prerequisite for this hike.

But I am content, for the moment, to stop and rest a while. My sapling is at wood's edge, away from the hubbub of troops stretched out on the ground between me and the sand road in the distance where the trucks will come.

The late afternoon sun is warm and the breeze is light. But it is strong enough to bend the sapling with my weight against its swaying trunk. I feel the breeze gently touching my face and reaching under my helmet. But I ignore the urge to take it off my head. I'm just too tired now. Later. I'll do it later.

Now, there are clouds drifting by overhead to follow, and see in them the unicorns and pigs with curly tails, and to see my Gypsy's golden smile. The clouds change hue as their shapes dissolve and I am flying, up there in the clouds. They rock me gently back and forth between them and I sleep.

I wake to fading light. The breeze has died. The sapling is still. The troops who were just there, moments ago, are gone. There are no trucks. I look at my watch and know the trucks have come and gone while I stood lulled to sleep by the gently swaying sapling. Remarkable, I thought, that I could sleep so soundly standing up and burdened with the combat gear I wore. But now I knew what faced me next.

I walked.

The twenty-mile trek back was so much longer, it seemed never to end. At times I thought I might be lost. But no. Judging by the sun, already set below the western horizon, I was right on course.

Now I know why it was so important in my early childhood not to go to bed, and sleep, for fear I would miss something important. And now, I had — twenty years later.

I am in the U.S. Army, serving my country. My country now, by choice not by inheritance, is the United States of America, and I serve in her armed forces by virtue of volunteer draft. I might have waited for the normal draft, but I went before my time so as to gain my discharge sooner and finish my education before I was too old to use it. But for the generosity of the newly enacted GI Bill, I could no more afford a college education than a trip to the moon.

There are occasional reminders of things past, reminders which would not surface if I were not in uniform, not trained and armed to be a soldier. Some bring to mind unpleasant things, but also curious and strange ones which I thought I had forgotten. The smell of cordite has not changed. It has the same bite in U.S. Infantry training as it did in the slit trenches of Germany. But training is now well behind me. I have a job which helps keep Infantry on the move.

My Transportation Corps unit is stationed in Fort Eustis. Before that, we were in Fort Story, also in Virginia, Fort Jackson in South Carolina, and in Fort Bragg when briefly attached to Airborne. Those, and other posts where I stayed during my tour of duty, all bear strong resemblance to military bases in another world, of another time. Long gone now, they are etched deeply in my memory, when I was a DP.

Ignoble Title

To many Germans, we were still *Flüchtlinge* (runaways). A less demeaning title was *Heimatlose Ausländer* (homeless foreigner). At war's end we gained a new title. We became DPs, Displaced Persons. It was a ridiculous, diplomatic term, hardly adequate to define the scale of human tragedy which earned us the title. DPs or refugees, we were herded into detention camps, grouped by nationality, in preparation for future repatriation to our own countries. It had not occurred to the Allied occupation forces that for many, whose countries were now under Russian control, such repatriation meant certain death. This applied to everyone from Poland, Lithuania, Latvia, Estonia, and the Ukraine, and included many liberated Nazi concentration camp inmates.

Russian view of fleeing westward was an admission of guilt — guilt of treason against the Soviet state, punishable by death. This included their own soldiers who surrendered in battle and returned home at war's end. Accused of treason, they suffered execution along with DPs who also chose to return. Fate visited on clergy of all faiths, whether they stayed or fled and returned, was worse than death itself.

Information released after dissolution of the Soviet Union disclosed documents, presented in 1955 by the Commission for Rehabilitation of Victims of Political Repression, include records of nuns, monks, ministers, and priests having been crucified, strangled, scalped, burned, drowned, and shot in the basements of NKVD, and KGB office buildings. The commission's report concluded that 200,000 clergy were tortured and murdered under Soviet rule. This included Russian nationals who never left as well as returning DPs. Of 50,000 churches a scant 5,000 remained.

In spite of wartime horrors just past, the endemic brutality, disregard of human rights, and casual waste of human life routinely practiced by the Soviets, were beyond the comprehension of Western Allies. DPs, in fact, were encouraged to return home, and some were persuaded to do so. Most were never heard from again. Before DP camps were established, some two million were forcibly sent back to their homelands to end their days in prisons, Siberian slave labor camps, or the execution block.

We were fortunate to have reached the Allied occupied zone later, after the need for emigration elsewhere had been recognized. It was another stroke of fate which saved the surviving members of our family in no way brought about by our own knowledge or intuition.

Numbering in the millions, we became a huge problem for the defeated Germans as well as the Allies. In view of disease which plagued the Nazi concentration camps, it was assumed every DP was a carrier of influenza, diphtheria or typhus. Fear of epidemic labeled us unclean and dangerous. Perhaps to satisfy themselves, as well as the German population, the Americans administered DDT to combat typhus. Everyone was dusted head to foot via nozzles passed down our necks and up our skirts and trousers. If few approved, most found it a demeaning process, reinforcing the idea of DPs as undesirables.

The U.S. War Department allowed that no American soldier could be expected to understand, let alone deal with, millions of uprooted, homeless, desperate people who fought for food, spoke no English, and stared with mistrustful eyes at any foreigner in uniform. General George Patton thought DPs were *'baser than animals'* He suggested we all be held behind barbed wire.

According to Capt. C.E. Jack in his 1945 memo *DPs vs. German Authorities*, DPs lived in barracks and barns, shared common, public sanitary facilities. A DP had little clothing beyond what he wore, resorted to petty theft, and had a highly defensive attitude toward authority. He learned to distrust promises and pieces of paper. His world revolved around food and shelter. In American eyes, he looked and acted like a bum. By contrast, Germans were well dressed, better fed, lived in homes with families, and treated Americans with respect. This simple contrast made the Military Government believe German complaints and discount those of the DPs. *(Abzug - Inside the Vicious Heart, 1985)**

If we were misunderstood by the Allies, we were despised by the Germans for allegedly living like animals, for being thieves, and carriers of the plague. This attitude was most common in Schlezwig-Holstein where most DP camps were being established. The camps were under military jurisdiction and off-limits to all Germans including their police. This magnified their resentment.

DPs, in general, were blamed for disruption of law and order in post-war Germany. Deservedly or not the Poles, in particular, were singled out as the worst of the lot. They quickly gained a reputation for criminal activity of all kinds against the Germans. Some reasoned it was payback for Sobibor, Auschwitz, and so many other chambers of horror having been sited in their homeland. Just outside the gates of one DP camp, a German policeman shot a Polish DP for some undisclosed reason. Infuriated, other Poles lynched him on the spot. No legal action against the lynch mob was ever taken.

There is no denying that black market was perpetuated in DP camps as it was throughout Germany. It grew out of need, as black market always does. There were many who profited by it. It continued unabated until the need was diminished by British and American relief efforts through CARE, UNRRA (United Nations Relief and Rehabilitation Administration), IRO (International Relief Organization), and the Swiss Red Cross. Later years of occupation saw the German population soften towards the DP presence.

By the end of 1947 escape from the camps to a new life elsewhere was on everyone's mind. Emigration to Canada, Australia, Brazil, Sweden and England was sought by everyone who could get work and sponsorship there. This meant the young and the strong went first.

America's outdated isolationist immigration policy of the 1920s was responsible for Congress procrastination on the DP issue. Annual quotas were set for each country of interest, and no longer applied to post-World War Two. In round numbers, these were 26,000 from Germany, 6,500 from Poland, 110 from Estonia, and so on. At that rate, it would take 300 years to absorb all the DPs from Estonia alone.

Nevertheless, in 1948 Congress passed the Displaced Persons Act. It allowed immigration of 10,000 DPs per month. Security demands made the process slow and convoluted. Fewer than 40,000 reached the U.S. by mid-1949. By the end of the year, however, 82,000 arrived. Before it ended, rehabilitation of war refugees to the U.S. reached an unprecedented 400,000 people.

Efforts to be accepted for immigration began the day it was learned some countries were opening their doors to refugees. For us the process consumed three years. In the interim, Russian NKVD agents swept through every DP camp to persuade residents to return to Eastern Europe and the Baltics. Assembly camps were established to facilitate repatriation to Russia and elsewhere in the Soviet Union. This move may have succeeded had British authorities not been in Germany at the time. They looked on the Americans, even at the highest echelons of command, as being completely ignorant of Russian methods and political doctrines toward not only their captives, but their own people.

The often quoted exchange between General Eisenhower and Marshal Zhukov was repeated to show they were not far wrong. When Eisenhower expressed dismay at Russian commanders marching their infantry across minefields to clear a path for tanks, Zhukov explained: "Casualties are casualties whether from enemy guns or enemy mines. What's the difference?"

We were terrified of repatriation. When we were approached to enter one such camp near Celle, father was adamant about our Lithuanian citizenship and freedom to live where we chose. Celle had once housed political prisoners who worked the salt mines there. The guard towers and barbed wire fences surrounding the camp were still there. General Patton would have been pleased.

The NKVD did everything it could to spread propaganda damning DPs in German eyes as well as American. But it soon backfired. American authorities eventually recognized the propaganda for what it was, and became increasingly protective toward us. Forcible return of refugees to their homelands was no longer tolerated. It was our first hint of America's generosity which we later found quite astounding.

After delaying as long as possible, the first internment camp we entered was at Lingen, and the experience was as unpleasant as we had expected.

Saxony

Before we reached the point where further independent wandering in Germany no longer made sense, we continued westward across Lower Saxony to delay, as long as possible, entry into one of the DP camps established by the Allied military government. It was another of those decisions made by instinct. Mistrust of any military administration in general, even of the friendly side; ingrained over the years of flight from oppression; saw us through this one last time.

To be in a DP camp before our plight was understood by the Allies, meant risking repatriation. And repatriation to a home country under Red Army occupation was a death warrant. The British already had an appreciation of this conundrum, but American military and political administration took more convincing of its reality. We were in the British Zone, but we didn't know what the various attitudes were among the Allies. The decision was made out of ignorance more than anything else, but it probably saved our lives.

We passed several more camps after Fallingbostel and Celle-Winsen. The largest occupied an abandoned German Army base in Diepholz. The barracks of brick and concrete appeared relatively new and well maintained. Roads were paved, there were sidewalks, and the grounds were landscaped. In spite of the attractive appearance and British administration, father continued on toward the Dutch border, another 120 kilometers west. Leaving Germany as soon as practicable seemed best.

While in Celle, we took the opportunity to have Displaced Person identification papers drawn up by British authorities at the camp. They would save us a great deal of red tape if we ever did enter a DP camp. The Celle *Arbeitsamt* (employment office) issued *Arbeitskarten* (work permits) and *Kennekarten* (ID cards). The Bürgermeister provided us with food ration coupon booklets, required to purchase groceries in German stores, and merchandise cards for other needed goods. We would not have DP camp privileges until we were registered residents. We were now, however, legal refugee residents of Germany's British Zone. Although we had spent considerable time traveling through areas held by American forces, the American zone of occupation was established well south of us.

Our visit to Ovelgen camp near Celle revealed it was exclusively Lithuanian. Internment by nationality made the new authorities' job of administration easier. It also benefited the occupants. There was an elementary school and a volleyball league. A small theater group was already active. We attended their first play, presented in the large cafeteria of what only three months before had been a German Wehrmacht barracks.

When we walked into the cafeteria to see the play, someone tapped my father on the shoulder and called him by name. Without a word spoken, the two men embraced in the doorway. They blocked others, but everyone stopped to wait, and watched in eloquent silence until they broke apart. It was a simple show of respect for a personal event repeated countless times by countless thousands throughout the war.

It was father's old friend and schoolmate from his birthplace in Biržai. Mother and I did not know him, but he and father were so obviously close we felt at home in his presence. Of all that happened during our visit to Celle, the most heartwarming thing was meeting friends from home whom we had not seen for more than four years, and did not know if they were dead or alive. One of them was my elementary school teacher from Raseiniai, now teaching class at the camp. Another was a district court judge who was a neighbor in Kaunas before I was born.

All of them lived in the camp and said things were improving every day. But as there were still no official steps being taken for permanent resettlement elsewhere, and threat of repatriation still loomed, we decided to go on. Perhaps we would return later, or find another Lithuanian camp farther west. Uncertainty of the future tempered our joy that we no longer felt hunted and were free to move where and when we chose. But we were not yet safe from Russian persecution. Nor were our family members who stayed behind. Word of their survival would trickle in, in small doses, many years apart. The fate of some is still unknown.

A day did not go by when I didn't think of my cousins, Arūnas and Gintautas in Raseiniai, aunt Elena and uncle Mike. Did his bees still produce honey, or did they flee the war like many people did? What was it like to have the Red Army come to their homes? Did they come to harm? Were uncle Jonas, aunt Ona, cousins Vida, Olė and Dana all right? Did they stay on the farm or have they, too, left home? Would I ever see them again?

I thought of them often, late at night, when sleep wouldn't come. I anguished over their fate when the Russians came. I missed them all, and most of all I missed my Gypsy's golden smile.

* * *

Foraging for food was becoming more and more difficult. It would only get worse until the fall harvest. Although we never starved, we were always hungry. Some were said to have used the amphetamine Benzedrine to suppress hunger. We did it by osmosis. Slowly, gradually, almost subconsciously, the stomach pains of hunger; so frightening and so severe at first; had dissipated. But I suffered with it rarely. My parents saw to it that I always had food even when there wasn't enough for all of us.

Reconnaissance by bicycle was now of longer duration. Father was away from dawn to supper time. Mother and I trundled along in the wagon a few kilometers behind him. The mare plodded on without urging, resigned to her task, tossing her head to get at the last of her feed in the muzzle bag. Her mane billowed up and down in time with her gait as her tail whipped the flies off her flanks. When passing a wooded stretch of the road, swallows often helped keep her comfortable as they darted after the pesky flies.

"Tomorrow, I'll need some help," father said gazing at me expectantly one evening. Then to mother: "This little bit took hours." He pointed at the small bucket of blueberries he picked that afternoon. "Two of us can pick twice that much now that I know where they are. We can start early in the morning. When you catch up, we'll all pick."

Next day we straddled the bicycle and went on ahead. The large blueberry field was on a steep slope right along the road. It looked like it had been abandoned years ago, so overgrown with weeds and underbrush it was. I was amazed father found it at all.

By late afternoon our buckets were full, but our wagon was still not in sight. The road was straight for some distance and we would see it well off. Father said mother should have been here by now. He didn't seem worried, but we got on the bicycle and started back. It wasn't long before we saw the wagon.

"There's mom," I pointed.

The wagon was still far enough to be obscured by the summer haze. As we drew near, we saw the wagon was by the roadside, reins laced around a sapling, the mare still hitched.

Something was wrong. Was mother inside?

We approached, calling for her. No reply. We looked in the wagon. Then we searched the woods, calling for her constantly.

Nothing.

The grove of ash and maple was not very large. We completed our search in minutes. Still nothing. Mother wasn't here. Now we worried. Leaving the wagon was synonymous with losing it along with everything we owned. Why would mother do such a thing? In concerned silence, we tied the bicycle back onto the rear of the wagon and set off retracing her morning route. There was no traffic.

"Did mom run away?" I wondered out loud.

"Of course not. Don't be silly."

"Then were is she?"

"Something happened. We'll find her. Don't worry." But I could see his concern.

Looking left and right along roadsides, hoping to spot some clue, we continued as our concern mounted. Mother may have gone back to the last farm she passed. But she would never leave the wagon when there was nothing wrong with it, would she?

We turned into the farm's gate and father ran to the house. An old woman opened the door. They spoke briefly, then father ran back. "She hasn't been here," he said.

There were no other farms before the last town, and Wietze was at least ten kilometers away. Mother would never just walk away. Maybe something happened. Maybe she had to go back. Maybe someone gave her a ride. We continued to town.

A car was approaching from Wietze. We recognized a British army staff car. It stopped when it reached us. Mother burst out the door and stumbled hurriedly toward us. She was limping badly.

"I'm sorry. So sorry," she said, fighting back tears. Our concern was overflowing. "I'm fine. I'm not hurt," she added between sobs she could no longer contain.

Two British officers got out the other door. They spoke in apologetic tones. We all stood in a small circle in the middle of the road, both car doors left ajar. It didn't matter. The road was deserted. We had had it to ourselves for hours. No one was using it before the British army car came along.

Hard as they tried to explain, it was useless. None of us understood a word of English. Mother tried to stop them and tell her own story, but they seemed embarrassed, and obligated to us. They just kept on talking. The older of the two pointed to the left front wheel on our wagon and said something, his fist punching his open palm, and shook his head, face marked by a heavy frown. To our complete surprise, we realized the wheel was new. With so much on our minds we hadn't noticed.

They were unwilling to leave. Mother urged them on in every language at her command. They nodded, spoke without much help of gestures or body language, but showed some signs of understanding.

"*Danke. Danke shön,*" she thanked them. "*Thank you very much,*" she spoke in a language we didn't understand — her first words spoken in English.

At last, they made reluctant motions to leave us, but not before one of them produced a piece of paper, wrote something down, and handed it to my father. We stood there, totally confused — except for mother — as they drove away.

She started her story for us before we got back in the wagon. Father examined the wheel, shaking his head, but with a smile on lips. He asked again what was wrong with mom's leg. She assured us it was fine. Nothing was broken, only a bruise. I wasn't concerned. After all, mother had nurse's training, she would know if it was serious. To my mind she might as well have been a doctor.

Her story was strange.

The car passed her too close. Although it wasn't moving very fast when it just touched the front wheel, the wooden spokes broke and the wheel collapsed. Mother was bending down, looking over her shoulder, lost her balance and fell off the wagon just as it jolted to a sudden stop. The two men helped her into the car. One drove her back to town while the other one used the car's jack to remove the broken wheel.

Taken to the town clinic, mother was immediately checked by a German doctor. She said the clinic staff seemed very frightened to have a British officer on the premises. The attention she received was better than she was used to at home. As there was an English speaker on the staff, and mother's German was passable, communication was not a problem. The British officer said he would go help fix the wagon while mother was being tended to, then return to take her back.

He returned hours later, after picking up his companion at the wagon, getting the wheel to a blacksmith in Wietze, and returning to put the new one on. They had made four trips back and forth, between the wagon and the town, and then one more to bring mother back once they got the doctor's OK. They paid the clinic for all services and insisted that mother accept additional money as compensation for the harm they caused.

After they departed, father showed us the piece of paper the officer had given him. On it were the names and rank of both men, the name of their unit and location of its headquarters. These two British soldiers left us with a lasting good impression.

Mother refused to show us her injury. It was her left thigh and was bound up with bandages, she said. It was well taken care of and would heel in no time, she claimed. Her knee was barely touched. She said that was important. The only other injury was a scraped elbow when she hit the ground. Even I had injuries like that. She was very lucky and father no longer worried.

What concerned us more was that now our whereabouts were available to anyone seeking this information. The information we gave British authorities was protected, and Celle's civilian office records were under British administration. But medical files at the clinic in Wietze had no such protection. Father said they were probably safe, because we were in the British occupied zone, and the fact that British army personnel were involved made it all the more secure.

Father felt it was safe to stop for a while and find work.

Cows, not horses, pulled the plows on farms here. There were no horses. He thought our mare could speed up the work and be cheaper to use. If work could be found nearby, we could enjoy the company of friends in the Ovelgen DP Camp, and make plans for a more stable future.

Camping

The Aller River, at Ortze's confluence, was dammed by several locks to control flooding and provide irrigation for the planted fields between Wietze and Winsen. What was left of the small Wehrmacht artillery base was in ruins, except for a large, solitary brick and concrete barracks still standing. Exterior wall damage looked pretty bad, but inside the barracks was still usable. It was to be our "home" while in the Celle-Winsen area. Permission to use it came from civic authorities which also operated the Aller River locks. Maintenance of the locks fell to a Ukrainian family of four who already occupied the damaged building.

They extended us a warm welcome and helped us get established. The two sons were in their late teens, and older than I by several years, but we hit it off even without a common language. Their German was very limited. Our conversations were like extended charades. To my benefit, I learned more Ukrainian in the process to supplement what little I had already learned from Alla. They also spoke Russian. Father knew enough of the latter to form a neighborly association with the family.

Another welcome neighbor was the farm adjacent to the artillery base. Our mare had a fenced grazing pasture all to herself and we were allowed to use the farm's bath and toilet facilities. Defecating in the woods, at which we had all become expert, was a thing of the past. We could even take a bath in a real bathtub indoors! But plumbing in the barracks was not functioning and there was no water or electricity. Mother used our camping stove to heat river water for washing and cooking, and the Ukrainians had built a brick and mortar grill. It was a reasonable arrangement for a longer stay.

One morning, the older of the two Ukrainian boys took me by the elbow and led me behind their grill, saying he needed my help. He handed me a spade and pointed to the ground where he wanted me to dig. Our communication was mostly by way of pointing and showing, as my Ukrainian had not progressed beyond a few words. His Lithuanian was no better. His explanation of what we were doing fell far short of my understanding.

He pushed his spade into the ground and turned the soil urging me to do the same. We did this in several spots when suddenly he stopped me and got on his knees to scoop the dirt up in his hands. That's when I realized what we were after. Worms!

His brother arrived with several sardine cans into which we put all the worms we had unearthed. We were going fishing, he said. We each had a wooden stick with a long string on one end. The older boy tied the hooks to it. These were made by bending heavy wire and filing deep serrations into the sharpened curved end. With worms impaled on them, we stood on the bank of the Aller River and waited for the fish to bite. This was the first time I had stayed in one place near water long enough to go fishing since we left home. We didn't do well the first day, but we changed location later and caught enough for a grilled fish dinner to feed everyone in our bombed out barracks. We fished three times a week from then on, and ate well the whole time we lived there. Father returned to the Celle Arbeitsamt and registered for whatever work was available. Our mare enjoyed a well deserved rest. No work was needed from the beast.

I attended the Lithuanian school in Ovelgen DP Camp. Although it comprised only elementary school curriculum, my former teacher from Raseiniai, who taught the small class, provided work at a higher level for me. I found sitting in a classroom of much younger children a very uncomfortable experience at first. Soon, they realized I knew more than they did and enlisted me, one by one, to help with their studies and their home assignments. Our teacher encouraged it. I found myself very busy.

Before long, I felt obligated to them and considered this the most important work I had ever done. I tried my mother's patience with questions about handling these children's academic problems. She often referred me to father who found the whole thing quite amusing. Looking back to this unorthodox experience, I realize I learned more in less time at this school than I ever had in my previous formal education.

Although we were still non-residents of the camp, we took part in community activities there whenever we could. I played soccer in pick-up games at least two or three times a week and renewed my membership in the Lithuanian Boy Scouts in exile. There were several others at the camp who were members before the war, all older than I except the three who joined after me. Interest in scouting was enhanced by rumors of a Jamboree of scouts displaced from countries overrun by war. It was to be organized somewhere in the British Zone by the Boy Scouts of England. This was an event I looked forward to with great anticipation.

Despite British protection under which the British Zone DP camps functioned, NKVD/KGB agents cruised these communities with intent to repatriate as many DPs to Soviet occupied territories as they could. Our Ukrainian neighbors were visited by one of those agents. They didn't talk about it and we didn't pry. But we knew what it meant. Within a week, they packed their meager belongings and moved out without a word. We didn't know what hold the KGB had over them. Perhaps family members still in the Ukraine were subject to political persecution as were so many families of voluntarily repatriating DPs. It was a typical KGB ploy not always recognized by American intelligence. But the British were thoroughly familiar with such tactics. We were therefore puzzled by our neighbors' predicament. Losing them was particularly painful for us as our friendship was the first new one extended over several months since we left home more than three years ago.

This first, of several incidents in quick succession, signaled the need to reevaluate our safety. We had made ourselves more comfortable here than we had since crossing the border into East Prussia, but staying much longer in Wietze was unwise. We bid our goodbyes to new and old acquaintances at Ovelgen camp and commenced our trek westward.

Father's decision was based on his suspicions confirmed later. At war's end the Russians made no distinction between Nazis and anti-Nazis, or between POWs and civilian refugees. Their imprisonment was marked by total chaos. Most of them were taken to Russia as slave laborers. They numbered in the millions. Only a few returned. Of the 90,000 taken prisoner at Stalingrad, for example, only 5,000 returned. If captives escaped, their numbers were made up by random arrests of civilians along the route to Russia.

The only formal education to have come my way since leaving home was being left behind. On my last day at school, our teacher told the children I was leaving in the morning. Their sad, questioning faces turned to me in puzzlement. The teacher explained that my family had to go to another camp. Perhaps some of their families would soon follow. This calmed their concern. We weren't friends. They were all much too young for me. But I, too, was saddened with the prospect of never seeing them again — a very likely possibility.

There was a large Polish DP camp in Lingen, where Lithuanians were also accepted. Lingen was only 20 kilometers from the Dutch border which was our next target.

At our last overnight stop, in Furstenau, we heard that a Lithuanian refugee family was staying in a monastery there. No one knew who they were, but father decided to pay them a visit before we continued. We were rewarded with a huge surprise. The man who opened the door was a Lithuanian Air Force lieutenant whose family had known ours for years. Neither of us knew whether we had survived the war until that moment.

He worked as gardener at the monastery and also waited for prospects of emigrating overseas, to Canada or the U.S. His wife was the eminent Lithuanian artist, Stančikaitė-Abraitienė. Her work in book illustration was known throughout Europe, and her painting exhibitions were sited in many neighboring countries as well as Lithuania before the war.

Father's decision to visit our unknown countrymen, flung far from home by the war, could not have been more welcome. This joyful reunion was repeated nine years later in the United States, where we had all emigrated. When we met there to celebrate our mutual survival, she presented us with one of her original oils. It is a moody shoreline view of an old, weather beaten oak overlooking a lake pier. She called it *Sargybinis* (Sentinel). Pride of place is reserved for this painting today in my living room.

* * *

The Lingen DP Camp was sited in another Wehrmacht military base, as was the one we saw in Diepholz, and the Polish DPs were accommodated in large brick barracks. Administrator of the camp was a Polish Army major with an unpleasant air of superiority and prejudice against those of other nationalities. Lithuanians were treated as second class citizens.

By his directive, the Lithuanian section was in recently abandoned huts. Ours was 12 by 20 feet, which we shared with a young couple and their 4-month old child. A tarpaulin curtain, draped over a rope attached to the ceiling between our quarters, provided a modicum of privacy. The tarred shingle roof overhang provided outdoor space sheltered from the rain for possessions not needed on a daily basis. We kept them in two large trunks. Two smaller ones fit indoors and served as tables. Aside from the five bunks, there was no other furniture. Cooking was over open fire outdoors — a method we were well acquainted with. We wore overcoats indoors and out. There was no heat.

On the coldest nights the fire outside served a double purpose. The young people who shared our accommodations always helped with collecting wood for the fire, but I was charged with a special task. When it was burning hot enough, it was my job to collect large stones and toss them into the flames. The shower of sparks each one sent spraying skyward was a fireworks spectacle. After hours in the flames, they were ready for removal. This I was never allowed to do. Father used a pair of tongs and collected the heated rocks into a heavy metal bucket. This bucket of hot rocks kept our room warm for most of the night.

Morning was always the same. Frost formed in small starbursts on the window glass — inside! Stones in the bucket were cold. Time to get up and stamp our feet — put life into them so we could walk.

We were permitted to keep horses in stables on camp grounds under the care of a Lithuanian cavalry officer. He was amazed we managed to keep a horse the whole way across Germany without it being requisitioned by the retreating Nazi army. Very few had come this far with horses. He said we were very lucky. Luck may have smiled on us on occasion, but I know it was father's good planning that we traveled where and when horses were needed in farms which supplied food to that retreating army.

Both our young cohabitants worked daily shifts, in turns to care for the baby, as did both my parents. Procurement of milk for the baby fell to me. After much reluctance, a local farmer agreed to sell milk. It was my task to walk to the farm four times a week to pick up the milk. This was an easy task when I was not in school — this one, a class of children more my age. It was taught by Henrikas Stasas and his wife Stefanija, teachers from Šiauliai. They made it all the way from Lithuania in a two-wheel cart drawn by a mule. Although younger than I, their two daughters were my newfound friends and schoolmates.

So far, every new friend I found had been a girl. The only exception were the two Ukrainians in Wietze, and they were much older. I began to wonder where the boys were — another reason I could hardly wait for the long promised Boy Scout Jamboree. Earlier rumors were now substantiated and plans were drawn to participate. Scout uniforms were being made for the Polish boys at the camp haberdashery. Mother's fluency in Polish helped her get the materials needed and I was soon outfitted in a spiffy Boy Scout uniform as sharp looking as anyone else's.

Anticipation of the event deprived me of rest. I collected the things I would need and packed them days ahead of time. The compass my godfather gave me, which guided father and me on our mushroom picking ventures in the forests of Mecklenburg, was in my hand and godfather was in my heart. I stopped packing and sat on my bunk, my hero clear as if he were standing on the parade ground right here in this room.

Where was he now? Did he survive? Or did he perish? Will I ever know? And godmother, the Gypsy with the Golden Smile, where was she? Will I ever see her again? Will I enjoy the Jamboree without either one knowing that I went? Will I ever be able to tell them about it?

* * *

Because it originated in Holland, the train was not as crowded and noticeably cleaner than the German norm of postwar trains. Due to lack of coal, this train was pulled by a wood fired engine. It meant frequent stops were needed to replenish the fast burning wood. It was a slow ride for the boy scouts from Meppen, Lingen, Diepholz, and Apeldoorn in Holland, who were bound for the Jamboree. Fast or slow, I was on my way to the long anticipated event at last.

The train stopped in Celle. I found myself in country I knew well. The Jamboree was being held in a large pine forest near Wietze where we once lived. The Scouts, perhaps two hundred Polish, Estonian, Lithuanian, Czech, Ukrainian, Hungarian, Latvian, Danish, and Dutch, marched the seven kilometers to meet our English hosts at the site.

The welcome we received came in the form of English boys meeting us before the campground was in sight. They intermingled with the group, breaking our formation to shake hands and pound us on our shoulders with much cheering, chatter and huzzahs in a language none us knew, but all of us understood. They relieved us of our backpacks and carried them the remaining distance.

A group of small children scattered into the woods as we approached. I was told to walk on and ignore them, or they would come begging later and steal everything they could. This was not news to me. I already knew that small bands of German orphans, living in the wild, had turned feral. I had seen them before. They always scattered like wild animals when approached by adults. But they were dangerous to other children.

Outside this minor incident, it was a marvelous beginning to a week of learning new things, making new friends, and happy competition in sports, trail finding, crafting, nature study, and singing songs in languages I had never heard before. Gathered around campfires, we learned the national anthem of every country represented at the Jamboree. One evening, someone started a parody of the German anthem:

Deutschland, Deutschland, über alles. Zwei kartofeln, das ist alles. (Germany, Germany, above all. Two potatoes, that is all.) Some of us tried to join in, but were immediately scolded to silence by the scout masters for our impertinence.

There was only one Boy Scout from France among us. He strode to the campfire clearing, stood there silently for a bit, commanding attention by his presence alone. We waited. Then he began to sing:

Allons, enfants de la patrie
Le jour de gloire est arrivé...

It was the *Marseillaise*. And he sang it all alone. We listened in silence. No one else knew it. Then he started from the beginning and sang it again — over and over again. Another voice soon followed his lead. Then, a few more joined in. He continued singing until the entire troop around the fire learned it and joined in. It was a most rousing display of patriotism. I can still see that boy's beaming smile when all of us sang the French anthem as if we had known it for years.

My first participatory exposure to English came in a song. It was called *America the Beautiful*. We learned to sing it in English. When we heard it translated to languages we already knew, we were sure it had to be the national anthem of the United States. I am still disappointed that it isn't.

Religious education was rare in my academic curricula, but at this Jamboree was a Lithuanian Jesuit priest who had escaped the NKVD torture chambers and had been without a congregation ever since. Perhaps Jesuits didn't lead congregations. Perhaps their work was teaching. But he was the spiritual leader at the Jamboree. My limited understanding fell short of his teaching. He tried to convince us to fear God's wrath when we knowingly did wrong, and to welcome His blessing when we did right. But I already knew that God does not punish, only the devil does. I've known that ever since my adventure in the sauna hut when we lived in Raseiniai.

He convinced me to respect all living things, as father had already done when I was younger, and Vida showed me that it was worthwhile. But then, our Jesuit teacher said that humankind was guaranteed eternal life as no other living thing was, that we were better than the rest. He said we were superior to all because we had a soul, and when we died, our soul continued to eternity. How did he know? Was this not disrespectful to other living things? Wasn't such arrogance spiteful?

He spoke to us about God's commandments and about sin. But then, in contradiction, he said God should be praised. Yet, seeking praise made men proud and pride was a sin. Why would God want to be praised? I also wondered why it was that when good things happened, people thanked God, but whenever bad things happened, people were blamed. If God was almighty, didn't He have the power to make bad things happen as well as good? And if He did — why, to what purpose? And why was He never blamed?

Our spiritual leader tried his best, but failed to answer these questions to my satisfaction and convince me of God's vengeful nature, or His existence for the good of mankind. His strange habit of uttering words in Latin and carving a cross in the air didn't help. But he taught us the basic Christian ideals and showed us their value in our daily lives. Much admired for his courage and his work with the resistance, he was also looked upon to mend our doubts and our confusion. But he confused me farther when I learned he was returning to Lithuania to continue his work there. Weren't members of our clergy the first victims of Russian savagery? Wasn't this priest going back to certain death?

Many years later, I read about a Jesuit who had returned to resume his teaching while under Soviet oppression, was arrested and deported to the Siberian wasteland from which he never returned. Was this the man I met in Wietze, at the Jamboree?

Another meeting was of particular delight. The two sons of the Ukrainian family with whom we shared accommodations in the war torn artillery base, were at the Jamboree. They had returned to the same barracks and still tended the Aller River locks. The KGB/NKVD agent had been careless. Word reached the British military governor that Celle-Winsen was losing its caretakers of the locks needed for farming and intervened to stop their repatriation.

It had been a close call, but they were now safe and planned to stay until they could return to the Ukraine after the Russians left. I was very happy for them, as were my parents when I returned and told them the good news. Who was to know the Ukraine would endure the same tragedies of Russian oppression our own homeland would for the next 45 years.

But now, the news we heard substantiated rumors that this encampment was the staging ground and prelude to the first postwar World Scout Jamboree being held in France. The French boy's *Marsellaise* at the campfire took on a whole new meaning. We were coached in conversational French and learned a little of French history.

Once assembled, which took the entire week, we were on the way to France. Women of the Swiss Red Cross passed each of us a modest packed lunch to be taken on the train as we boarded. As expected, the train was crowded. It was dirty, hot and ripe with the odor of hundreds of noisy, happy people. Although the ride was tiring and uncomfortable, we hardly noticed. Many hours and river crossings later, it seemed no time at all before we were near the Belgian border near Aachen. Border crossing documents were accepted without question. They were provided by the British military government and guaranteed our legitimacy.

The countryside changed little after Aachen, but when the rail line began its way along the Meuse River, forests grew denser and we saw mountains in the distance. The 180 kilometers across Belgium went by quickly. We were told there would be another train waiting for us at Jeumont. We were to change trains before entering France.

Our excitement grew in direct proportion to our shrinking proximity to the Jamboree site. Everyone speculated on what it would be like to be in France, the country about which we had heard so much during the war. To no one's surprise, changing trains was a revelation.

French trains were far superior to any I had ever seen. The wood benches were padded, windows had pull up shades, there were separate compartments to seat six or eight, and the floor was rubber coated for better footing on the jostling ride. I also discovered I could walk from one rail car to another through short, accordion baffled passageways between them. This was a new experience. The first time I tried it the noise and instability at the rail car junction gave me a fright. Treading the metal floor plate, which moved unpredictably under my feet, I once lost my balance and was thrown into one of the soft canvas baffles. But it didn't take long to learn how to adjust my balance to the sway and jostling of the moving train and the bucking floor plate. It soon became second nature and I roamed the train from one end to the other with no fear of a tumble. In fact, I enjoyed these long walks so much I could hardly stay seated more than a few minutes at a time.

That's how I met many other Lithuanian boy scouts on the train. National patches on our uniforms were easy to spot and I was stopped many times by boys who saw my patch before I saw theirs. We were all eager to meet as many of our countrymen as we could before our destination.

The train stopped in Rouen, the nearest station to Moisson where the Jamboree was being held. The railroad station was a crowded, noisy place. It was a vast building with ceilings higher than any I had ever seen. They were bordered in glass through which the midday sun cast bright daggers of light onto the walls and the white brick floor. The building was so large that trains could enter. Steam from their engines rose to the ceiling and out the open glass windows there. Vendors sold flowers from two-wheel carts pushed like wheel barrows. Several booths, built into the walls displayed knick knacks, books and newspapers.

Buses were soon filled with excited, chattering boy scouts from all over Europe. We rolled down the wide road leading to the encampment. The road was fringed with national flags of the countries represented at the Jamboree. It was disheartening that the flags of Lithuania, Latvia and Estonia were not among them. Instead, the contrived DP flag combining all three was displayed. We looked on it with disdain. Apparently France did not want to offend their Russian ally by recognizing the three Baltic countries as separate from the Soviet Union.

Grounds of the Jamboree were teeming with scouts in a variety of national uniforms from twenty or more different countries. Among them were war refugee scouts from the British, the American, and the French zones of occupation in Germany. In an open field a huge crowd — 10,000 someone said — packed in shoulder to shoulder, were rolling a giant world globe over their heads. It was painted green to represent the earth's continents and pale blue its oceans. It was more than twenty feet in diameter, but it bounced lightly over their heads, hand to hand — an eye catching demonstration of postwar solidarity among nations.

All around the perimeter of the encampment a small train moved at walking speed, discharging and embarking passengers without stopping. People hopped on and off at will wherever they wished. It was a great way to get around. We were issued French Jamboree badges of a square knot superimposed over a fleur-de-lis surrounded by the words *Jamboree Mondial de Paix* (World Peace Jamboree). They were to be worn on our uniforms at all times.

The first campfire we attended was a cornucopia of entertainment from all over the world. On a raised stage, scouts of various nationalities performed songs, dances, and skits of the kind I had never seen before. The Hungarians danced the *Chardash*, and Arabian mimes had us rolling with laughter at their amazing antics. We sang along with the Greek choir, and the Americans whooped it up to drum rhythms dressed as Indians.

International competitions and cooperative projects of all kinds followed in the days to come. Nature study, archery, wood crafts, survival trials, and games brought everyone together, no matter our nationality, race, creed, or political heritage. On the day the Jamboree was visited by the Parisian cardinal and other French dignitaries, there was a parade of nations. To our dismay, free nations only. We were not permitted to represent ourselves. It would have been politically incorrect for France to recognize us apart from Russia; one of her allies during the war just won; never mind that Russia invaded our country and was not represented at the Jamboree.

To our great joy the American contingent marching in the parade carried the Lithuanian flag. They received our boisterous cheers as they passed. We were incredibly grateful to them for this expression of support and invited them later to our own modest campfire. This was my first opportunity to interact with Americans of my own age, at my own level. We conversed in gestures and a smattering of foreign words we each had learned. But the exchange was difficult and not very productive. Unfortunately, the time spent together was insufficient to learn more than a few words of English.

Nor was there enough time to learn any other of the dozens of languages spoken at the Jamboree. I did manage to learn some polite words in Polish, but that was it. I remember them well, however, and use them when the occasion arises. *Dzien dobry, dzienkuye,* and *dovidzenya* may roll off my tongue without effort, but any Pole will spot me for a foreigner after the first syllable.

This Jamboree was the brightest eye opening experience of my young life. It restored faith in the innate gallantry and goodness of people in time of war after that war itself had conspired to fling them asunder. It was the experience to which I would rally many times in the years to come.

Wind

Canyon walls rise sixty feet above me. Wind howls upstream between them. It whips the spray full in my face hindering my ability to read the river ahead. But read it I must. Class IV rapids can be unforgiving if taken lightly. My knees must steer the kayak in the right direction and my paddle strokes must balance the mistakes I make. The speed of the river is stronger than the canyon wind. But the wind slaps me hard for every error and reminds me how insignificant I am in nature's grasp.

Is this dangerous? Not if I read the river well. When I'm uncertain, I scout from shore. If indications are I may be in over my head, I carry around. But if I want a challenge, I will study the river, not merely read it as I go. Then I'll take the challenge and I'll soar!

Kayaking whitewater allows me a studied look at myself, from the outside. I know how awkward a sight I present when the next haystack wave pitches me downward into the trough below. If I'm deceived by a line of haystacks, frothing downstream like ducklings taking flight, into thinking that's all they are, I feel a momentary fear when suddenly faced with the unexpected explosion wave instead.

I can steer around it. There is time enough when I first see what the last haystack becomes. But I may choose to take it on and blast my way through. When I do, the wind slaps me in earnest. The frothy spray stops only when I submerge, then rise to a torrent of water streaming down my face.

I will continue this way for hours, enjoying nature's awesome power at first hand, up close and personal. When I tire, a brief rest is always available in the next eddy. But I must work to gain its relative calm. My knees will have to rotate the kayak as my shoulder dips into the water while I lean on the paddle blade and let fast water spin the boat upstream into the peaceful waters of the eddy.

209

This is not easy. But things achieved with little effort give little satisfaction. What I learn from this river today I can use on another tomorrow. My knowledge builds on itself, but I will never be an expert. That demands dedication I do not possess. Dedication requires stability, a luxury which came my way long after rivers were in the distant past of younger days.

Hiding

Triggered by familiar smells or sounds, not experienced for a long time, are the myriad mental images of scenes long forgotten. Such occasions unexpectedly surface in unrelated ventures.

My wife and I were picking apples in a Pennsylvania orchard. There were bees in the air. It brought to mind my uncle's beehives in his orchard and how his two sons, my younger cousins, and I were out to pick ourselves an apple to taste. This was another of those things not to be done — not before the fruit were ripe and permission was given. We three were sneaking up on the one gnarled apple tree with branches low enough to reach. Sneaking up so as not to be noticed. And who, but uncle Mike himself, would venture out on the back porch just as we picked an apple off the lowest branch. This was trouble, we knew.

Being the oldest, it was my responsibility to save the situation as best I could. My immediate suggestion was to cover our faces with our hands, so as not to be recognized, and run. The amazing thing is that all three of us actually did, in all seriousness, cover our faces as we ran. What humiliation I felt when I realized how absurd an idea this was now escapes me, but it does bring an inward smile on reflection.

A later hiding episode, though equally childish, was not quite so amusing.

In the depressing atmosphere of DP camps, we brightened our days with detritus of war which we converted into playthings. But for the priceless few things fashioned from wood scraps which our fathers made for us, those were the only toys. We often found discarded ammunition of all kinds. Much of it we didn't recognize, but bullets were familiar to everyone. We tossed loose rifle rounds into bonfires, ran for cover, and watched them go off in all directions at once.

One day, I came across a full belt of machine gun caliber rounds. This was cause for celebration. The most inventive among us suggested a more elaborate display. The belt was laid out and pinned to the ground, facing a well chosen direction. The bonfire was then built over it. Certain the bullets would fly where directed, we stood in the open behind them and lit the fire. We knew this was dangerous, but that was the whole point. We were wary, however, of abandoned minefields marked with signs proclaiming "*Achtung! Minen*" and bearing the scull and crossbones of pirate lore. Where the unmarked minefields were nobody knew. Fortunately, no one in our camp ever stumbled into one.

Our older peers were more inventive than we and did not discourage our interest. Kazys was one whose company I sought on those occasions when adventuring was in the wind. I was unaware of his fatal fascination with explosives.

On one occasion, three of us went diving for treasure in a local pond. It was an operation not without a plan. Kazys had dived the shallow pond before and knew exactly where the treasure was. We were flattered he was willing to share such secrets with 13-year olds. We had never seen such treasure as he described. Treasure, there, at the bottom of the pond. Treasure abandoned by the retreating Nazi army which passed here just months before.

Down into the murky waters we went. Our first attempts were fruitless. Then, on the third dive, my hand found the round shape Kazys described — a large, disk-like, metal thing too heavy to lift even under water. I tied the rope around it and rushed back up for air. I still had no idea what it was.

There was another, but it was too far gone, said Kazys.

"That one doesn't have the *Zupzünder* switch," he told us. That, evidently was important to his purpose whatever it was. We wiped the mud off, washed the dark hard surface in pond water and read the numbers on its side. Kazys identified it as a *Tellermine*, an anti-tank mine. And he knew exactly how it worked.

"This one has the switch, see," he pointed. "When I take it apart, and dry it out, it'll work like new."

Work like new? What was he planning to do? Kill a tank?

Not wishing to betray our ignorance, we didn't ask. He took the thing to the old camp barracks where we lived, there to render it operable in a day or two. When he told us it was ready, curiosity and sense of adventure spurred us on to whatever Kazys had in mind.

There was a farm three kilometers beyond the north gate of the camp. Carrying Kazys's modified mine in a net sling, and rotating relief by each of us in turn, it was an easy walk. The second spring harvest of hay was stacked across the field in typical German fashion – huge hemispherical stacks eight meters high and more than ten round, bound lightly with string and capped with canvas.

First job was cutting the string. We all had knives — standard pocket equipment for teenagers then — and cut short lengths to tie into one long string, long enough to reach the next haystack. Kazys instructed and told us we would make rain. If we did as he said, it would rain. A skeptic before I was seven, I had my doubts, but held my tongue. I was about to be proven wrong.

We burrowed deep inside the haystack and buried the *Tellermine* just below ground under the hay. Then we led the string behind another haystack and took cover there. The string attached to that all-important switch was in Kazys' hand. The hay behind which we crouched was our protection.

"With the *Zupzünder* switch, you don't need the weight of a tank to set it off." That's alright, I thought, not all that anxious to see tanks.

"Ready?" he asked. We nodded. Serious voices now. No laughing.

We covered our ears and he jerked the string.

The deafening blast sent the earth spewing up in the air. Dirt and roots and stones descended on us like hail. We charged into anther haystack. A pause, and then we dared a look. It still rained hay long after all else had returned to earth. Kazys was right. He never said it would rain water.

We marveled at the sight. But not for long.

The barn door in the distance opened, and out came the farmer a'gallop on his horse. My friend and Kazys fled. I froze in fear. Perhaps I wasn't seen. Without a second thought, I scrambled back into the haystack and stuffed hay back in the hole. I heard the hoof beats passing and fading away. I thought to take a peek, see if I could get away, when voices stopped me. German voices, coming closer. I stayed put and held my breath. The voices came within clear earshot, alarmed, angry voices.

"I hope he catches him this time," one said.

"Those damned DPs should all be skinned alive!" threatened another.

"Last time it was a grenade. What now?" wondered a third.

I heard the voices recede and return as if looking around the area, stack to stack. What if they find me? I felt trapped. My skin crawled. Would they really do that? Then I remembered the string. What if they see it? I dared not look, or move, or breathe. Activity around me continued for some time. Voices became more numerous and other sounds were heard. It was an hour, maybe ten, before things quieted down and I ventured to push a plug of hay out into daylight. No one was near. There was a hay wagon where the stack had been. Hay had been raked and loaded into it. No horses. Alongside was a crater, how deep I couldn't tell — the sun was setting. At dusk, I moved stealthily away, haystack to haystack, and back to the camp.

This convoluted route was not an original idea. I knew that downed Allied airmen used haystacks in this manner to hide from German searchers. Sometimes they, too, moved from haystack to haystack, between fields, for days on end before finding a more suitable hideout or being caught.

No news reached me about Kazys, but the other boy was caught. A hue and cry was heard for days about the hooligans and delinquents from the DP camp causing all manner of grief to the farmers, the same farmers who supplied us with much needed food in exchange for farm work or Red Cross goods they couldn't get otherwise. Shame was only a small part of what I felt. Stronger was the apprehension with which I approached my task two days later.

It was my job to walk to the farm four times a week and refill two small milk cans with milk which the family we shared our room with needed for their baby. They paid for the milk and I saw to it they received it on schedule. Without refrigeration, this was important. So, now I was to return to the scene of the crime. What awaited me there? Would I give myself away? Will I be recognized, had I been seen? What will I do?

I need not have worried. The milk maid, an old grouch who never spoke a single word to me, or any DP for that matter, was true to her habit. She filled my cans with milk, still warm from the cow's udder, and pocketed the money I handed her as always. It was of my return walk that I should have been wary.

Word had spread about exploding haystacks. Everyone knew the culprits were DPs. Local German boys, my age and somewhat older, barred my way. I was the intruder. This was their home. And I was a DP, of those DPs who blow up haystacks. These thoughts came later. At the moment, I was terrified. Not because I might be hurt, but because the milk might spill. They pelted me with insults and with rocks. I didn't feel that I deserved that. Yet, self defense was not an option. My sense of obligation was too strong.

I ran. I did not spill the milk.

A later repetition of this harassment, on my way to the farm with empty milk cans this time, ended on a different note. Double-handled, three-litre, metal cans can be formidable weapons. I was never bothered again.

This unpleasant experience was as nothing when set alongside the tragedy only a month later. Kazys' fascination with explosives, so readily available to children of war, prompted him to experiment with discarded ammunition he knew nothing about. A "potato masher" grenade exploded in his hands. He lost both arms. Rushed first to the camp clinic, where no anesthetic was available, he died in agony in his own mother's arms before they reached the hospital.

School

Our stay in the Lingen DP Camp came to a welcome end when it was learned that a new Lithuanian DP Camp was just opened a mere 16 kilometers away and 4 kilometers from the Dutch border. Major Greenwood, the British Army representative of UNRRA (United Nations Relief and Rehabilitation Administration) made it known that Lithuanians transferring to this camp would be responsible for its operation and free to structure the community whatever way was best for us. We were assured United Nations would stand behind our decisions in the administration of the camp and UNRRA would support the venture in every way.

Of the 3400 residents in the Lingen camp, nearly 1500 were Lithuanian. With additional DPs from other areas, the number would grow to more than 2000. The new camp at the village of Gross Hesepe was ready to support a community that size.

On the date set by UNRRA, a wagon train of impressive size rolled out of the Lingen DP Camp, bound for the first all Lithuanian community in exile. This was one of four very large prison camps along the Dutch border where Russian POWs worked the peat mines. Peat growing industry was concentrated on both sides of the border, and Gross Hesepe had the most extensive peat bogs. They stretched 250 km along Germany's western borders.

Everything was left in working order when the POWs were released. Sod already cut and stacked to dry was still awaiting its turn under roof. Piles of dried peat, cut to briquettes, were scattered about after falling from their original height of ten feet and more. Small wooden sheds, spaced some distance apart across the bog, still contained slanes and other peat cutting tools used to harvest the product of this scarred land. The winning of peat required hard manual labor, and the surface of the land bore it witness. Landscape color was a haphazard mix of mottled shades of brown and olive drab and, nearly always, there was musty ground fog hanging low over the bog.

Peat production had left the land furrowed in zigzag patterns of trench-like, flat bottomed gullies. Some were deep enough to form water filled basins at the foot of the lowest terraced cuts in the bog. Trees were few, and those that still thrived were scrubby and thin. Here were the first birch bushes I had ever seen. I didn't know such things existed. Birches at home were straight, proud, beautiful trees, prized for their clean white bark and their shade. There was something bright and clean about a birch forest in the snow. Here, they were little more than overgrown weeds.

In this bleak and dreary countryside were rows and rows of small, single level, wooden barracks. Two large buildings behind one row were used for peat storage. An even larger one housed a stage and more than 500 chairs. Under the same roof were the community kitchens, the cafeteria, a huge pantry, and the community baths. There were other large buildings which originally served as hospital and jail.

Those of us who still had horses were allowed to use the extensive pastures just east of the camp. Keeping them was to become a burden, as work animals were no longer needed. Before the first winter came, most of the horses were sold to area farmers or traded for food, tools and other necessary items. Parting with our small mare which, except for distance traveled by rail, had pulled our wagon well over a thousand kilometers, was especially sad for me. I missed our gelding, which we lost earlier, but the mare was my mount when learning to ride. She never complained when I pulled her mane mercilessly trying to keep my balance, and never left me when I fell off and lay there nursing my bruises.

Our assigned accommodations were in one of the small barracks, which we shared with another family, partitioned off by a movable plywood wall. There was even indoor plumbing with water supplied from the peat bogs via underground pipes and steam driven pumps fired by peat. Peat was also used for heating and cooking. We did not have to cut our own peat or dry it for burning. Seasoned, dry briquettes were stored in abundance under several huge roofs supported by steel I-beams.

I never got used to sleeping in a room heated with these briquettes. Peat makes a smoky, bilious fire, pungent and sweet. The strong aroma did not follow the smoke up the chimney. It stayed in the room through the night and kept me awake for hours. But I was always warm, even on the coldest nights.

Several barracks stood abandoned for what appeared an extended time. They were run down beyond repair. Permission was granted to tear them down. The men and boys in camp pooled our resources and not only leveled the old buildings to the ground, but used the wood to make furniture for everyone in the camp. In the next few weeks, we supplied 2000 residents with all the basic furnishings needed. They were crude but functional.

Among these abandoned barracks was a smaller building which still functioned and was a godsend to the new residents of the camp. It was a washroom used almost daily by men and women, in turn, with assigned hours for each. Its interior was one large room with metal walls, and a cement floor which sloped downward from the center of the room to a trough the whole way around its perimeter. This trough carried off waste water from the showerheads mounted on the walls. In the center, on the highest point of the floor, was a huge, wood-fired kettle for boiling laundry — the best way to clean garments without soap or detergent. It also served to keep the room warm while we showered.

Boys my age were said to have made holes in the metal walls through which they could observe the interior during women's washroom hours. But they were never caught in the act. I wouldn't have dared.

We lived in reasonable comfort. Many adults worked outside the camp, in German owned industry, and provided everyone with food bought for the meager wages they earned. Those working in administration of the camp were provided for cost free. The Lithuanian-American organization BALF, still active today, sent clothing donated by Lithuanians in the U.S. The occasional Red Cross and CARE packages from the United States helped and no one starved — a new luxury for some. Everything was in cans, and made me think all American food was canned. But hunger was universal. Refugees, resident Germans, even allied soldiers went hungry every day.

There were occasions when I was taken along to buy food at the neighboring farms. My teacher, Henrikas Stasas, sometimes came with us. Father managed to communicate with the farmers well enough, but Mr. Stasas was fluent in German. This made our task so much easier, especially at first, when farmers refused to admit us. This lack of trust was attributed to Polish refugees who not only refused to pay the farmers, but demanded they be given food as their due. It was my teacher's patient explanation that we were not Polish that won their trust.

It was illegal for farmers to sell or trade livestock and for us to keep it on camp grounds. It was done, on a limited scale, nevertheless. DP camps were outside German police jurisdiction which made this activity easier. Major Greenwood, the British administrator of the Gross Hesepe DP Camp, is another case in point. "When I'm in camp, the pigs must be quiet and chickens must stay out of my way," he said and turned a blind eye.

We also traded soap, cigarettes, coffee, and other non-perishables, which we received from the Red Cross, for food. I accompanied father often, but one day he said no. "Not today. I must go alone. There is no room on the bicycle for you."

When he returned, I learned why. The bicycle was loaded with sausages, smoked hams, bricks of pickled pork fat, tubs of lard and portions of meat I didn't recognize, some forty kilograms in all. There was so much, we shared with the Stasas family and other neighbors. All this was taken in trade for our mare. A nearby farmer had been using the beast to help work his farm. In return, the animal was well looked after and was no longer our concern. We also received eggs and a quart of milk every other day.

When the farmer offered to buy the mare, father traded her for a pig which the farmer rendered into the bounty on the bicycle. It was a most welcome development in view of the stale cornbread, gristle laden meat, and old liverwurst we usually received from German authorities. They were required by the British military administration to help supply the DP camps and produced only the minimum to meet the requirement. When IRO took over from UNRRA, food improved, but there was never enough.

This camp was the first place conducive to social and cultural endeavors that we had seen since leaving home. My return to formal education, after its long interruption since leaving home, was at this Lithuanian refugee camp in Gross Hesepe. My haphazard, catch-as-catch-can education came to an end, replaced by a structured curriculum modeled after Lithuanian schools at home. One of the larger barracks was converted to school use. Henrikas Stasas and his wife, Stefanija, the teachers we had first met in Lingen, were instrumental in making our school the success it was to become over the next two years. Its administration fell to them as much by their own choice as did teaching class — there were only three other qualified teachers in our new community.

At my age, it was difficult to appreciate the Stasas' dedication, but I understood the community respect they soon garnered. Their two daughters were my only friends on arrival in Gross Hesepe. Although both were younger than I, we played together and exchanged banter as if we had known one another for years. It was another confirmation of my experience on uncle Jonas' farm that even girls could be good friends.

The day school started I gained more friends than I could count. Every Lithuanian child in camp attended — aged six to sixteen — and new friendships came as naturally as breathing.

Books were still a luxury. What few were collected from donations and saved library volumes were shared by everyone in class. Home study was impractical. We stayed after class and studied in small groups we formed and rotated ourselves. In winter, we were to stop feeding peat briquettes into the classroom stove as soon as class ended to prevent an accidental fire with no one in attendance. The last hour, or so, of each day we all wore gloves, hats and coats in the classroom. Our school day was six hours long. Assigned homework was light, and consumed little additional time. But it had to be done before nightfall because candles, made by an adult hobby crafts class, were rationed. It still left more than five hours a day to get into trouble before bed time.

Peat bogs are hazardous by nature, but the itch for adventure never gave it a second thought. Harvested peat in peat bogs leaves deep, water filled holes hidden under thin new growth of sphagnum — ready made for drowning. The black water surface was like oiled silk harboring mosquitoes. Diphtheria and typhus were an ever present threat that never occurred to us in our quest for adventure. Seemingly dry ground could be undermined by soft, mossy mesh of soggy matt, afloat over a deep, water filled gully. If not as dangerous as quicksand, it comes a close second.

Drowning in one of those never occurred to us. But quickly learning from experience, we tested the ground gingerly before we allowed it to bear our full weight.

In summer, when we weren't needed to restock our daily supply of briquettes for heating, we roamed the bogs with bow and arrow hunting muskrat. Our home made bows were crude, but not all that bad. We had our fathers' help. Arrows were another matter. After repeatedly losing them, it was embarrassing to seek help in making more. We made our own. And few of them ever flew straight. Needless to say we never bagged a muskrat, although we scared many.

We sought other pursuits in hopes they would be more productive. Open waters of the bog were inaccessible on foot. What we needed was a boat. Building one was to fill our time throughout the entire summer. It was complicated by need for secrecy; our parents absolutely forbade playing in the bogs. Nevertheless, we succeeded in building more than one. Unfortunately, we never succeeded in building one that did not sink or turn over. After more than a few evenings of slinking home soaked through head to foot, and trying to explain how such a thing could happen, our noble project died.

In one of my solitary wanderings over the peat bogs I came across a large, untended, overgrown graveyard surrounded by a broken fence. The crosses were marked with recent dates, but I could not read the names. They were inscribed in an alphabet I did not recognize. Father later told me the names were written in Cyrillic. The graveyard was the burial ground of 35,000 Russian POWs who worked the peat mines here. Over 100,000 of them had been held in the Gross Hesepe camp.

In addition to concerts by singers and musicians exchanged with other Lithuanian refugee camps, a varied concert program by our local entertainers continued throughout the year. Social dances were held monthly for children as well as the adults. During our second year there, a well received international chess tournament was held in Gross Hesepe, the first of its kind among refugees. Estonia, Poland, Hungary, Czechoslovakia, Latvia, and the Ukraine were represented. Participants roomed and boarded with residents of the camp. This event inspired me to learn chess which I still enjoy on a regular basis. I persuaded father to teach me. He did a good job, but I was never able to win a game against him.

Although the community did not lack sports minded youngsters my age and older, sports equipment was available only to British military personnel, and there wasn't enough to share with the camp. Our administration knew the value of sporting pursuits and set out to make it happen.

In nearby Osnabrück was the British Zone's YMCA/YWCA central office. One of the officers there was a lieutenant Maksvytis, a Lithuanian. He was approached with request to help start a sports program at the Gross Hesepe camp. Coaching and organization needed no help, but sporting goods and equipment were badly needed. These were soon provided at no cost. My father was quick to recognize this generosity and took it upon himself to rally the community behind this idea. He worked directly with the YMCA/YWCA in Osnabrück.

In a matter of weeks, teams for volleyball, football (soccer), and basketball were competing in tournaments attended and cheered by the whole population of the camp. Although American football and baseball did not attract participants (there were no coaches for these unfamiliar games), a tennis court was built and non-team sports had a start.

I tried my hand at all the available sports and soon found myself ill-suited for basketball. I was too short. Volleyball was a girl's game, and I was no sissy. There was no way I would play it. That left soccer. And that's where I went. In fact, I enjoyed the game enough to continue playing it right through high school. But the game I excelled in was table tennis in which I won the camp's junior title.

Thanks to the small frozen stream between our barracks and our school, I learned to ice skate. No ice skates were available. We made them ourselves and, much as our bows and arrows, they served us well. Tied on to our boots were foot-long wood boards, with steel rails cut from a variety of war wreckage, attached to the bottom. Although they broke frequently, we skated to school every day and even played hockey with curved sticks and a flat stone for puck.

Thanks to Mr. Stasas and his small school, I was prepared for high school when the time came. It came after two years in Gross Hesepe, when we learned the camp was to be liquidated. Everyone was to be moved to the old Luftwaffe base in Diepholz, which we passed on the way to Lingen, 100 kilometers east of the Dutch border. Father's hopes of leaving Germany were dashed when it was learned that Canadian military administration in Holland imposed a no-entry policy on DPs.

Father's health took a downward plunge shortly before the move. He was taken to Meppen Mariestenkloster hospital. There, without bothering to electrocardiogram, he was diagnosed with what was called *Myocardschaden* (coronary heart disease? angina?) The Lithuanian camp doctor prescribed *Traubenzucker* (grape sugar?) ampoules. After filling the prescription the first time, the pharmacist in Meppen said he had no more. On a subsequent visit father slipped him a bag of coffee beans saved from a CARE package. Prescriptions were filled for months to come without question.

Coffee was virtually unobtainable in Germany, even on the black market. On the rare occasions when we had it, we never drank coffee. It was a more valuable currency than money or even cigarettes. Only nylon stockings commanded higher value. Ersatz coffee made from acorns and roots was the only coffee drunk by DPs — those who could stomach it.

Until the Währangs Reform in 1948, two packs of cigarettes were enough to cross Germany by train. One cigarette was good for ten Reichsmark or a smoked herring. That ended when one Deutsche Mark replaced ten Reichsmark, but that cigarette was still good.

Mother and I worried about father's health daily, but seldom spoke of it. Our concern was borne in silence. I still remember watching him carefully filing a groove around the glass ampoule's neck to snap it off, then inserting the syringe to withdraw the drug and inject himself. Years later, after more precise diagnoses, medication of choice was nitroglycerin tablets. This relieved the angina, but did not cure the disease. He suffered with it for the rest of his life.

Shortly before departure for Diepholz, we received a most unexpected and welcome visitor. Out of nowhere, on our doorstep was uncle Jurgis' son, my cousin Narimantas from Biržai. We had no knowledge of his having fled the country. While we were in Mecklenburg, father had contacted several relief organizations in Germany seeking information about our family members' whereabouts, and whether anyone else had left home during the war. Nothing was known. Narimantas had done the same, found out where we were, and wrote to us in Hallalit. By then, we had moved on and the letter never reached us. He had enrolled at the UNRRA University in Munich, in the American Zone, after war ended. There he met a conference attendee from the Lingen DP camp from whom he learned we had moved to Gross Hesepe.

I remembered him only vaguely from my visit in Biržai; our age difference of twelve years played a big part in mutual disinterest. Now, seeing him here, after years of wandering independently, overwhelmed me to tears. I could not have been happier.

His stay at the University in Munich to graduation was in jeopardy due to lack of funds. Cost of education was funded by UNRRA, but it was still up to the students to provide for themselves. Full time studies did not leave much time to earn enough to maintain a livelihood. He was on his way to Pinneberg, where the Baltic University had been established for students from Estonia, Latvia and Lithuania whose studies were interrupted by war. This fully accredited university functioned three and a half happy years. On the strength of some 180 Estonian, Latvian and Lithuanian college professors and more than 2000 college age students in the British Zone alone, permission was secured from the United Nations to establish the only refugee institution of higher learning in exile in Europe. It stood as testament to the lasting solidarity of the three Baltic countries. Its contribution to our cultural stability cannot be measured in words.

Currency of the day was American cigarettes, which paid for Narimantas' train travel to see us. The only "currency" valued higher was nylon stockings, and they were hard to come by. Father packed a carton of Lucky Strikes and accompanied him to see if he could enroll there and finish his studies at lower cost. It was not to be. For reasons I don't remember, he left the University in Munich and enrolled in a technical college. Our poor financial situation notwithstanding, my parents agreed without question, whatever could be done to ensure their nephew's graduation would be done. For the next two years, with father's financial support, Narimantas pursued a degree in electrical engineering.

This kindness was repaid tenfold years later when he had emigrated to the U.S. before us. Younger, able bodied, educated applicants were the first ones accepted for immigration and he was already overseas bound when father first entertained the idea of leaving Europe.

Narimantas visited us several times after we moved to the Lithuanian DP camp in Diepholz, and told us many stories of his long trek from home to Bavaria. He was the only one of my father's side of the family who chose to leave home before the Russians returned. His escape from Lithuania was even more convoluted than ours. He tried to leave the country by truck with six coworkers and friends. They were stopped by German military police before they reached the border. Two escaped and two were released, but Narimantas and the remaining two were taken to join a work brigade to dig trenches where the SS Grossdeutschland division was in retreat. When the work brigade was attacked by Russians, he escaped.

Traveling on foot, he reached Berlin. He told us that if it hadn't been for the documents he had made out for him at the Lithuanian Embassy there, he probably wouldn't have gotten out. Unlike our movement along the rural northern edge of Germany, his route took him from one urban area to another. Although the consequences of our travels were similar, the details were vastly different.

Before DP camps were established by the Allies, living in Germany without a job was illegal. Any kind of work, no matter what it was, was a godsend. My cousin's jobs were of even greater variety than my father's. He worked at a paper mill alongside Russian POWs once. From them, he learned to sneak out to a farmer's field next door and dig up potatoes to be roasted over their heating stove. Food shortage was universal.

He later escaped from this labor brigade as well, but was caught and delivered to the Gestapo. Through a lucky break and his clever tongue, he walked away from the Gestapo and ended up on a train to Czechoslovakia. But because he traveled without a ticket, he was detained at the border and turned over to the Gestapo again. A Latvian refugee, who worked at the local Arbeitsamt, saved his skin this time. She sent him to work at a farm. When this farm was bombed, he joined a group of Ukrainian refugees in Czechoslovakia. With this group, on foot and by bicycle, he traveled all the way to Bavaria.

After the Americans came, he had a business going along the Rhine river valley, the valley known for its vineyards. It seems a wine maker was impressed with the U.S. Army boots my cousin was wearing, took him to his wine cellar and let him choose some wine in trade. Narimantas offered the wine to American GIs for more boots. The wine maker sold the boots and sometimes let him take a cut of the profits. This unorthodox business thrived for months.

I listened to his tales with childish fascination, but was old enough to know how serious and tragic all those stories were. The differences between his experiences and ours were many, but the similarities weaved an unbroken pattern. His stories deserve to be heard and, like those of the bicycling pair who crossed the Elbe River on a barn door, could fill another book. I regret not having had the opportunity to persuade him to publish his experiences. I did not know he kept a journal until after his death in 2007. But he left it for his grandchildren to read. And that is all he wanted.

Many years later, when we were all in America, he was one of the very few people with whom I shared my feelings about the war. Doing so with others would have been meaningless, for no one can understand war without having experienced it first hand.

Diepholz

Arrival in our next temporary home was by train. There were no horses or wagons to load this time. They were sold to the farmers of Lower Saxony who needed them now more than we.

As everyone who was there fondly remembers, post-war train travel in Germany was an uncomfortable, trying experience. It had no time to improve in the months immediately following the war. There were still the usual crushing masses of people being packed into the train and anxious crowds jostling for their turn in the station. But there were no armed guards. German police kept order under the watchful eyes British administration.

We were herded into a car already filled — standing room only. People held on to the overhead straps which I couldn't reach. I held on to father's belt. Our crude luggage was stacked helter-skelter in a freight car. It would be a 4-hour ride to Diepholz.

Now that it was over, fear of war was replaced by new uncertainty. The war had ended, and we were people without a country. Would we become a nation of nomads?

Very few possessions from Lithuania remained. Most had been sold or traded for items needed to survive the war years. Kept were only small things of value and mementoes of home. The few books, which father saved for me when I grew older, were packed in a small trunk he made from wood collected in bombed out buildings. Two larger trunks, made the same way, contained clothing, blankets, cooking utensils, bedding, and canned goods. Everything made of metal vanished. There were no nails. I learned to pull rusty ones out of burned wreckage so father could use them in making the trunks.Food no longer needed to be carried in quantity. The IRO (International Refugee Organization), which replaced UNRRA, proved more capable of supplying the 600,000 refugees in Germany with basic needs and our lot continued to improve after we reached the new camp.

Diepholz was to be a more structured residence. While there, we were to await development of the Allies' new policies regarding refugees. Implementing those policies would take time. No one knew how long. We were still DPs, still unable to shake off that ignoble title, and we were still as homeless as we were when we first crossed the border into East Prussia. Nevertheless, everyone looked forward to a more stable environment in which to plan for the future. This was a new luxury with connotations of permanency.

After the tiring but uneventful train ride — itself a novelty — we arrived in flat open country surrounding the vacated Wermacht army base four kilometers from Diepholz. We walked those last four kilometers along the Hunte River. British military authorities arranged for German postal service vans to transport our luggage of hundreds of trunks, suitcases, bags, bedrolls, and other assorted packages. There was no room for the 1200 people.

Our procession wound slowly along the town's narrow, winding streets. Some were cobble-stoned, and there was even an old castle. Diepholz was a picturesque old town harking back to Germany's more glorious times. Church bells were ringing in celebration of our arrival, we thought. Turns out they rang in Diepholtz at noon every day.

The camp buildings were visible a fair distance ahead, behind a columned gate flanked by a small gatehouse — our future police station. There were no enclosing fences. We were met by Lieutenant Colonel Brady, the camp director himself, and welcomed to our next temporary home.

Behind the main brick, block and mortar barracks area were smaller, and newer, wooden buildings. These were later used to accommodate arrivals from the Uchte DP camp and the hundred or so Latvians and Ukrainians. A short distance farther were the remains of a military airfield, its runways peppered with bomb craters and its buildings destroyed, except the largest one which Father Kirvelaitis, a Lithuanian priest, had set up as a church. Mother and I went to the first service a week after our arrival. It was impressive — complete with incense and alter boys in red cassocks and white cottas — but it failed to advance my spiritual education. Church was on the second floor. A farmer kept cattle downstairs.

Another treasure, discovered in one of the airfield sheds, was a boon to camp women's fashions. The building was used to store parachutes. Those who knew how to sew tailored all manner of garments from the silk. Within a week or two, the camp was filled with well dressed women outfitted in spiffy blouses, silk dresses and skirts. Some even painted a thin dark line down the back of their calves where the seam would be, to make it look like they wore nylon stockings. It did wonders for everyone's morale.

Miles of nylon parachute cord found endless uses throughout the camp. Rubber containment straps from parachute packing attracted my attention. We used them to make the most powerful slingshots of all time. As for clothes I was rapidly outgrowing, father bought me several new shirts, another pair of pants, and a pair of shoes. Funds for these purchases were raised by the sale of his bicycle, which had served us the whole way across Europe. Due to his declining health, he was advised to stop riding it, and I had no interest in learning how. I still had the scooter he made for me in Vollrathsruhe.

Addition of people from the Lithuanian DP camp at Dedelstorf swelled our numbers to well over 2000. They were moved because of Dedelstorf's close proximity to the Russian Zone of Occupation and incessant visits to the camp by NKVD agents. This was correctly viewed as subversive and dangerous by British authorities. When it couldn't be stopped, the camp was closed down.

Larger number of inhabitants meant more organized activities. It was also the first time we had our own police force. The large, two-story building in the center of the base, which had been the officers' club, was used as theater, dance hall, and movie house. Films were borrowed from the British Army or donated via the IRO. This is where I saw my first Hollywood movie in English, with German subtitles. It was *"Der Dritte Man"* (The Third Man) with Orson Wells and Joseph Cotten. The Harry Lime character left me with a decidedly poor impression of Hollywood. But then, I didn't know what a *film noir* was.

Several craft oriented courses were started by those with useful skills, but sports activity was slow. There were no playing fields and the bombed runways were in no condition to be used. A YMCA chapter still functioned in that role, but father no longer worked there. He was now the welfare administrator and served on various committees as need arose. It was a full time occupation with less time for procuring food and other family needs. Then he suffered a heart attack and was bedridden nearly two months. Medication prescribed in Meppen was not available in Diepholz and only the care of Dr. Ažubalis, the camp clinic director, saw him through to recovery. We were very concerned for him. Father told me years later that he was even more concerned about his limitations in physical work in the future, in a foreign country whose language he did not speak, where physical labor would be his only option.

Most ominous was the likelihood of disqualification to relocate permanently overseas to Canada, Australia, Brazil, or the United States. We did not know how stringent the health requirements were. Those details were still in our future. But more and more people were leaving for transient camps to proceed with emigration. We had no relatives or friends outside Germany and Lithuania. It would be difficult, if not impossible, to secure sponsorship and job guarantees in order to satisfy U.S. directives. We didn't know what they were for Australia or Brazil. My view of the problem was that no matter where we went, I would have to start learning all over again. My limited familiarity with German, Ukrainian, French and Dutch would be of little use. Neither Portuguese nor English were ever offered in the schools I had attended, and there was never an opportunity to learn them on my own.

But my education continued uninterrupted from Gross Hesepe. Henrikas Stasas was head of the elementary school in Diepholz as he had been in Gross Hesepe. The school I attended here was a full curricula high school under the direction of Pranas Šileika. Set up on independent Lithuania's Board of Education model, it proved to be on higher level than American high schools of the same period. I learned this when applying to a public school in Maryland on my arrival in the U.S. Had my knowledge of English been stronger, I would have been accepted into the senior year, having completed only two years in the Diepholz school.

As in other DP camps, our schools thrived in spite of camp administration efforts to discourage their establishment and encourage return to our homeland. Some American authorities still refused to believe conditions in Soviet occupied countries were as bad as they were. To that end Lithuanian organizations in the U.S. already functioned to build world awareness of our plight. ALT (*Amerikos Lietuvių Taryba* — American Lithuanian Council) was instrumental in promoting new understanding of the DP predicament. Its representatives were received at the White House while war still raged.

After reading the council's report concerning Russian occupation and petition to effect its removal, President Roosevelt's words are remembered as follows: *I am pleased to know that you, American citizens of Lithuanian descent, are so genuinely concerned with the fate of your homeland. But let me point out an error in the report you have presented. It states that Lithuania has lost her independence. You are mistaken. Lithuania has not lost her independence. Her independence is only temporarily suspended. Lithuania will be free again and it may happen sooner than you expect.*

This statement helped gain the American and British post-war leadership's attention to the unique situation in the Baltic countries at war's end and better understanding of the DP dilemma.

Our school administrators were more concerned with our education than the political climate in which it functioned. High school classes in Diepholz began at 8 AM. We stood when the teacher entered and remained standing for the morning prayer. There was a ten minute break between classes, and each class was 45 minutes' duration. Lunch was 20 minutes. There were usually six classes per day.

There was a shortage of everything — books, pencils, ink, paper, and furniture. When there were not enough desks for everyone in class, we took turns sitting on wooden boxes or on the floor. Things improved over time, but shortages were never quite filled. There was no shortage of teachers or the desire to learn. We pursued our assignments with passion. The drive to learn was born of past experience with the temerity of our education during the war, and we could never be sure how long this new stability would last.

We lacked many things, and many more had already been taken away from us. But the knowledge we gained through education could never be taken away. Education was a priceless treasure and every student knew that. If it was directly related to getting a better paying job in the future, it was a concept which never occurred to us at the time. My cousin Violeta came to mind, and how important it had been to know what she knew — to know more. So the purpose of education being education seemed perfectly normal. If not, the words by one of our teachers resonates another: "… *you will have to fix and build the houses, bridges, ships, roads and trains which war had destroyed, and you will have to know how to do it*".

On Sunday mornings, there was an invaluable addition to my high school curriculum. I sat on the sill and listened to the lessons under my open window. A group of men, perhaps a dozen or so, gathered there after church to discuss current events and their imminent impact on our future. They stood in a circle and spoke quietly, perhaps an hour or more. If weather threatened, they didn't stay long. On rainy Sundays they did not appear under my window. But whenever fair weather graced our camp, I could depend on getting an education.

I came to know aspects of our condition never mentioned in school, things which never entered the minds of my teenaged friends. I learned about black market schemes to supply those unable to fend for themselves. I also heard about DPs who had forged documents and misrepresented themselves as allied nationals eligible for support. Some were even found to be Soviet undercover agents who infiltrated DP ranks. It intrigued me to learn that knowledge of Esperanto, the language about to be taught in all schools, would serve no purpose in the future in spite of the common belief all the world's people would speak it soon. And there was talk of methods to persuade the British administration to donate army blankets for use in sewing classes organized for all those willing to learn. It wasn't long before we all had warm winter coats made from those blankets.

If there were harmful or pointless rumors being circulated, it was here they were discredited and snuffed out. It was also here that I learned about conditions elsewhere in our realm and first heard plans to pool resources overseas toward improving the odds for emigration. And so, although the war had ended, I knew we would still be fighting on a different level for a while.

I usually left the window sill saddened. There were seldom any good news. The discussion circle never strayed far from matters of concern which were sometimes beyond my understanding. My questions later puzzled my father and teachers alike, not because they did not have the answers, but because I knew to ask them.

New friendships progressed rapidly. I was never at a loss for something to do, and there was more free time now than I had ever had. Exploring new hobbies to which my friends introduced me occupied much of that time. Extracurricular activities were limited to theater and an art club, neither of which I found to my liking, although I did do the lead part in a school play. There was no sports activity.

Every morning the Lithuanian national flag was raised on a tall flagpole near the main gate. High-schoolers were detailed to perform this ritual as well as its reverse every evening. My rotation came once a week. This task engendered national pride and never failed to remind me of the Scout Jamboree in France. It also introduced us to military style precision and discipline. Our group carried the flag in formation from the school to the gatehouse under the leadership of our physical education teacher or one of the police officers. It was the highlight of the day often watched by a hundred and more. In the evening, the reverse ceremony was followed by the singing of the national anthem.

After years of friends who were exclusively girls, my new friendships here included none. I came to view girls as something more than that, and my troubles began. In view of past experience, this was a confusing discovery. It made me uncomfortable. I purposely avoided them. The older ones saw right through it and teased me mercilessly. That was worse than being bullied by boys. There, at least, I knew the form of effective defense.

But I had a protector. She was the only exception I made, because her language preference intrigued me. Whenever she spoke to me she insisted on using French, one of the foreign languages we were learning in school. This helped my schoolwork, but her persistence puzzled me no end. No explanation was forthcoming. Many years later I learned to appreciate the complex and devious female mind which rendered all women challenging and intriguing.

I was crushed when her family emigrated overseas.

As the number of emigrations grew, Lithuanian schools in Germany began to close with regularity. Even though DPs were not permitted to relocate freely from one camp to another, especially between the established post-war Occupation Zones, many of high school age arrived in Diepholz to continue their studies. American and British authorities charitably turned a blind eye.

When the larger schools in Lübeck and Neustadt shut down, we saw the last influx of students to Diepholz and expected our school to close soon. It was the last Lithuanian school in exile. But it did not close. It was formally renamed *"Vasario 16-tos Gimnazija"* (February 16th High School) after Lithuania's Independence Day, and survives to the present day. This school still functions on an old estate with its own castle in Hüttenfeld, and is attended by Lithuanian students from all over the world, as well as numerous local Germans. It remains a unique phenomenon in Europe and stands as testament to the enduring Lithuanian tradition of educational pursuit.

Our prospects for emigration did not improve until my cousin Narimantas had established himself in America. We now had a voice overseas and our choice narrowed down to the United States. In return for our support when he was at the University in Munich, his generosity was boundless. Having gotten to know him better in later years, I don't doubt his generosity would have been the same, school support or not. We received packages of canned goods and special treats from him on a regular basis. Trading work for food with German farmers was no longer necessary. In view of father's declining health, it was a godsend. We ate better than we had in years. But his generosity went way beyond food. After he married, he secured temporary housing for us with his in-laws. Julija Kezenius (Keženienė), his mother-in-law, volunteered her support as our sponsor.

Now that basic requirements were met, it was time to pursue emigration to the U.S. along formal channels. To that end, father prepared for months, collecting documents and information. When ready, he was called to Wentorf (near Hamburg) for questioning by American authorities to establish suitability for resettlement in the U.S.

This interrogation went on for three full days. His activities before and during the war were examined in detail. Every important statement of fact had to be supported by documents, witnesses or their written affidavits — hence his long preparation for the event. His health, although questioned; and much worried over by mother and me; did not become a hurdle. Nevertheless, when he returned he appeared to have aged overnight. But nothing prepared us for what was to follow.

Wind

I stand on the beach facing east across the Atlantic. It is still summer — late, but summer — yet the wind is cold and cutting. There is a hurricane blowing offshore, still miles away, but the wind heralds its coming in the frothing white spew of spray off the tops of breaking waves as they charge the deserted beach. They rise to heights I had seldom seen. The noise they make combines with the brave wind, but does not harmonize. There is conflict between them, the wind and the sea. There is also beauty in their violence.

If the sky shares my view, he doesn't show it. His clouds are dark. Angry. They rush along to keep up with the wind. They fail. Their anger grows as wind leaves them behind to stretch thin over the sea. The clouds above them are calmer, but just as dark, and they, too, will take their turn to close with the restless sea. They'll be at the wind's mercy when they do. Waves will pound the beach and mock the angry sky. They are the messengers. They bring the news, news of the hurricane out there, over the sea, still out of sight but coming.

I stand on the beach facing the confrontation. I am close enough to feel its power, close enough to taste salt water on my tongue. But it is wind that makes it happen. Without wind there are no waves, no spray, no hurricane.

I do not wait for it to come. I turn and walk off the beach inland, into the trees. The sound they make is more soothing. There is harmony between them and the wind. Wind plays the trees like a musician plays the strings. And like the strings and like the sea, they bend and give in to the wind. I give in too. I retreat deeper into the trees. I don't fear the coming storm, but I am comfortable among the trees. They shield me from the wind's full fury. The land whereon they grow has spoiled me. Everything here is comfortable. And safe. Risk is no longer casual, no longer necessary, no longer risk. For I have crossed the Atlantic long before this hurricane and long after storms enough to humble any tempest.

The Last Act

The stacks and cranes of Bremerhaven fade from sight in the distance. We stand along the rail and watch smoke dissipate over the city. The tugboats have departed. The ship's long, phosphorescent wake, like a road paved in broken glass, stretches behind us, pointing the way back. But we are not returning. This is the last act. We are on the way to a new world, a new life — the ultimate unknown — like death.

Before we boarded there was time to walk in the city, one of the few which survived largely intact. It was time to rid ourselves of German marks we had not yet spent. We bought small things for the Atlantic crossing — small, useful things to take to our new home. Father bought me a self-winding wristwatch. It was the greatest marvel I had ever seen.

In addition to the three small trunks of belongings, we had American dollars — a surprise reserved for our arrival in New York. Father had set aside each bill of American money he received during our stay in DP camps. There were $72 — a veritable fortune!

The ship was an American freighter converted to serve as troop transport. It had survived Dönitz's U-boats and was filled with DPs from nine nations invaded by the Red Army. We heard Romanian, Hungarian, Polish, Ukrainian, and Czech spoken alongside Estonian, Latvian, and our own. A floating Tower of Babel was our ark to salvation.

Among us were also Germans who escaped with their lives when the Allies crushed the Nazi army. Squeezed from the east by Russia and west by the other Allies, the Wehrmacht's last gasp came at great cost to the German people. Caught in the battlefields, silenced only hours before we reached them, the German burghers, farmers, villagers, and tradesmen suffered losses no lighter than our own. Still, they were the lucky ones, the old men and children who were not recruited by the Nazis for the last ditch effort to resist.

Each family on board already had a job and temporary home in the U.S. These were secured by sponsors enlisted by friends and relatives who preceded us to the land of promise. A requirement for entry at New York, they were arranged months, even years, in advance. The United Nations, IRO, NCWC, and the Swiss Red Cross, all had a hand in making these things possible. But nothing could have been done without the kindness of people in the U.S. who devoted their time and energy to process each complexity at however great an inconvenience to themselves. They understood our plight.

My family was fortunate to have Uncle Jurgis' son, my cousin Narimantas, already in America. He made initial contacts in order to meet U.S. Immigration requirements and secure employment guarantees. His mother-in-law volunteered, without being asked, and became our sponsor.

Seeing these arrangements through the usual government bureaucracy was a daunting task. Involved were foreign governments reduced to ruin by war, unwilling to help foreign nationals in light of their own problems. If this points to the need for political savvy to make a success of these efforts, then people in position to fill that need were as important as anyone else in this convoluted process.

In our case, the learned individual who saw to it was Emilija Raila. She emigrated from Lithuania to the U.S. in 1921, remained a staunch supporter of Lithuanian interests in this country, and single-handedly helped more than 100 families get established here after World War Two. Beyond her efforts to navigate through the bureaucratic maze, she even helped with the basic material needs long lost to all who lived through the war years in Europe. She saw to it that we had furniture for our first apartment in the U.S. It came from another widow who was moving to a nursing home. Born and raised in my father's birthplace of Biržai, Emilija Raila may have had a personal interest in our case, but we were the exception rather than the rule. When it came to helping others, it made no difference where they were from. Like my parents, she firmly believed Lithuania would be free again. Unlike my parents, she lived to see it happen. She died in 1998 at the age of 95.

Sadly, most of the remarkable people who guided my convoluted education during the war years, and many others who helped us later, did not see our country break free from Russian oppression. But Henrikas Stasas, my most memorable post-war teacher in Germany who emigrated to the U.S., also lived to age 95 and saw his beloved Lithuania regain her independence.

* * *

As tugboats guided our ship away from Bremerhaven's docks, and the port cranes grew smaller in the distance, I wonder what my parents felt. Was this the final blow of war that they would suffer? Or was this a new beginning?

Departing Europe was my second, and last, act of grand proportion. The first, although equally life changing, seemed small in comparison. Crossing the East Prussian border and leaving our home behind was a more gradual process, slowed by the visit in Jurbarkas and by my uncles' last farewell when they caught up with us in Sudargas.

Uncles Mike and Kostas reached Jurbarkas only two weeks after we had left home. They knew our plans and reached us as we waited for the fishing boats to be lashed together to take the wagons across Nemunas River. They brought us smoked sausage, preserves made by aunt Elena, and the last butter we would see for the next six years. Kostas' daughter, Violeta sent me a book of Grimm's fairytales which kept me amused until I reached the United States and found the same fairytales in English here — such a small world we live in.

Violeta's book of fairytales was a tie binding the familiar world I left behind and the new world I had entered. It spoke positively for my transition, the first of many aids in acclimating to surroundings in America. When I received the book, I thought no more of new worlds than I did of old. It was only a book then.

More important were news from home. Within a week of our departure, Red Army had advanced to the Nemunas River in the south and was firmly entrenched east of the Dubysa. Daily fighting was all around our home in Raseiniai. German soldiers had taken over Uncle Mike's home and destroyed his bees. He had to move his family in with uncle Kostas. Grandma Marcė stayed in our house, but the synagogue next door was looted and stripped of everything useful. Regina, the young woman who rented our apartment and had been my nanny when mother still worked as nurse's aide in the local hospital, still lived in the neighborhood. She was taken away by Russian soldiers — deported, raped, murdered — who knows?

German counterattacks around Kaunas slowed Russian advance. Fighting was said to be bloody. Our capital, Vilnius, was in Russian hands, being harassed by partisan units from the forests south of the city.

There was no word from Biržai and my uncle Jonas' farm, only that they stayed home when the fighting started and uncle Petras' family was still there. This small news was a glint of hope that Dana, Olė, and Vida, my country cousins, had survived. Worst news from Raseiniai was about my Gypsy with the Golden Smile. Her husband, who once showed me how to drive a horse drawn sleigh, disappeared without a trace in late summer, and their home was burned to the ground. Nothing else was known about him. She went away to search for him. No one knows if she ever found him.

My uncles stayed with us beyond Sudargas. They wanted to accompany us farther, but border guards turned them back even when told they planned to return before sundown. Our last parting was more tearful than it had been in Raseiniai. It was more permanent now.

Kostas would die young, way before his time. Uncle Mike would live to see the new world before he, too, would be taken before his.

Aunt Elena lived long enough to correspond with me for several years after I came to America. Her letters arrived cut and blacked out by postal censors in Moscow where letters were detoured for screening and search for reason to detain the authors. We wrote in code, known only to the family, and learned to read between the lines. It was 1989 before I received a letter unmarked by Russian censors.

Two years later, letters from cousins carried Lithuanian postage stamps. That was when I first learned my cousins in the country had survived the war. But their parents' farms were taken from them, without compensation, and they lived in Vilnius. They were glad to be alive. Beginning in May 1948, and continuing thru 1981, fifty percent of the listed deportees to Siberia were farmers who owned land incorporated into collectivization which made up ninety percent of Lithuanian farm land. Those few who survived to return to their homeland had nothing to come back to.

Relentless attempts at persecution of emigrants by the Soviet regime did not stop at its borders. It reached out to every country which sheltered former DPs in the free world. Personal encounter with this anomaly came to me in the most unexpected way, unexpected because I had grown blasé and took my freedom for granted.

I should have known better.

Uncle Mike expressed his desire to visit his sister (my mother) in the U.S. We were to make the necessary arrangements for his stay of several months. He also wished to visit acquaintances in Chicago and New York.

Before his visit could be scheduled, documents of support and sponsorship had to be executed in Cyrillic, an alphabet certainly more foreign to us than the English language. By then I managed English in reasonable comfort. That is why it fell to me not only to secure their translation, but also to deliver them to the Russian embassy in Washington. I still count this among my more unpleasant experiences. But I never suspected the consequences.

My daily motorcycle ride to work and back lost its routine when I noticed a car following me home to my apartment several days in succession. It was a different car each time and it always stopped and waited outside after I came home. It aroused my curiosity, but I suppressed the urge to investigate, thinking I was imagining things.

For several weeks, the car did not appear. I relaxed, sure I had been seeing things. Then it returned when on my way to a weekly gathering of friends. It was then that I became suspicious. I was followed quite openly. The car waited, then followed me home when I left late at night. I made up my mind then: if I saw the car following me again, I would investigate.

I didn't have to wait long. Two days later another strange car was behind me on the way to work in the morning. Again, quite openly, it stopped in the parking lot within 50 feet of my motorcycle. Although my employer did not yet have a guarded entrance gate, security personnel were present around the clock. I reported the car to security and had one of the guards accompany me to the parking lot.

When asked what the two men in the car were doing following me, we were told they were working. When asked for whom, they said they couldn't tell us. I asked what it was they were looking for and offered to save them time and trouble, and tell them whatever it was they wanted to know. The reply was the same. The security guard suggested they leave, as they had no visitor's pass and no company parking permit. They left without comment.

On another occasion, I approached the man in the car and asked the same questions. The answers were also the same. But this time I noticed the man's wristwatch. Its face was inscribed in Cyrillic. This, in itself, meant nothing, and my ignorance of Soviet covert activity abroad raised no suspicions. But I couldn't let this rest.

Not wishing to alarm anyone needlessly, I was not about to start asking friends and family if they, too, were being followed. I merely hinted in general conversation about unrelated subjects. It was then I learned my parents had noticed a strange car and so had a friend whom I visited often. In his case it was a private detective. (Years later, I found out that my cousin Narimantas, who lived out of state, had also been watched during the same period).

This was enough to take action. It was time to clear this up one way or another. My suspicions were confirmed without question at my next, and last, document filing visit to the Russian embassy. When asked about it, the attaché voiced no denials, became visibly upset, and had me escorted out of the embassy.

I suddenly recognized my mistake. Did I just jeopardize Uncle Mike's visit? Or was this not related to it at all? And that is, perhaps, the first time in my life that I became afraid. I don't recall experiencing the same feeling ever before. Not in childhood, not during the war, not in strange foreign lands since. Not even when strafed by machine gun fire, shelled by artillery, or bombed from the air. Of course, I had often been startled. Or frightened in a rush of adrenalin, a sensation of "my heart in my throat", a sudden pang which passed seconds after inception, or even that burn in my throat that meant I wanted to cry but couldn't.

This was different. This was fear. A silent, nagging anxiety which interrupted my concentration and disturbed my sleep. This realization was slow in coming. I thought it was something I ate. But, of course, it was the knowledge my uncle was not yet free of Soviet oppression even here in America, not yet free to enjoy the hospitality of relatives in a free country. If the arm of the KGB was long enough to reach with impunity all the way to the U.S. and follow him to his benefactors and sponsors without censure, wasn't it also long enough to find those who had once worked against the regime which it served?

Have I effectively closed the door to my uncle's visit?

I wouldn't know for two more years. The diligence of KGB work across international borders was demonstrated in the time it took to process the documents and arrange a schedule. It was two years later that uncle Mike was cleared to visit the U.S.

Russian persecution changes only in method, never in intent. It breeds fear even in those who have left their homes to live in the free world. It is pervasive the world over. I had occasion to work in the same department with a recent immigrant from Moscow. He reminded me of the absolute power of Russia's government over its citizens — the stifling infliction of fear I had forgotten after four decades in a free country. Whenever I broached the subject of Russian politics or its government shortcomings, this (I thought liberated) Russian immediately took on a defensive posture. Fear of being overheard was so obvious it was physically present in his face and body language. He cut the conversation short when within earshot of a third party. If not, he promptly changed the subject. If I persisted, he became visibly distressed. The idea of free speech was still beyond his comprehension. The KGB was listening. And this was in America, in 1998!

* * *

Uncle Mike's visit to the U.S. turned out to be our first reliable source of information about what happened at home when the Russians came.

Within a few short months of invasion, farmers were subjected to heavy taxes and harvest obligations to the new Soviet state. The ones who resisted were punished by impromptu raids by the NKVD sent to loot and pillage their property. Those farmers who were not deported to concentration camps in Siberia were evicted from their own farms. Grain already harvested was seized and shipped to Russia. Livestock was slaughtered to feed the Red Army. Everything of value was taken without compensation. Land was later incorporated into the *Kolkhoz* system of collective farms where its previous owners were forced to work without enough pay to feed themselves.

This was the fate of my uncle Jonas' farm, where I first learned that girls could be good friends. Uncle Petras' daughters, Vida, Olė and Dana, survived. They stayed on the family farm until evicted, then moved to Vilnius.

Urban life was no better. In the cities, looting and robbery went on in grand scale. A day did not pass without at least one murder during a robbery by Russian agents or NKVD troops. Soviet concept of law and order was geared to the protection of the looters. There was no legal defense. Victims were thankful to be left alive.

The synagogue next door to our home in Raseiniai was burned to the ground after the war. Its fire also destroyed every building on our property.

Food, clothing, appliances; even furniture; were trucked to rail terminals along with industrial goods and machinery to be shipped east on trains which were not transporting deportees. Damage to industry was so extensive, it could no longer function. Uncle Mike lost his accounting job with a local manufacturing plant. His brother, my uncle Kostas, lost everything he owned to looters, and they both moved their families to Vilnius.

City dwellers kept vegetable gardens to help feed themselves because food produced by collective farming was being shipped to Russia. Food shortages were common, as if the war never ended, and black market was rampant. Nothing official could be done without a bribe. Corruption was wide spread.

My cousins were being taught by people who did not speak our language. They were brought in from Russia to replace the

Lithuanian teachers who were deported to Siberia during the first purges of our intelligentsia. Everyone was expected to learn Russian and school curricula was filled with Soviet propaganda.

People were being arrested with no reason given — simply for being in the wrong place at the wrong time. One of those was my godmother's husband, the man who showed me how to drive a sleigh. He was never heard from again.

Young men were mobilized all across the country. They were pressed into serving with the Soviet armed forces. Many escaped and joined the partisans. The Lithuanian Freedom Council, a political resistance organization, gave way to the Lithuanian Partisan Movement and armed resistance was organized to be more effective. There was ongoing fighting against NKVD troops and other Soviet organs of terror. These actions sometimes even reached into the cities. Barbaric retaliatory measures by the Russians continued unabated under the guise of cleansing the country of "bandits". The general population could not believe that Westerners could be so naïve and so blind that they didn't see through Kremlin propaganda. But civilian support of the partisans remained strong and the conflict continued for years.

For people like my uncles and their families, both in the country and city alike, life was difficult, unpredictable and dangerous.

Before uncle Mike boarded the plane to fly home at the end of his visit, he impressed upon us that to return to Lithuania now would surely put my father and the rest of us in peril. He also said that if he, himself, did *not* return, his own family would be in peril. We understood exactly what that meant.

Chicago

Father and I were attending a convention of our countrymen who also survived the war and found a new home in a foreign land. For years we did not know whether our friends and neighbors lived or died. And if living, who could know where? People seeking acquaintances, friends and family continued their efforts for many years after the war ended. Search often spanned continents from Australia to the Canadian West.

When a letter arrived from Antanas Gantautas, it was the most unexpected surprise. He, too, had survived and lived in the U.S. He was my father's best friend from before I was born, and treated me to fresh berries of all kinds with every visit to our home during my pre-school years and on to when the war began. He was the man I came to call *Ponas Uoga* (Mister Berry).

Father arranged to meet him in Chicago.

It was on the occasion of the first formal convention of Lithuanian émigrés in a foreign country, on the broad steps of the convention hall, that we saw Gantautas waiting for us at the appointed time. I recognized him long before we were within arm's reach. It had been such a long time. I was twenty-two, and hadn't seen him for thirteen years, years when I had been so sure that, like so many family members and friends, he had been lost to us forever in the war. Yet here he was, shaking hands with me, a child no longer. I was so moved I wept like one, his hand in mine. I called him *Ponas Uoga* and he expressed regret he had no berries to offer. His tears of joy matched mine as we embraced.

This reunion was not unlike that of many others who had lost touch during the war. They were all around us here, thronged on the steps of a convention hall thousands of miles from home, feeling the same emotions I felt then. Celebrating life, survival; if even for a while; and remembering those who no longer could.

Had my father's, my godfather's and Antanas' obligations to family not been in the forefront of their priorities, all three would have surely been part of the resistance. And all three would probably have not survived. Most resisters did not. Many died at the hands of the Russians in the most horrific ways imaginable.

Among thousands of examples, postwar findings include Russian records describing the physical condition of KGB prisoner, and last commanding general of Lithuania's armed resistance, the American born Adolfas Ramanauskas (code name *Vanagas*) several days after his arrest in 1957, the same year we were in Chicago, eleven years after the World War Two ended:

> *"The right eyelid is covered with a hematoma. On the eyelid there are six stab wounds made, judging by their diameter, by thin wire or nail projecting deep into the eyeball. Multiple hematomi in the area of the stomach and a cut wound on a finger of the left hand. The genitalia reveal a large tear wound on the right side of the scrotum and a wound on the left side. Both testicles and spermatic ducts are missing."* (GRRCL)*

* * *

Although the fighting ended, the war for us had not. Everything had a temporary air. We still could not believe these blessings were to last. What-if discussions were the norm. Options for future action were explored much as they were during the war in occupied Europe. The feeling of security in our new homes, our adopted country, had not yet been gained, not yet realized. The care with which we had been screened by U.S. Immigration should have been sufficient indication of stability in this hospitable new land. But our general lack of understanding not only of the language, but also the most basic appreciation of a life style so alien to us and so seemingly fantastic, stifled all our efforts to tie it to reality. The world we had known was buried under the rubble of Europe's ruins. For many, the reality of ordinary life was unsupportable.

At first sight everything here was huge, awesome, gigantic. Skyscrapers, the blinding brightness of neon lights, so many cars, and so much noise, and so much land. No unfinished buildings, no great mounds of disgorged earth, no bomb craters, no piles of broken bricks and half burned wood, no muddy trenches with planks set over them for crossing.

Our arrival in New York was preceded by worry-filled months of waiting, red tape, interrogations and endless paper chase for documents and proofs of activity before our DP (Displaced Person) status.

It began with hope.

We lived in barracks abandoned by defeated German forces, a DP camp in Diepholz, Hannover. This, after six years of transit westward, much of it on foot and on horseback, the rest by rail and wagon train. East Prussia, Pomerania, Mecklenburg and Altmark behind us, there were short stays in farms with need of helping hands for harvest, and stops in places beyond number, before the British Zone of Occupation extended us official refugee status. We passed through several DP camps before Diepholz, and would pass two more transient ones before boarding a ship for North America. In the meantime, the paper chase kept us sequestered in Hannover.

We didn't know which foreign country would accept us, who would provide refuge, and for how long. Every effort was being made to prove we deserved the refugee status. The questioning and interrogation went on for months.

No, we were not Communist. We were not Nazi, not Fascist and not revolutionaries or deserters. No, we did not take part as soldiers in the fighting and were, therefore, not prisoners of war. We had no connection to the retreating German troops. We had no collaborators among relatives who stayed behind. No, we had no friends who sympathized with either side.

Guilt by association was a very real threat. That, alone, could block our emigration to a country in the West. And then there was the question of health. Communicable diseases, dependence on medication, family medical histories. The list went on.

All had to be proven, supported by documents, witnesses, medical examinations, state records. War or no war, they had to be produced. Father's military career was questioned from the start. Where had he been during such and such time? How long did he stay? Who was in command? What did he do during the first

Russian occupation? The second? What were his responsibilities under German occupation? How did he escape the second invasion by the Red Army? Why did he leave? What prompted his choice to go where he did? How long had he planned it? Who helped him? And why?

The required written statement of my father's military service had to be presented in English to the U.S. Army Special Security Investigation Department where his file was being processed. The fact that it still had not reached the U.S. Immigration Department could become a major roadblock. This statement was sent to my cousin Narimantas in the U.S. for translation, because no one could be sure the few who could have done that in Diepholz or Wentorf could be trusted.

Months of work could not produce documents to prove all the answers. Names were exchanged with those who might. It was only this reciprocal cooperation among ex-DPs here and abroad that eventually enabled those thousands of us to emigrate to Canada, Great Britain, Australia, the U.S. and elsewhere.

Resident sponsors were required. Warranty of financial support, gainful employment and housing had to be secured before immigrant status could replace the refugee stigma. Our predecessors, who established homes abroad, took on that responsibility without hesitation whether they were relatives or not. But one false statement, one mistake, one oversight, and we might be sent back to our peril.

The stress of living under such daily tension for two years did nothing to alleviate my father's suspected heart condition and medical treatments could no longer be put off. Our hope of emigration to the west was dashed. The roller coaster ride of ups and downs was over. The legal way was barred. Sweden by boat, pursued by some, was not considered — a risk my father would not have us take. To establish a new life it had to be done aboveboard. Anything less was unacceptable. So, his fight continued, and through help of people we barely knew, his heart condition was tamed. He fought and won.

Medical requirements of immigration met, promissory note to repay the NCWC loan for the transatlantic voyage filed, and by another miracle of survival, we boarded the USS *General Taylor*, a military freighter out of Bremerhaven, for New York.

Now that we were here, normality took on a new meaning. It meant we were free to enjoy assembly of our peers and countrymen, revel in our own survival, pursue our culture and our art, denied so long by war. It also meant that today, in Chicago, we could forget that other time, if only for a while, and lose ourselves in the first production of the Lithuanian National Opera in exile.

The grandeur of the stage set, aglow in lights casting flickering shadows over the singers resplendent in their costumes, earned my awe as fully as the music. That we were here to witness this miracle was a surreal experience. Each member of the cast, all those backstage, all those there in the light, all those in the orchestra pit, all lived through the same horrors as we. Yet, here they were, continuing their art with only temporary interruption. That they found one another, that they rebuilt the company, that they were guaranteed an audience, was proof of the glory of human endeavor. And opera was the West's highest art form.

How appropriate to have chosen Rossini's *Barber of Seville*. How fitting to express, in its light-hearted mood, their passion for music, for theater, for spectacle, so recently forsaken, so recently trivialized in the face of emotions far removed from the niceties of humanity. The contrast, if not intentional, was unmistakable. A celebration of survival was this performance of Rossini's master work. And yes, a celebration of life itself.

And I..? I gloried in their accomplishment. And more than that. This performance affected me in ways I scarcely suspected at the time. With father's support and encouragement I found myself at the Peabody Conservatory of Music. That I later sang with an American opera company, under the exalted critical eye of Rosa Ponselle, bears witness to what that performance in Chicago really meant.

❧

Wind

It ruffles my hair, this cold March wind. Cold, soothing and clean. I stand in the American cemetery where my father lies. His death, sudden and unexpected, sent my way a loneliness like one I've never known. It passed in time, but the late summer wind of Hurricane David that accompanied him to his grave I remember well. It came up from the south the day after he died, and stayed with us until he was buried. That howling tempest was a reminder of his stormy life. But it was late. He was gone the day before another storm could claim him, the day I will always remember: 2 September 1979.

This visit has purpose, a more meaningful one than visits before it. I have news. Important news.

Perhaps this late March wind already brought the news, but I must be sure he knows. So I stay a while, and speak the words he has waited so long to hear.

My father always believed that Lithuania would be free again. He never doubted. And he was certain it would happen in his lifetime; if not his, then mine. Nothing could shake this conviction, this faith. But he never imagined that his homeland would find that freedom by toppling the first domino in the fall of the USSR, and be followed by every enslaved country in Europe.

His life's work was the business of keeping our homeland free, secure, and safe from neighbors with belligerent intent. When that became impossible, his work changed. His profound love for his country found ways to become proactive in efforts which sought to promote world awareness of Lithuania's plight under Soviet rule and to help regain her freedom.

Now, freedom is hers. He didn't live to see it, but his prediction was correct and his life's work was not in vain. If he couldn't witness it on site in person, I know his heart would soar were he here with me, seeing it happen on the screen, hearing about it on the air waves. News of jubilation are broadcast daily. The world has noticed, at last. Lithuania was free.

It is March the 14th, 1990, three days after independence was reclaimed. That it cost so many lives, so much hardship and so many tears is the inescapable truth. Father would have understood. He knew the price of freedom.

I stand alone at his grave. My new American family does not understand the meaning of this visit. I stand alone. But I am here to tell him.

He should know.

Home

I find myself looking to the sky and listening for approaching aircraft overhead each time I see a car dealer's search lights advertising a sale. Longest lasting impressions are those from childhood, yet the older I get, the closer I feel to the war years, and it occurs to me how lucky we were. Although often hungry, we did not starve. Although persecution was near, we escaped. Although threatened with death, we survived. Although there were no schools, my education continued. After nine years of wandering across war torn Europe without the luxury of living even day to day — we lived hour to hour — doing whatever needed to be done to keep hunger at bay, depending on the goodness of strangers to shelter us, and fearing for our lives every step of the way, I am home at last.

It is not the home I left behind, not the home I hoped to return to, but a home so different, so strange, so foreign to my thinking, yet hospitable and safe as a mother's embrace. When the need arose, I was too young to defend the home I left behind, but I am not too old now to defend the home I have discovered. It is worthy of my efforts as I am worthy of its protection. I have earned my place and value the freedom I have found in return. No longer strange, no longer foreign, I am truly home again.

Being physically removed from foreign oppression does not free us from the pain of knowledge that others suffered worse horrors than we to survive and see our country free and independent again. Our joy on March 11, 1990 was boundless. We celebrated more than life then. The Soviet fiend was dead, its death brought about by its own path of horror and annihilation. The Berlin Wall fell. The Iron Curtain was in shreds. The world was jubilant. Germany was reunited, rebuilt in body and in spirit from the smoldering skeleton it became under the Nazi swastika. Lithuania was free. Other countries under the Russian boot followed her example and threw off the bloody red yoke. Russia was viewed in a new light. It would change for the better. It would earn its place in the civilized world again as Germany had done.

Alas, we are still waiting for that to happen.

Russia's designs on the Baltic States and other lands Russia invaded in the 1940s never changed. The rewriting of "history" continues as state policy, upheld and encouraged by the Kremlin. Claims to land rights never established and insistence that the Baltic States joined the Soviet Union voluntarily continues to this day. It took three years for Russian troops to leave Lithuania after its own government officially recognized Lithuanian independence — a ready admittance of Russia's lies.

In Kaliningrad, the Prussian land alternately ruled by Germany, Lithuania and Poland, and in Russian hands only by armed conquest, now harbors Russian troops with no reason beyond a clenched fist to threaten Poland and the Baltics. Our airspace is routinely violated in the name of supporting Kaliningrad. Military presence there is guarded with malicious determination. For what reason? Will Russian imperial ambitions by force of arms ever end?

The KGB weaned Russian president, Vladimir Putin, went to extreme ends to prevent Lithuania from joining the NATO Alliance. Russian propaganda and manufactured "history" notwithstanding, Lithuania was invited to join nevertheless. Once NATO had a direct interest in the Baltics, Putin was devising new ways to resurrect Stalinist ideals. But his repeated attempts to install communist party politicians into the elected government of Lithuania were recognized before they took root.

Chechnya is a living example of continuing aggression against people conquered by force of arms, where Stalinist methods couldn't be more marked. Putin failed in Afghanistan, but left the country in ruin and discontent. Being out of office did not stop him from pursuing his goals of domination by fear. To maintain his power, the puppets he installed at the 2008 elections were put in office to do his bidding for years to come. What fate awaits Chechnya, or Belarus, or the Ukraine, or Poland, or any other neighbor, if Russian imperial ambitions are not thwarted? In World War Two Russia took, by force of arms, 80,000 square miles of foreign land. It compares closely with the 70,000 taken by Nazi Germany.

Those who have seen previous results first hand can predict Russia's direction with some certainty. Those who have not, find those predictions hard to believe. But who is to say history will not repeat itself? It always has.

I hesitate to lay responsibility at the Kremlin's door alone. Pursuit of better quality of life in Russia, with its vast land mass and virtually unlimited natural and human resources, always failed, by wide margin, in comparison to that of countries a mere fraction its size. It is hardly puzzling that Russian people work against their own welfare, and make ill effort to improve their own lot. Complicity with their government's policies is induced by fear. This is a nation of illusion, delusion and collusion, a country where people disappear without trace, and all evidence of their existence disappears with them.

Russia's intelligentsia, which recognizes the Kremlin for what it is, is a powerless minority against the rest of the population. But people get the government they deserve. We all know what befell the countries Russia invaded, and we all know the scope of ongoing effort to rebuild the economies it had ruined.

I take learned interest in my new home and am perplexed by the widespread American xenophobia. Why this is so, I cannot say. People here extend a warm welcome to the thousands who come every year to better their lives if not to save them. My own was saved by the kindness of Americans whom I now consider my countrymen as much as the Lithuanians left behind. This great nation of immigrants embraced me as her own. She is my home now. And I was always taught the value of understanding countries and cultures other than our own. So my perplexity remains, no less in counterpole to my own failure to grasp the significance of the jobless and homeless on the streets of the most prosperous country in the world.

Surrounded by the bustling indifference of Americans for many years, I've come to understand why not one member of my adopted American family, into which I married, expressed concern for my relatives in Lithuania during the world shaking events there in the spring of 1990. It was not because they are cold, insensitive people, but because they were unaware of the upheavals in my homeland and the price paid to regain her freedom.

Disappointment of long standing is Washington's caution and fear of offending Moscow during the cold war. It engendered American disregard of recent European history, which only served to help the Kremlin with its customary falsification of facts to advance its own interests at the expense of every nation Russia had invaded.

In Lithuanian and other Baltic immigrant communities, and their organizations, the cold war was spent in protracted activity aimed at convincing Washington of the falsehood of history written by Soviet Russia. The difficulty of this task is illustrated by statements in *A World Transformed* by George Bush and Brent Scowcroft. They complained that political pressure exerted by Baltic American activist organizations to recognize Lithuanian independence in 1990 was so strong it was difficult to continue American support of Gorbachev's new policies.

It begs the question how long would it have taken for the U.S. to declare this recognition had it not been for the Baltic Freedom League and other Latvian, Lithuanian, and Estonian political interest groups with influence in Congress. U.S. recognition of Estonia's and Latvia's reestablishment of their independence was easier to enact by following the precedent already set by Lithuania, but still required the stimulus of special interest groups in the U.S.

That these steps needed to be taken by the collective immigrant community in the U.S. proves America's unwillingness to stand behind its official non-recognition of the Baltic countries' incorporation into the Soviet Union. Offending Moscow is still perceived as counterproductive to national interests.

There are times when I find the arrogance and ignorance of the recent leadership of my adoptive country as disturbing as the rhetoric of future belligerents in pre-war Europe was to my parents. But because I now live in the United States of America I am free to make that comparison and express opinion which would have put them in jeopardy of their lives had they done likewise in regard to the belligerents of their time.

I write these words without fear of persecution. Criticism of our own government is a confirmation of the freedoms we enjoy here. If it is not by my own choice that the U.S. is now my home because I was too young to make it, then that choice would have been the same had I been older. Now that I am, and have made that choice, I know I cannot have done better.

Wind

In Samogitia, where I attended my first school, there is a saying: *It is better to be bold than cautious, because the time and manner of our death is decreed at birth.*

The seed of death is planted at the same moment as the seed of life — the rule of the game we cannot change. Nor can we undo mistakes once they are behind us.

There are only two unavoidable tragedies in the game of life — the mistakes we make and the passage of time. We all make them and we all grow old. Mine were many. But good fortune saw me through them all and I miraculously breezed by unscathed.

I did not plan my lot, but I am thankful for the course my winds have taken. They define who I am. They help me deal with my newfound home and grow comfortable here. If I miss what might have been, it is only what I can never know. And that, no wind can define.

"What you are is always more important than what you have," were words spoken to me by the Gypsy with the Golden Smile before I understood what those words meant. I must not mourn her, those words now tell me, any more than mourn the other good people I have lost who spoke words as meaningful as hers. They did not give me what I have. They made me what I am.

And I no longer mourn.

But I miss the Gypsy's golden smile, the dance never learned.

The game goes on.

Kryžių Kalnas

Near the city where my favorite teacher was born is a popular, but little known, tourist attraction. At first glance, from a distance, it looks like a giant porcupine. When approached closer, it appears to be a cemetery. On a hill overlooking the verdant rolling countryside there is a forest of crosses. They rise and fall with the lay of the land. They crowd one another so closely they intertwine. The forest they make is too dense to walk through. But there are paths left open so we can admire the artistry of each one. They appear to have grown out of the ground of their own accord. No two are alike. They are carved out of wood, formed in metal and chiseled in stone — each one, a work of art.

The history of The Hill of Crosses (Kryžių Kalnas) is long and meaningful, but it is only now attracting world attention via tourism. Thanks to Russia's ongoing falsification of history for the purpose of propaganda, foreign tourist guides and the news media seldom get it right.

First, it is not a cemetery. No one is buried there. It is a symbolic site to commemorate Christianity's arrival in Lithuania in the 14th century when, presumably, the first crosses were erected on this hill. Now, it also commemorates resistance to Russian occupation.

For centuries, people erected hand carved wooden crosses at road intersections to bless and protect travelers — each one the quintessential expression of Lithuanian folk art. This 400-year old tradition was as strong in the 1940s as it was in the mid-1500s, or whenever the raising of crosses on this hill became a tradition.

Soviet Russian oppressors had them torn down as they did all expression of ethnicity, nationhood, and religion. They were soon replaced by new ones at every road crossing where they had been destroyed. These were also torn down. Eventually, as part of peaceful resistance against the invaders, these crosses — thousands of them — were being assembled in one place for more effective demonstration, on this single hill. In short order they, too, were torn down.

Within a week, they were back, outnumbering their predecessors tenfold. Again, the Russians destroyed them. Then, tens of thousands appeared on the hill almost overnight. This continued for years. Torn down repeatedly, they reappeared, more numerous each time, even after the invader's attempt to level the hill itself.

As in other instances of persistent demonstration, Russian authorities were slow to give in. Nevertheless, the hill sprouted more and more crosses, until they numbered in the hundreds of thousands, and became the tourist attraction it is today.

UNESCO (United Nations Educational, Scientific & Cultural Organization) has identified and inscribed it into the list of protected World Heritage Sites.

The Hill of Crosses remains a unique exhibit of Lithuanian folk art. It also remains a thorn in Russia's side, a thorn of its own making.

Epilogue

Omission of people's names is intentional. This is because some people in this story are still not free from Russia's persecution. Some have requested their names to be withheld. Others are not named because their fate is still uncertain. There is no guarantee that doing otherwise will not harm someone else by association.

Such is the nature of Russian oppression, Soviet or not. Even today, the risk is not worth taking. Unlike Germany's rise from the ashes to return to civilized statehood and the welcoming embrace of nations, no sign of similar direction by Russia is in evidence. The Kremlin continues persecution of its own people. Its preoccupation with KGB style deception, secrecy and conspiracy, and pursuit of Stalinist ideals is ongoing. The world's trust is repeatedly betrayed.

To preserve ongoing propaganda and falsification of history, the Duma (Russian Parliament) enacted a new law, in 2010, to prohibit any criticism of the Soviet version of World War Two history. Under the clever guise of anti-Nazi legislation, this law is aimed at anyone disagreeing with such "history", as set down by the Kremlin, which seeks to decriminalize the Soviet past. It means to prosecute scholars and historians not only within Russia's borders, but world wide. The press was informed that *all* Latvian historians are terrorists subject to criminal prosecution. In other words, this law provides the constitutional base for prosecuting historians of *any* nationality. Scholars, academics and journalists also fall within its broad definition of "terrorists". As if that were not enough, Russia is in process of passing a bill in 2010/2011, specifically targeting Estonia, Latvia and Lithuania, which will make it illegal to say that Soviet Union unlawfully occupied the Baltic countries.

This book burning and witch hunting legislation is aggressive, intrusive, intellectually bankrupt, and morally perverted. It sets the free nations of Europe against the autocratic Russia and makes criminals of people who search for and speak the truth. But that is the Russian way. Free speech remains a crime in Russia.

Government sanctioned political murder and assassination continues unabated. In 2006 alone there were Alexander Litvinenko, the ex-KGB Kremlin critic, poisoned in London; Andrey Koslov, chairman of Central Bank of Russia, shot in Moscow; and Vytautas Pociūnas, chief of Lithuania's Home Security, thrown out of a 9th floor hotel window in Belarus. The year before there were Paul Klebuikov, American editor of *Forbes Russia;* and Sergey Yushenkov, member of the Duma no less. Another democratically minded Duma member and human rights advocate, Galina Starovoitova, was murdered in 1998.

In more recent times the international journalist and Putin critic Anna Politkovskaya was gunned down in St. Petersburg, and Yuri Shchekochikhin, liberal opposition editor of *Novaya Gezeta,* met a similar fate. Even Zelinkhan Yandarbiev, past president of Chechnya, could not escape the reach of Kremlin's assassins. He was murdered in Qatar in February 2004 while on vacation.

Forty six journalists, reporters, editors, writers, and photographers have been murdered in Russia since 1992. All were contract killings, a third of that count during Vladimir Putin's presidency.

Convenient premise of war was used to do away with Afghan president and *Mujahedin* supporter Hafizullah Amin when he was gunned down by KGB troops in his own palace in 1979, followed by widespread and systematic torture of men, women, and children to combat "ideological sabotage".

The poisoned umbrella tip execution of the dissident Bulgarian BBC broadcaster, Georgy Markov, is one of the more sensational incidents of 1978, but we can also look back to Stepan Bandera's murder in Germany in 1959, to the murder of Hungary's Prime Minister Imre Nagy in 1958, and Czech anti-communist leader Jan Masaryk's assassination in 1948, and compile an endless list of victims throughout Russia's recent history. The Kremlin's barbaric methods of maintaining government control have not changed since World War Two, and still include gruesome murders of its own highest placed servants just as it did in Stalin's time, when one of his top military leaders, who displeased him, was loaded alive into a crematorium.

That many of Kremlin's political targets have been Russian nationals in the service of their own government surprises no one, but the loss of non-Russians opposed to state policies number in the thousands. In Stalin's view, whoever served the interests of the state deserved praise, whoever did not deserved death, be they Russian nationals or not. This view remains entrenched in the Kremlin today. It is perpetrated by a government made up of past KGB leadership when, after its reform and dissolution into the *new* FSB, Vladimir Putin installed its members into the highest echelons of that government. When Putin's term in office was transposed to Prime Ministry, it changed nothing. His puppets still dance to his tune.

The tragic loss of Poland's president Lech Kaczynski, his wife, and many members of the country's military and political elite, in the air disaster of 2010 was never investigated by any agency from Poland or any other country because the Kremlin would not allow it. Putin personally assumed charge of the investigation. After all, it happened in Russian air space, and it was no one else's business. Pilot error was cited as the cause of the crash. No proof of this claim was provided. The bizarre events at the crash site were never explained. Even in view of Russia's many disagreements with Kaczynski's government, and veiled threats to his administration, political implications have been discounted in the West.

* * *

I lost count of the people that I had met, known, befriended, or was related to, who died or disappeared at the hands of the Russians. During the war years alone there are the 27 mentioned in this book. Countless others lost everything short only of their lives. Many more are among those who died by Russian hand in the nine years *after* war ended. And I am only one of the millions whose stories are, in many cases, more harrowing than mine.

Historical Note

Much of this memoir is from the immediate post-war years in Europe, post-war as traditionally accepted in the West because 1945 marks the end of World War Two. Although the Nazis, Fascists and Japanese were defeated, war against Soviet Russia continued in the Baltics for nine more years.

The 1944 Soviet "liberation" of Estonia, Latvia and Lithuania did not restore freedom and peace any more than did the Nazi version of 1941. The first put an end to massacres and deportations only to be replaced by the Nazi substitute. The second spawned national resistance to the Soviet horrors already endured three years earlier. The non-aggression treaty of 1933 between Lithuania and Russia was violated as the slaughter committed in the cities and towns horrified the population. In addition to countless deportations to Gulag concentration camps, 4,200 political prisoners were executed by the retreating Russians in the most horrific manner ever seen in the 20th century. In neighboring Poland 22,000 prisoners of war were massacred by the NKVD (*Narodnyi Kommisssariat Vnutrennikh*).

This organization, hatched by the Revolution of 1917, still stands as Russia's instrument of tyranny and symbol of oppression today. *Cheka*, as it was first named, did not change its methods when the name was changed, first to OGPU, then to NKVD and MSB, followed by MGB/MVD, any more than it did in our own time when it was known as KGB (Soviet Security and Intelligence Service), and FSB (Russian Security and Intelligence Service) after 1995.

Although it changed its name many times, its headquarters never left the infamous Lubyanka prison building in Moscow. This place was no ordinary jail. Behind its walls thousands of real and imagined enemies of Soviet rule were subjected to prolonged interrogation and hideous torture before execution.

In addition to their operational divisions, these agencies had their own prisons and torture chambers and fielded their own, specially trained, armed forces. No other civilized country has ever possessed anything to compare with the political police forces and security agencies of Russia. They operated with the same intensity in peacetime as they did in war, and were executors of all the deportations conducted since the Revolution. Supressing armed as well as passive resistance by terrorism was their specialty. Attributed to them are also the 25,000 prisoners of war who disappeared without trace in the USSR in 1940.

Confirmed stories of atrocities committed by this Soviet state organ prompted hundreds of thousands of Estonians, Latvians and Lithuanians to flee with the defeated Germans when the threat of a second Russian invasion loomed.

The German Blitzkrieg in 1941 brought a temporary halt to Russian atrocities. The country was jubilant to be rid of the Bolsheviks. Lithuanian Army units, which still survived, successfully defeated Russian forces and reclaimed the capital city of Vilnius on June 22, 1941, a year and a week after the first Red Army invasion and in anticipation of the German advance. It was generally believed that independence would be restored with the German arrival.

Nazi authorities demanded 100,000 men for German service. Lithuania refused and remained the only occupied country never to field a foreign SS legion. This refusal came with a price. Lithuanian Army command staff was replaced, its units disarmed and disbanded. Before they could be arrested or detained many officers and men, who were relieved of duty, dispersed with weapons into the heavily forested country. Thousands later organized into a partisan army of freedom fighters to oppose both, the Russian and the German, invaders.

Behind the Wehrmacht (German army) came the Brownshirts (*Sturmabteilung*), the SS (*Schutzmanschaft*), *Einsatzegruppen*, Gestapo (*Geheime Staatspolizei*), and even trained teenage gangs called *Hitlerjugend*. No better than the Red Army occupation before them, the Nazi plague ravaged Lithuania anew.

Baltic countries were to be a protectorate of the Third Reich with limited self-governments. Many came out of hiding with renewed hope of rebuilding the government institutions of the recent past. Once more it came to naught. Unlike his campaigns in the West,

Hitler conducted his Eastern Front as a *Vernichtungskrieg* (war of eradication), and told his generals International Law would be disregarded here. (*GRRCL*)*

This surprised no one as Hitler's long list of deceptive propaganda, broken promises, violated treaties and lies, second only to Stalin's, harked back to the early 1930s, when Italy and Germany signed the Anti-Commintern Pact vs. Russia and departed from the League of Nations. In direct defiance of the Versailles Accords (set down at the end of the First World War), the *Luftwaffe* (German air force) was secretly rebuilt in Russia. Civilian aero clubs in Germany trained pilots throughout the 1930s and the need for Lebensraum was being preached as reason for action.

Before the Spanish Civil War ended in 1939, and after Franco took power, Spain served as test ground for German, Russian, and Italian weapons and tactics. Military support of the war, in the form of both matériel and manpower, was provided by Hitler as well as Stalin for Loyalists on one side and Republicans on the other. It was a dress rehearsal for the conflict yet to come.

Even before this could bear fruit, Austria was invaded and annexed in March 1938. Then Hungary was forced into alliance. A year later Czechoslovakia fell to Nazi invasion and Sudetenland was occupied. Czech mineral resources and Romanian oil fields came under German control and nothing blocked the seizure of Poland. On September 1, 1939, in blatant disregard of the 1934 Polish-German Non-aggression Pact, western Poland was attacked and occupied. At the same time, Russia invaded Poland's eastern half.

Spheres of influence over neighboring countries were established for Germany and Russia behind closed doors, without the knowledge or participation of the affected countries. The Winter War came to a proud end for Finland when armistice was signed with Russia after the loss of nearly one third of the country. But capitulation of Norway, Holland, Belgium and Denmark forced their governments into exile in Britain — Europe's last hope, seen as such after her Royal Navy reduced German sea power to a U-boat fleet. But the U-boats were a menace to U.S. supply convoys to Britain and her ground forces were being battered by Rommel's Afrika Korps.

Before the summer of 1940, French and British troops were pushed back to the sea at Dunkirk. In March 1941, Bulgaria fell and Greece surrendered to Italy. Then, in July 1941, Hitler hatched Operation Barbarossa and attacked Russia, his own ally!

When Musollini's army fell apart after British/Canadian landings in Italy, the remaining Italian Navy ships joined the Allies to secure the Mediterranean. It was then that the tide of war began to turn. The Battle of Britain was fought and won, establishing air superiority over the English Channel and coastal France. Hitler's invasion plans were dashed.

In December 1941, Pearl Harbor was attacked by the Japanese. It was no longer an European war. America was now involved. But it was another two and a half years before the Normandy landings heralded the last gasp for the Third Reich.

When Operation Bagration began on July 22, 1944 (three years to the day after Barbarossa), the German Army was outnumbered two to one in manpower and four to one in matériel. Russian forces mustered 5 million in 166 divisions, with 30,000 guns, 5,000 tanks and 6,000 aircraft. It was the largest army ever assembled and put in the field. The handwriting was on the wall.

On July 13, the Red Army reentered Vilnius and the protracted reign of terror began anew. Their units disarmed and disbanded twice by the enemy, Lithuania's military forces were reduced to wan hope of resistance. But they were not defeated. Surviving members of the Lithuanian Army, National Guard and Police continued organized guerilla warfare against the Soviets for another nine years. These partisans had no illusions about driving the invaders out all by themselves. Their hope was to continue armed and passive resistance only long enough for the West to come to their aid. But their efforts were *vox clamantis in deserto*. The West saw Russia as an ally and had already closed the book on World War Two.

After Roosevelt's death, neither Harry Truman nor Clement Atlee, who replaced Winston Churchill, were experienced in world affairs. Stalin was a seasoned, crafty, and ruthless leader at the apex of his power. There was no question who would win the war in Europe after the Third Reich surrendered.

The Molotov/Ribbentrop Pact at the start of hostilities, drawn up behind closed doors without participation of the countries affected by its accords, divided Poland and placed Estonia, Latvia, and Lithuania into Stalin's sphere of influence leaving the door open for armed invasion and absorption into the Soviet Union. To this day, Russia claims all three Baltic States joined voluntarily! And, to this day, Russian government seeks to glorify Stalin while celebrating the anniversary of the end of World War Two and the defeat of Nazi Germany. Vladimir Putin even had the gall to formally invite the Baltic heads of state to the unveiling of monuments erected to enshrine Josef Stalin on the occasion.

Geared to justify her invasion of the Baltics, Russia's claims to land rights are ongoing. Such claims are in keeping with Russian guidelines to create "history" with the aim of showing the USSR as always the victim, never the aggressor, in military conflicts which Russia herself had instigated. A prime example of this in World War Two is the Winter War of 1939/1940. In this conflict, the Russian behemoth of 250 million people assaulted Finland in an undeclared war against a country of three million, and still claims Finland was the aggressor. This points to the now recognized array of deception, truth twisting, disinformation, and propaganda, as perpetrated by the Kremlin, which has never seen its equal. It is the reason so much is known about 20th century German belligerence, and so little about Russia's aggressions against the world.

While nothing can justify Nazi war crimes against humanity, German guilt is confined to the two World Wars (1914-1918 and 1939-1946). Russian (and Soviet) war making fills a list spanning a hundred years in addition to the two World Wars: Revolution (1917), Spanish Civil War (1936-1939), Winter War in Finland (1939/1940), Berlin blockade (1948), Korean War (1950-1953), invasion of Hungary (1956), Vietnam War (1964-1975), invasion of Czechoslovakia (1968), the Afghan War (1979-1989), the 1994 launch of ongoing hostilities against Chechnya, and the attack of Georgia in 2008. This list does not take into account limited actions in Angola, Syria, Mozambique, Bosnia, Ethiopia and Yemen, among others; including Cuba, where Russia brought the world to the very brink of nuclear war during the Kennedy administration in 1962.

Russia's warmongering continues unabated today in what was once East Prussia (now Kaliningrad), on the southwestern border of Lithuania, which Russia occupies and claims illegally. The region was overrun by the Red Army during World War Two when it fell victim to invasion along with Poland and the three Baltic States. After reestablishment of their independence, and four years of political pressure, Red Army troops eventually departed from all except East Prussia.

No postwar documents exist to show agreement of the Allies to cede the region to Soviet Russia. They are not to be found in the Churchill Archives at Cambridge University, the National Archives in Washington, or those in London, because no such agreement was ever made. Russia claims otherwise. In fact, East Prussia was occupied by force of arms and remains under Russian control. International law makes it clear this occupation is illegal.

In terms of military threat, a parallel to the 1962 Cuban missile crisis can be drawn here, when Krushchev tried to arm Cuba with weapons to threaten the United States. Where Krushchev failed in Cuba, Vladimir Putin has succeeded in Kaliningrad. The threat to Europe is very real today. Russian arms buildup in the region within easy reach of eastern and central Europe continues. There are currently eighteen SS-21 short range ballistic rockets capable of delivering a nuclear warhead 120 kilometers away. Eight more SS-C1-B rockets, mounted on transport vehicles and also nuclear warhead capable, have a range of 750 kilometers.

In addition, permanently stationed are 837 Russian tanks, 1085 armored vehicles, 530 self propelled artillery weapons, 77 jet fighters and a dozen MIG-24 attack helicopters. This count does not include infantry and transport. The latest is the intention to add 500 kilometer range, nuclear warhead, Iskander rockets to the arsenal. (*Pasaulio Lietuvis, 2008.01/457*)*

What is all this for?

It is clear that the INF Treaty signed by Gorbachev and President Reagan is not being honored in Kaliningrad. The demilitarization question has been repeatedly raised since the first weeks of independence restoration of the neighboring states. In 1993 the United Nations aired the problem and Russia began a gradual arms reduction in Kaliningrad. But during Putin's term in office, arms escalation began anew.

East-West relations are sufficiently strained to prompt the West's refusal to acknowledge Soviet Union's role in international terrorism for political reasons alone, never mind the moral implications. The Kremlin knows where to draw the line and is clever enough to provide western leaders the opportunity to close their eyes. One of many examples is the erstwhile KGB link to Black September, the terrorist group responsible for the 1972 murders of Israeli Olympians in Munich.

There is positive proof that after the Soviet Union broke up, Russia was selling arms to mid-eastern terrorists to keep Russian military from starving. In fact, the major Islamic terrorist organizations are being armed with Russian weapons to day.

Soviet practice of inciting unrest to weaken a foreign political adversary is well known. If no fanatics surfaced, they would create them. They knew if the NKVD/KGB trained and supplied enough violent extremists, and let them loose, havoc was sure to follow. In wartime, these practices escalated.

Nazi concentration camps consumed millions, yet were outdone tenfold by the Russian version. The Russian counterpart was different. Lethal medical experiments on the living were conducted in some camps, but there were no crematoria, no gas chambers. For extermination purposes, there was no need. Vorkuta's winter temperature of -80°F was normal, and camps farther north often recorded -98°F. These are temperatures at which uncovered eyeballs freeze solid. Prisoners worked 16 hours a day and lived in huts without heat, in cold beyond human endurance. Siberian camps saw at least a million deaths each year. This means some seven or eight million people died in Russian labor camps alone during the war from 1939 to 1945. (*Gulag, 2004. Kizny*)*

These people comprised Ukrainians, Poles, Lithuanians, Latvians, Estonians, Finns, and Russian nationals. Even British and American deaths were counted among them.

The horrific aspect of Russian captivity can be found in the use abandoned Nazi concentration camps saw after German retreat. The Russians did not destroy them. Here, they detained and tortured countless German POWs and those unfortunates who fell into political captivity because they did not fit in with Stalin's new regime.

They died there by the thousands long after the war had ended. We know little about these crimes against humanity because the West is still reluctant to accept and digest indictment of a regime which was the ally of western powers in the war against Hitler.

At the end of World War Two, the Kremlin's propaganda was still not penetrated. Allied with the West, Russia continued her deceptions as before. The Yalta Conference (between Roosevelt, Churchill and Stalin at war's end) came to be the ultimate betrayal of the Baltic States. Its political rhetoric with no supporting action rendered the immediate post-war status quo a *fait accompli*. U.S. State Department gave Stalin everything but the west lawn of the White House. The fact that the U.S. and its allies never recognized Estonia's, Latvia's and Lithuania's incorporation into the Soviet Union changed nothing. Their embassies in Washington were downgraded to foreign legations and status quo endured until the fall of the Berlin Wall. For all the diplomatic rhetoric of the Bush administration, it was slow to acknowledge Lithuanian independence in 1990. United States was the 37th country to do so.

From 1944 to 1954, the struggle against the invaders cost the lives of 50,000 Lithuanian Freedom Fighters and 80,000 Soviet occupation forces and Russian NKVD troops. Although 1944 is regarded as the year of Soviet occupation it was, in fact, the beginning of an undeclared war against the Lithuanian people which continued until freedom and independence were restored in 1990. This war after the war cost even more Lithuanian lives through mass murders and deportations of civilians numbering over 340,000 including women and children. At least 8,000 officers of the Lithuanian Army were tortured and murdered by the Russians. All told, the country lost nearly a third of its population to genocide — the worst human disaster in her entire thousand-year history — all vehemently denied by the Kremlin. (*GRRCL*)*

An indication how pervasive Soviet/Russian (and I make no distinction between them in this case) attempts at rewriting history came to me in the form of TV entertainment which bills itself as "documentary".

I recently watched the celebrated 2009 BBC production *"Behind Closed Doors - Stalin, the Nazis and the West"* on DVD. This is a six hour epic series of grand proportion. It incorporates newsreels, propaganda footage, and staged scenes with professional actors - a truly superb presentation. It is so well done, in fact, that what is *not* shown and what is *not* said never falls under suspicion that it may have been influenced by what the Kremlin wanted known and what it did not want known.

It would have been more appropriately titled "Stalin on Poland", because that is the only emphasis of the *entire* six hours, and includes only those aspects of Soviet crimes to which the Kremlin has already admitted. Every war map shown on screen is incorrect in the Baltic region and depicts borders as set down by Stalin, before the fact, to indicate what he wanted them to be not only as war progressed, but also after it ended.

The Molotov/Ribbentrop pact is glossed over, never mentioning the division of Europe beyond Poland. The Yalta Conference between Churchill, Roosevelt and Stalin is depicted as nothing more than a controversial discussion of Polish government in exile! The list goes on... How could BBC consider such trash?

This so-called documentary has short changed every country which the Red Army invaded. No one watching this series would suspect what happened in Finland, Estonia, Latvia, Lithuania, Czechoslovakia, Romania, Hungary, Bulgaria, or the Ukraine, unless they were already well informed about the history of World War Two.

In the end, the program contributes nothing to the knowledge and understanding of the war except in Poland. But it does imply that the West is just as naïve today as it was while war still raged in Europe 65 years ago, and demonstrates just how pervasive Kremlin propaganda can be.

On the other hand, it does not fool those who take the time to do their own research. An example is another current video production. *"The Soviet Story"*, the documentary by Edvins Snore is a more truthful treatment of this subject on DVD. It is a shocking recounting of the truth. It is not entertainment. Less than two hours long, it is a more complete story than BBC's six hour marathon, and it shames the BBC production in its accuracy. Small wonder it was officially condemned by Russia even before its release to the public, and its producer burned in effigy in Moscow.

* * *

Lithuania was surrounded for centuries by powerful neighbors with imperial ambitions. But she was once the largest and most respected country in Europe. Her borders extended from the Baltic Sea in the north to the Black Sea in the south. In her entire thousand-year history those borders dissolved altogether only during the postwar years of World War Two. The Soviet "Red Tide" swept over her, trying to extinguish the last flames of nationhood with blood soaked storms. But the attempt failed.

In spite of relentless Soviet efforts, the repopulation and russification of Lithuania was slow and unsuccessful. It failed due to underground resistance and the determined efforts of Lithuania's Freedom Fighters. Thanks to their sacrifice, only 7% of Lithuania's population today is ethnic Russian, as compared with 22% in Estonia and 30% in Latvia. For obvious reasons, Russians were more reluctant to emigrate to Lithuania than other occupied countries.

When independence was restored on March 11, 1990, national government institutions were reestablished in remarkably short order, thanks to the resistance efforts by the underground and their support by organized emigrant Lithuanian agencies abroad.

This momentous example was soon followed by Estonia and Latvia, and fifty years of war and oppression in the Baltics ended at last.

* Note on references

The most recent references cited are marked *GRRCL* to indicate the Genocide and Resistance Research Center of Lithuania (www. genocid.lt) in Vilnius, Lithuania, which produces numerous publications and research reports about the Soviet and Nazi occupations and the resistance movement during and after World War Two.

Other references are noted in the text.

Older historical references are redundant and not given. This information is readily available in countless scholarly publications covering the history of the Second World War. Those of more recent publication make use of previously unavailable Soviet archival material and deserve more credence than some previous works.

It is useful to note that the newest Kremlin regime has now closed all state archives. Russia's crimes are once again being swept under the carpet.

Further Reading

A selection of recent publications

Adamczyk, Wesley	*When God Looked the Other Way*	(University of Chicago 2004)
Butler, Rupert	*Stalin's Instruments of Terror*	(Amber 2006)
Davies, Norman	*No Simple Victory*	(Viking 2007)
Duffy, Christopher	*Red Storm on the Reich*	(Castle 2002)
Eksteins, Modris	*Walking Since Daybreak*	(Mariner 2000)
Gaidis, Henry	*A History of the Lithuanian Military Forces in World War II*	(Lithuanian Research & Studies Center 2001)
Judt, Tony	*Postwar, A History of Europe Since 1945*	(Penguin 2005)
Kizny, Tomasz	*Gulag*	(Firefly 2004)
Lukša, Juozas	*Forest Brothers*	(Central European Univ. Press 2009)
MacDonogh, Giles	*After the Reich*	(Basic 2007)

www.ingramcontent.com/pod-product-compliance
Lightning Source LLC
Chambersburg PA
CBHW051942090426
42741CB00008B/1241